The Dead
Have
No Need
of
Ethics

Fred Blackburn
Assistant Professor of Philosophy and Religion
Christian Heritage/San Diego Christian College

Dedicated to

Don and Linda Blackburn
who laid the foundation
for my life and ethics.

Also, to
Sam and Betsy Burton
who greatly encouraged me
in this project
and in my daily life.

Part 2

Personal Journey & a Mystical Approach to Ethics and Morality

§

The Dead Have No Need of Ethics

Preface

This is the most difficult topic I have ever attempted to come to terms with; not simply because of the depth of the subject matter, but also because of its implications. Writing a book on ethics would be a relatively simple project if it were being done as an academic or intellectual exercise. We would only need to research the material and present the facts regarding various ethical theories and then critique those theories based on their relative strengths and shortcomings. However, when the pursuit of ethics is done in an existential manner, when the findings result in life changing applications which affect our morality, the task can be daunting.

The first thing I noticed while trying to write this work was the incredible sense of presumption on my part to tackle a topic that has engaged the brightest minds and purest souls in human history. To say that I felt a bit intimidated and under qualified, both in the realms of intellect and purity, would be a gross understatement. To come to terms with my own shortcomings and moral failings has made the task of writing a work on Ethics into a pilgrimage of my own depravity and dark introspections along with the frailties of being human. Since the time I have tried to record my thoughts and musings on this subject, it is as though my whole life has become a proving ground and every action, a test of moral veracity. I have been confronted on a daily basis with my own faults and weaknesses as well as the struggles or apathy of those around me. My life has become a crucible and a test study for these things which I hope to share with you. By God's grace, I pray that what you read here will pierce your very soul and that together we may be purged of all dross and impurities, thus presented as pure vessels, tempered by the blood of Christ and presented flawless to the service of the King.

SUMMARY OF ETHICS

Ethics is a subcategory of philosophy. Philosophy is an approach to knowledge that seeks to find the foundational principles or reality behind a concept. Philosophy comes from the Greek root words *philo* (love) and *sophia* (wisdom); therefore, philosophy literally means the "love of wisdom." Philosophy can be applied to any topic under the sun, but there are several traditional fields which are of particular interest to the philosopher. The major categories of philosophical investigation would include: logic (the theory of right reasoning), aesthetics (the theory of critiquing, addressing what is *the Good, the True,* and *the Beautiful*), epistemology (the theory of knowledge), metaphysics (the underlying nature of reality), and ethics (the theory of right conduct). We will be focusing our study on the ethical branch of philosophical investigation, but the study of ethics will also include all the other major divisions of philosophy.

Ethics, defined as the theory of right conduct, investigates the very nature of what we mean by "right" or "good." Ethics begins by questioning if we are even in a position to know what the "right" or "good" is. If ethical knowledge is possible, then the question becomes, how do we go about determining right conduct? For now, I simply want to establish the distinction between ethics as a theory of right conduct, and morality as an application of ethical theory. Ethics is the theory, and morality is the practice. Yet, determining what is ethical and being able to live up to a given ethical theory becomes a task of monumental proportions with profound philosophical and practical ramifications.

Although a discipline in its own right, ethics must draw from the other major divisions of philosophy. Epistemology (theory of knowledge) investigates *if knowledge is even possible.* And if it is, then it seeks to understand *how things are known.* If knowledge isn't possible, then neither are ethics. And the way in which we believe will affect our theory of ethics. Logic investigates correct reasoning; yet, our epistemology will influence the logic and reasonableness of our ethic theory. Aesthetics (theory of critiquing) investigates the concepts and evaluation of ideas such as *the Good, the True, the Beautiful.* Are these objective, absolute, and universal qualities, or are they subjective, relative, and personal constructs? Metaphysics (beyond the physical) seeks to know the underlying nature of reality, and its sub-discipline of Ontology (theory of being) seeks to understand "what is *being*: what does it mean to be or not to be." Yet, these questions take us to the very core of what is real and what is not. Ethics must first establish a basis for reality, value, correct reasoning, and knowledge, before it can have any hope at discovering a theory for the right way to live. This leads us to a discussion of paradigms and worldviews and the effect they have on the study of ethics and reality.

SUMMARY OF WORLDVIEWS

A worldview, paradigm, is very much like a pair of glasses or a lens through which we perceive the world. It colors our perceptions and judgments of the world. It is a matrix by which we are able to interact with the world; but in many ways, it also becomes the cage which limits our perception of the world or reality that we are able to experience. There are many things which affect our perception of the world—from the language spoken to the food eat eaten. Our ethnicities, genders and ages can affect perceptions along with temperament, personality and intelligence. Culture, education, class, and caste, along with religion and politics can all affect one's view of what is real and what is not, or what is of value and what is worthless. All these filters affect the way we perceive reality which in turn will affect the way we determine ethics and morality. In addition to the above influences on our perception of reality, there are also deep philosophical foundational beliefs which affect our view of the underlying nature of things, including how things are known, valued, and evaluated. These worldviews provide a framework through which to answer the most basic of philosophical questions (*Figure 1*). They attempt to explain what is *real*, why we are here, what is the purpose of life, how we should live, and what happens to us when we die. Philosophy and religion essentially seek to answer such questions.

In my Philosophy of Origins class, I spend a lot of time talking about worldviews. I begin with Animism which, at least from an Anthropological perspective, is the oldest world view known to man. Animism is the belief that virtually everything is alive and has a soul or a spirit. I say *virtually* because some things are dead and the reason that they are dead is because they are no longer connected to their soul or spirit. Not only are organic life forms such as humans, animals, and plants thought to be alive, but even things considered to be inanimate by modern, western cultures. Not only are rocks, rivers, and clouds alive, but even tools, weapons, or cook ware could be considered *living things*, and were often named and treated with respect. This belief system is still found throughout the world in many indigenous and tribal societies. In fact, in many respects, it is still the foundational belief of many people who would align themselves with some of the broader worldviews I will be discussing.

Of the worldviews that I will be addressing, since they encompass majority of perspectives, can be traced back to animistic beginnings and usually a period of polytheism as well. Polytheism is the belief in *poly-* (many) *theism* (gods). Polytheism can be found throughout world history. In a polytheistic worldview, certain powerful spirits are elevated to the level of deities. For example, the spirit of the ocean could be personified or anthropomorphized (giving human traits to non-human things) into a deity such as Neptune or Poseidon. The spirit of the sky could be elevated to divine status in the form of Jupiter or Zeus. Even abstract concepts such as *love* or *war* could find personification in the deities of Venus or Mars. Polytheistic cultures produced large pantheons of gods and goddesses. It was not uncommon for a typical first century Roman village to have over ten thousand divinities, and the pantheons of India can reach into the millions of gods. The empires of Egypt, Sumer, Greece, and Rome, along with their Nordic, Celtic, Indian and Chinese counterparts all had elaborate lists of gods. Even the Biblical revelation of God begins with God as a primal creative Spirit brooding over the face of the waters: "And the earth was without form, and void; and darkness was upon the face of the deep. And the Spirit of God moved upon the face of the waters" (Genesis 1:2 KJV). Note that this book shall refer to the KJV, King James Version, of the Bible whenever verses are referenced. God is portrayed as a force of nature and manifested Himself in fire, smoke, earthquake and storm: "And mount Sinai was altogether on a smoke, because the Lord descended upon it in fire: and the smoke thereof ascended as the smoke of a furnace, and the whole mount quaked greatly" (Exodus 19:18).

Throughout the Old Testament, God declares Himself as the greatest of the gods and is jealous of His worshippers' affections. God often intervenes on behalf of the Israelites, not because of their obedience and devotion, but rather because of the mockery of His power by the devotees of other gods. I am not claiming that the Bible advocates polytheism, rather I am saying it was written to people living in polytheistic cultures. God revealed

Himself starting as a Creator Spirit, to the Greatest of the gods, and a jealous God, to a God of law and order, a shepherd and a judge, the King of Kings, and finally as the only True God. This monotheistic, *mono-* (one) *theist* (god), revelation is often called the gift of the Jews, and although there are some examples of it in non-Abrahamic traditions, it is the foundation of a Theistic worldview.

For additional explanation see the following video(s)

"Ethics Part 1: How worldview and presuppositions act as filters to our understanding." YouTube, recorded and uploaded by Fred Blackburn. 24 Jan. 2019, https://www.youtube.com/watch?v=3f1mtdFMzPY&feature=youtu.be

"Ethics Part 2: What is a human being?" YouTube, recorded and uploaded by Fred Blackburn. 6 Feb. 2019, https://www.youtube.com/watch?v=uK-pGLUui69c&feature=youtu.be

"Ethics Part 3: What is a Christian?" YouTube, recorded and uploaded by Fred Blackburn. 29 Jan. 2020, https://www.youtube.com/watch?v=nsM-w69RO8UY&feature=youtu.be

"Metaphysics and Philosophy of Origins Part 10: World views; Animism." YouTube, recorded and uploaded by Fred Blackburn. 27 Feb. 2020, https://www.youtube.com/watch?v=6v4xdfi_x_4&feature=youtu.be

"Metaphysics and Philosophy of Origins Part 11: Animism (continued) and Polytheism." YouTube, recorded and uploaded by Fred Blackburn. 4 March 2020, https://www.youtube.com/watch?v=iciR4xGuEwY&feature=youtu.be

For additional resources and biblical references

GENESIS 1:2 - "And the earth was without form, and void; and darkness was upon the face of the deep. And the Spirit of God moved upon the face of the waters."

EXODUS 19:18 - "And mount Sinai was altogether on a smoke, because the Lord descended upon it in fire: and the smoke thereof ascended as the smoke of a furnace, and the whole mount quaked greatly."

List of figures

Fig. 1. Diagram of worldviews.

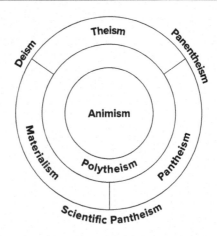

Figure 1. Diagram of major worldviews. – This is a simple matrix and template to help decipher the various competing perspectives; it illustrates the divisions of the leading worldviews.

II.A THEISM

In a theistic worldview, the foundation of reality is God. God is seen as singular in essence, yet infinite in attributes. Some of the more common attributes associated with God identify an omniscient, omnipresent, omnipotent, omnibenevolent being. At the beginning of the twenty-first century, theism is by far the most predominant world. The Abrahamic faiths alone—Judaism, Christianity, and Islam—make up over 54% of the world's population. All of these religions believe that God is also personal and has revealed His will on how humans should live. The ethic most associated with this worldview is Divine Command Theory, where the commands of God are equated with good, and the violation of God's commands or prohibitions are seen as evil.

Theists believe that God is both immanent (permeates creation) and transcendent (beyond creation). God is viewed as creator in the Abrahamic traditions and is seen as separate yet involved with His creation. As creator along with His attributes, God has the right, knowledge, and wisdom to determine proper conduct for His creatures and possesses the power to enforce His decrees. All of the Abrahamic Faiths believe God has revealed His will—both in a general and a special way. General revelation includes the creation itself, as well as the attributes and even concepts we share with God. This will be discussed in greater detail when I talk about what it means to be *made in the image of God* (Genesis 1:27). Special revelation is seen as information or truth revealed by God that is beyond the scope of human reason or experience. This type of revelation often came to people known as prophets and the record of their revelations is what comprises much or the Holy Writings or scriptures of the various Abrahamic Faiths.

In addition to divine revelation being ssdn bnrecorded in scriptures, many people within the Abrahamic Faiths, especially those from a more mystical end of the spectrum, also believe that God communicates through, signs, wonders, omens, and dreams. In some cases, God is even believed to communicate directly with humans ranging from an audible voice to impressions or promptings received in our own minds. Although there are many similarities between the Abrahamic Faiths, there are also irreconcilable differences. Each Faith teaches an exclusive knowledge of truth. With very little exception, the exclusivity of the Western Religious Traditions is often so intense that even sects within the various branches view others as heretical or unorthodox if they do not hold to all the same doctrines, creeds, and practices.

Theism is considered a dualistic worldview. What I mean by this is that theists believe in both a physical and a spiritual reality. This belief is applied to humans themselves with the idea that humans have a physical as well as an immaterial makeup. It also applies to the cosmos at large where there is a belief in natural laws and orderliness which can be predicted, but these laws can be acted upon by the creator and this supernatural intervention is what is known as a miracle. Due to this dual view of reality within theism, theists themselves hold to a wide range of beliefs. The more materialistically minded theists may find themselves on the deist end of the spectrum (God exists but is not active in the world), whereas the more spiritually minded theist may find themselves relating more to Panentheism (God is in all things or all things are in God).

For additional biblical references and resources
GENESIS 1:27 - "So God created man in his own image, in the image of God created he him; male and female created he them."

II.B PANTHEISM

Pantheism comes from the Greek root words *pan-* (all) and *theism* (god). This worldview believes that all is God and God is all. Unlike theism which sees God as being distinct from His creation, pantheism sees God and nature as one. Pantheism is the second largest worldview and is comprised of what is often referred to as the Eastern Religious Traditions. These include Hinduism, Buddhism, Jainism, and Taoism but would also be influential in the Sikh and Bhai Faiths. It also has made inroads into a variety of Western Religious Traditions (Abrahamic Faiths) and can be seen as the philosophical foundation of some ancient Gnostic sects as well as modern manifestations in what has been called the "New Age" movement. Pantheism has a broad range of beliefs and practices, and various groups would even agree with the attributes associated with God by their western counterparts. Other pantheists, however, would disregard a belief in a deity entirely and would simply state that the underlying nature of reality is simply ONE. This could be personified or seen as a more Naturalistic (all phenomena can be explained through natural processes) base for reality. It is harder to associate a specific ethical theory within pantheism than it is within theism because of the pantheist's view of reality and where individuals may be in their understanding of right conduct.

Pantheists range in their beliefs, concerning the nature of God, gods, or nature depending on the particular religion being discussed and the particular sect within that religious or philosophical context. Some Hindus believe in a monotheistic God which transcends all creation; yet, this God is also immanent and involved in creation. Some Hindus practice polytheism and have a variety of gods which they worship and consult, based on culture, location, and spiritual advancement. Other Hindus would see all the various gods, as manifestations of one God. Some Buddhists have personifications of the Divine, whereas others speak in terms much more akin to Atheism (the belief that there is no God). Among the pantheistic traditions, there is also widespread belief that God has revealed his will to man. This can take the form of revelation or inspiration as is seen in the Western Traditions, or it can be traced to personal insight, self-realization, and enlightenment. The writings of those who have been inspired or enlightened have also been collected and are viewed with varying degrees of authority depending on a person's particular sect or personal beliefs. The range of ethical beliefs that come out of a pantheistic system can take the form of legalism and a slavish sense of devotion to a prescribed set or rules as is often also found in the Abrahamic Faiths. Also, it can lead to a state of personal enlightenment and self-governed behavior for those who have realized their own divine natures.

Pantheism is considered a monistic worldview. What I mean by this is that pantheists believe the ultimate reality is spiritual. While it is true that some pantheists also believe in a physical world; this physicality is seen as impermanent at best. But by many sects the physical is seen as pure illusion. This places a pantheist's ethical concerns largely on the non-physical aspects of human behavior; although as mentioned above, some sects will have a very rule-based approach to how people should live their lives. Pantheism, with its foundational belief that *All is God* or *All is One*, often leads to a greater toleration for different approaches to religious belief as well as ethics and morality. Pantheism can also lead to higher degrees of empathy; if a person truly believes that all is ONE, then it is an illusion to distinguish "the other," thus serving another is serving oneself.

For additional explanation see the following video(s)
"A broad introduction to Pantheism Part 1." YouTube, recorded and uploaded by Fred Blackburn. 14 April 2020, https://www.youtube.com/watch?v=UrmS8jdJ1Bw&feature=youtu.be
"A broad introduction to Pantheism Part 2." YouTube, recorded and uploaded by Fred Blackburn. 14 April 2020, https://www.youtube.com/watch?v=EBvyhmlVpDU&feature=youtu.be
"A broad introduction to Pantheism Part 3." YouTube, recorded and uploaded by Fred Blackburn. 14 April 2020, https://www.youtube.com/watch?v=c-1dgjOYKIrA&feature=youtu.be

NATURALISM/MATERIALISM   *II.C*

In a materialistic worldview, the underlying nature of reality is matter. Philosophic materialism should not be confused with consumeristic materialism. This worldview is not stating that those who have the most things are the better off although the philosophic belief of materialism could lead to this conclusion. Materialism as a worldview is stating is that matter is all that exists, it is eternal. And although it may change form in its conjunction with energy, it can neither be created nor destroyed. Materialism is often associated with philosophic naturalism. Naturalism is the belief that all phenomena (things that appear to our senses) can be explained through natural processes. Although Naturalism/Materialism is by far the smallest worldview by population, it has a majority view in the fields of the hard sciences (biology, chemistry, geology, etc.) and dominates many of the social sciences, especially anthropology. Because materialism does not believe in non-material things, such as souls, spirits, ghosts and gods, it is often associated with atheism or agnosticism (the belief that there is not enough evidence to be an atheist or a theist). Some materialists may participate within more secularized versions of the religious beliefs of their community such as many mainline versions of Christianity have become or in a more open Universalist approach. Some sects of Judaism, such as Liberal Judaism, may participate in religious festivals and traditions, but for all intents and purposes hold to a naturalistic, materialist approach to understanding the nature of reality.

Materialism is a monistic worldview. What I mean by this is that it holds to only a physical reality. For a materialist, the physical world is all that is real; so, it is in the material realm where we should look for answers on *why we are here* and *what the meaning of life is*. This is why the scientific method and a naturalistic approach to knowledge are of such great interest to the materialist. From this perspective, it makes sense to study the body which we can observe, rather than to study the soul which no one has seen. As a society, we can map the brain, but how does a person examine the mind? We have an entire cosmos to explore and learn from, but if there is a creator, where is He?

Materialists in their naturalistic explanation are not influenced or concerned about values and ethics. Materialists and naturalist as people, however, are very concerned with the "right" way to live. Unlike their theistic or pantheistic counterparts, naturalist/materialist do not look for some divinely inspired truth or otherworldly revelation. The same tools used for trying to understand the cosmos can be used to understand ethics. Reason, utility, and the consequences of one's actions can all be used to formulate ethical theories of right conduct. Secular humanism is the view that man, rather than god, is the measure of all things. Humans, being the most evolved beings that we are aware of, get to determine for themselves what the best way to live is. This often results in care and concern for other humans because we are part of the same species, but it can also extend to plants and animals; for although they are not human, they are connected to us through a common ancestry and common destiny.

ADDRESSING THE CRUCIAL QUESTIONS   *III*

Now, to take this line of thought to a different level, we need to not only address what ethics and worldviews are, but also, we need to define what a human being is and what a Christian is. At this point I want to transition from what ethics are and the effect worldview has on ethics, to who ethics are for and why. Since many of the ethical topics we will be discussing later in this course deal with human life such as abortion, euthanasia, capital punishment, and war, I think it is important that we take the time to define what it means to be a *human being*. In addition, this text is concerned with Christian Ethics, so it seems important to take the time to talk about what a Christian is, if we have any hope of coming up with a Christian Ethic.

WHAT IS A HUMAN BEING?   *III.A*

The study of man is fascinating for it touches us so closely. Yet, it is also very difficult to define because of its close proximity. Most of us have simply assumed that we know what man is, but what does it really mean to be human? What separates and distinguishes human beings from all other types of beings whether they are angel or animal. Man has the unique distinction of all of God's creation to be made in the image and likeness of God. But what does that mean—to be made in God's image? I will be exploring those qualities and characteristics that are unique to God and man and examining that which separates us from the rest of the created order.

Some would say that human beings are unique and can be distinguished from other organisms by our D.N.A.; our genetic code is what makes us what we are. But a body could have a complete human D.N.A. but still not be a living breathing human. Man is more than a compilation of bodily parts made up of water and a vast array of minerals. Man is more than a physical creature and cannot be reduced to his chemical composition. What does it mean to be human? When does human life begin? When does human life end? What will be the final state of man? These and similar questions will be discussed in this section.

Man does have a physical frame, and this does seem to be an important part of being human. I do not believe, however, that our physical appearance is what is meant by being made in the image and likeness of God for God is Spirit. In many ways, man's physical appearance is truly animalistic; science has categorized humanity as a high order of primate. We have been designated as hominids because we stand erect; yet, even though we are classified as mammals within the animal kingdom, man is unique from all other earthly and heavenly species. While in our frame we may more or less look like animals, our true distinction comes from the immaterial part of man. It is in this immaterial element that we can see the image of God manifest.

Man has an immortal soul, and it is this that begins the inquiry of what man truly is and where our distinctiveness can be found. By soul, I mean, the immaterial part of man that is the core of his being. Soul is the collective term for the mind (reason), will (choice and volition), and emotion (feeling and passion). I also believe that each human being contains spirit which is his ultimate connection to the divine. This aspect will be discussed in greater depth when I cover the doctrine of salvation, but it is a part of what makes us human.

Now you may be thinking, there he goes, body, soul and spirit. Well, I must admit a trichotomy does allow for making nice illustrations and I will use it when discussing salvation. But it is only a model based on human reason, and Greek philosophical reasoning at that! I, along with the ancient Hebrews, hold to a more holistic view of man's being. I believe we were created as a unit, a whole, which was not meant to be divided into triads, but was meant to act in harmony together. A body without a soul or spirit is a dead body and is no longer recognized as a human being. But we do not cease to exist after the demise of our physical form. Paul draws the parallel of the tabernacle and our earthly bodies in 2 Corinthians 5:1: "For we know that if our earthly house of this tabernacle were dissolved, we have a building of God, an house not made with hands, eternal in the heavens." Similarly, Philippians 3 tells us that there is a persistent *us* that is given different bodies; "For our conversation is in heaven; from whence also we look for the Savior, the Lord Jesus Christ: Who shall change our vile body, that it may be fashioned like unto his glorious body, according to the working whereby he is able even to subdue all things unto himself" (20-1). God will give us a glorified body which we will inhabit throughout eternity. Man was meant to function within a frame. We were not meant to be disembodied spirits floating about, but to have both form and substance.

I would like to say that a soul is the intermediary between the realm of matter: the body and the spirit. This may work out philosophically; but at least scripturally *soul* and *spirit* and even *breath* are interchanged too readily to be dogmatic on the subject. The Hebrew word *ruwach* means breath but is also known to be translated into *wind, mind, soul* or *spirit,* thus echoing the interwoven essence of the word and its meaning. God is spoken of as having a soul but not as having a body, so it wouldn't be a mediator for Him. Souls and Spirits, however, are not unique to God and man. Angels are spiritual beings and they have been reported in the scriptures to take on human form when dealing with mankind. Animals also have spirits and/ or souls according to the Scriptures. In Ecclesiastes 3:21, Solomon is not questioning if animals have souls or spirits, but what happens to that soul or spirit after they die; "Who knoweth the spirit of man that goeth upward, and the spirit of the beast that goeth downward to the earth?"

If animals have bodies but also souls or spirits and if angels have spirits and can take human form, what distinguishes man from the rest of God's creation? What does, being *made in the image of God* really mean? We often think of human reason as a distinguishing factor. While we appear to be more intelligent than animals, we are most certainly less intelligent than angelic beings. Language may be considered a superior form of communication, but animals certainly communicate—some of them quite elaborately. Choice is a human trait. But did not Satan choose to rebel along with a third of the heavenly host (Revelations 12:4), and do not animals make all sorts of choices every day? Emotions may provide some sort of distinction since we are told of the heavenly host rejoicing and we know animals can show fear or pleasure. Yet, perhaps humans have a quality of emotions not shared by other beings besides God.

I believe if we look in the first chapters of the book of Genesis, we can find some of the unique qualities which are indicative of being made in God's image. In Genesis 2:15, we see the first task assigned to Adam, he was placed in Eden by God and told to dress and keep it. Man was given stewardship of the garden and of all creatures. He was given power and authority over the work of God's hands. Adam was awarded the headship of the human race and God made a covenant with him providing him with all his needs with the sole prohibition of not eating from the tree of knowledge of good and evil. Adam's headship was a type (an actual historical event that is a foreshadowing of an event to come) which would be shown again in its glory in Christ.

Adam's second task from God was to name all the animals (Genesis 2:19-20). During this process, we see several unique attributes of Adam. He created names and he observed patterns and completeness. It was after naming the animals that he noticed there was no helpmate for him. Patterns are a basic element in human intelligence and are a method of testing a person's intelligence quotient.

Other attributes that seem to be shared by only God and man are laughter and lamentation. I know of no recorded incident of either angels or animals laughing, but the scriptures speak of the laughter of God. Perhaps the laughter of God is a pressure relief for the pain caused him by the wicked; Psalm 2:4 states: "He that sitteth in the heavens shall laugh: the Lord shall have them in derision." Additionally, Psalm 37:13 adds that "The Lord shall laugh at him: for he seeth that his day is coming," thus echoing God's sadness towards the wicked. Laughter and weeping are both powerful emotional responses to overwhelming joy or pain. Man seems to share some type of unique emotional response with God that is either lacking or limited in comparison for other created beings.

The ultimate distinction that I have come across between man and any other created being is the concept of *Nous*. *Nous* (meaning mind or intellect) in Greek philosophy is the highest part of man; it can be associated with first principles, like the platonic forms or the ability to distinguish and make value judgments. *Nous* is the a-priori part of the mind; thus, it includes *the Good, the True, the Beautiful*. Although animals and angels both appear to have minds, wills, personalities and emotions, the part of man referred to as the *nous* seems to be a unique quality. This term is used throughout the New Testament when referring to the mind of God and man. Additionally, this is the part of man than is imprinted with the mind of God and allows us to think of concepts beyond human reason or experience. Ideas such as perfection, holiness, eternity, and even the very idea of God cannot be known through human understanding or investigation alone. If we as humans have these ideas, where did they come from? From a philosophical perspective this has been used as a proof for the existence of God as well as a theological confirmation that we were indeed created in God's image.

WHEN, WHERE, AND WHY HUMANS WERE CREATED AND WHAT WILL BE THEIR END?

III.A.1

With regards to humans, when, where, and why are words that lead to provoking conversations and even deeper questions concerning mankind's original state and final condition as well as, God's interaction and provision for humanity.

WHY WAS MAN MADE?

III.A.1.a

Man was made for the glory of God; "The Lord hath made all things for himself: yea, even the wicked for the day of evil" (Proverbs 16:4). Man was made to glorify God, not the other way around. Revelations 4:11 supports this saying, "Thou art worthy, O Lord, to receive glory and honour and power: for thou hast created all things, and for thy pleasure they are and were created."

III.A.1.b WHO MADE MAN?

God. "So God created man in his own image, in the image of God created he him; male and female created he them" (Genesis 1:27). This idea of God as creation is reinforced in Isaiah 45:12: "I have made the earth, and created man upon it: I, even my hands, have stretched out the heavens, and all their host have I commanded." Man was made by Christ; John 1:3-4 states, "All things were made by him; and without him was not anything made that was made. In him was life; and the life was the light of men." Another verse referring to the breath, spirit of man coming to be is Job 33:4: "The spirit of God hath made me, and the breath of the Almighty hath given me life." It is clearly accounted here that the Spirit created man, thus making it very clear that all members of the trinity contributed to the creation of man.

III.A.1.c WHEN WAS MAN MADE?

Genesis chapter 1 tells us that man was made on the sixth day of creation. Yet, Psalms 139:14-16 tells us that God knew us before any of our parts were made: "I will praise thee; for I am fearfully and wonderfully made: marvelous are thy works; and that my soul knoweth right well. My substance was not hid from thee, when I was made in secret, and curiously wrought in the lowest parts of the earth. Thine eyes did see my substance, yet being unperfect; and in thy book all my members were written, which in continuance were fashioned, when as yet there was none of them."

III.A.1.d HOW WAS MAN MADE?

Genesis 2:7 states, "And the Lord God formed man of the dust of the ground, and breathed into his nostrils the breath of life; and man became a living soul." In this verse, we are shown both the physical and immaterial aspects of human beings.

III.A.1.d.i PHYSICAL ATTRIBUTES OF MAN

Because of mankind's physical qualities, man is intimately connected to the physical and material world; "In the sweat of thy face shalt thou eat bread, till thou return unto the ground; for out of it wast thou taken: for dust thou art, and unto dust shalt thou return" (Genesis 3:19). People need the physical properties of food, rest, and shelter to sustain the physical frame.

IMMATERIAL ASPECTS OF MAN

III.A.1.d.ii

These are the parts of man that cannot be physically perceived. We have not only a brain, but also a mind, a heart as well as passion and feelings; we are not merely components of a machine, but rather possess will and volition. Jesus quotes Deuteronomy 6:5 saying the greatest commandment is "Thou shalt love the Lord thy God with all thy heart, and with all thy soul, and with all thy mind" (Matthew 22:37).

THE SOUL

III.A.1.d.ii.1

I believe the soul is our personality and temperament; it makes us different and unique from other human beings. The same word for breath, *neshamah,* which appears in Genesis 2:7 also refers to soul; so in breathing life, God imparted a soul. In Matthew 10:28, Jesus warns that we ought to be concerned for our whole being: "And fear not them which kill the body, but are not able to kill the soul: but rather fear him which is able to destroy both soul and body in hell" (Matthew 10:28). Whereas humans may have power over other human's bodies, only God has power over another being's soul.

THE HEART

III.A.1.d.ii.2

As an aspect of the soul, Deuteronomy 6:5 equates *lebab* (the word for heart) with soul, mind, thinking, conscious, appetites. We shall go into further detail later in this book. In Matthew 15, Jesus makes the point that it is not physical impurities that defile us, but rather what comes out of us: anger, jealousy, wrath, and bitterness (11,17-20). It is not the unwashed hands that makes us dirty, but the words that come out of our mouths.

THE MIND

III.A.1.d.ii.3

Mankind possesses a mind; this is the highest aspect of the soul. This is where we a priori knowledge (value judgments and platonic ideals which allow us to discuss *the Good, the True,* and *the Beautiful.* Romans 12:2

speaks to the transformation of one's mind through Christ: "And be not conformed to this world: but be ye transformed by the renewing of your mind, that ye may prove what is that good, and acceptable, and perfect, will of God."

<u>For further additional explanation see the following video(s)</u>
"Ethics Part 2: What is a human being?" *YouTube*, recorded and uploaded by Fred Blackburn. 6 Feb. 2019, https://www.youtube.com/watch?v=uKp-GLUui69c&feature=youtu.be

<u>For additional resources and biblical references</u>
PSALMS 8:4-6 - "What is man, that thou art mindful of him? and the son of man, that thou visitest him? for thou hast made him a little lower than the angels, and hast crowned him with glory and honour. Thou madest him to have dominion over the works of thy hands; thou hast put all things under his feet:"
ECCLESIASTES 7:29 - "Lo, this only have I found, that God hath made man upright; but they have sought out many inventions."
GENESIS 1:26-7 - "And God said, Let us make man in our image, after our likeness: and let them have dominion over the fish of the sea, and over the fowl of the air, and over the cattle, and over all the earth, and over every creeping thing that creepeth upon the earth. So God created man in his own image, in the image of God created he him; male and female created he them."
GENESIS 2:7 - "And the Lord God formed man of the dust of the ground, and breathed into his nostrils the breath of life; and man became a living soul."
2 CORINTHIANS 5:1 - "For we know that if our earthly house of this tabernacle were dissolved, we have a building of God, an house not made with hands, eternal in the heavens."
PHILIPPIANS 3:20-1 - "For our conversation is in heaven; from whence also we look for the Savior, the Lord Jesus Christ: Who shall change our vile body, that it may be fashioned like unto his glorious body, according to the working whereby he is able even to subdue all things unto himself."
ECCLESIASTES 3:21 - "Who knoweth the spirit of man that goeth upward, and the spirit of the beast that goeth downward to the earth?"
MATTHEW 10:28 - "And fear not them which kill the body, but are not able to kill the soul: but rather fear him which is able to destroy both soul and body in hell."

MATTHEW15:11, 17-20 - "Not that which goeth into the mouth defileth a man; but that which cometh out of the mouth, this defileth a man. [...] Do not ye yet understand, that whatsoever entereth in at the mouth goeth into the belly, and is cast out into the draught? But those things which proceed out of the mouth come forth from the heart; and they defile the man. For out of the heart proceed evil thoughts, murders, adulteries, fornications, thefts, false witness, blasphemies: These are the things which defile a man: but to eat with unwashen hands defileth not a man."

PHILIPPIANS 4:7 - "And the peace of God, which passeth all understanding, shall keep your hearts and minds through Christ Jesus."

1 CORINTHIANS 2:16 - "For who hath known the mind of the Lord, that he may instruct him? But we have the mind of Christ."

THE DOCTRINE OF SIN AND THE FALL OF MAN   *III.A.2*

The *doctrine of sin* has caused much confusion and much of it stems from an improper understanding of what sin is. First of all, sin is not a tangible, created thing! God did not create sin! *Sin* is more akin to an adjective or a verb than to a noun. Sin is the result of God creating a perfect standard and giving sentient beings the opportunity, free will, to either conform to God's standard or to rebel against it. In short, anything that is contrary to the will of God is sin.

However, this presents a theological, philosophical problem: if God is omnipotent (all powerful) and omnibenevolent (all-good all the time), how could anything be contrary to the will of God? If other beings could go against God's will, would that not limit His sovereignty? This dialogue is the great, *problem of evil* dilemma found in philosophy and theology. The problem is stated something like this:

Premise 1	God Exists
Premise 2	Evil Exists
Conclusion 1	Therefore, God is either all powerful, but not all good
Conclusion 2	Or, God is all good, but not all powerful

Figure 2. Problem of Evil.

This is very logical, but also very inaccurate. God is both all-powerful and all-good. To deal with this apparent contradiction, some have denied that there is evil or sin in the world and that it is nothing more than ignorance, due to our limited human perspective. Certainly, this accounts for some instances, but the scriptures are quite clear that evil and sin do exist, and there will be grave consequences for those that participate in rebellion against God either willfully or out of ignorance.

A better solution to this dilemma is to acknowledge God's gift of choice to His creation. Personally, I believe this ability to choose extends from the angelic host all the way down to plants and animals. I maintain that they can and do on a regular basis. If we think back to the original definition, that sin is anything contrary to the will of God, then anything that acts contrary to the way God created it, is in sin. All of creation groans and suffers under the curse, not because of iniquity, but because of the fall of man. Nature is in a fallen state and we can see the horror of "tooth and claw," all seen in "the survival of the fittest," that plagues our world. Romans 8 clearly states that even creation has been effected by the consequences of sin, but it will also be redeemed: "For the creature was made subject to vanity, not willingly, but by reason of him who hath subjected the same in hope, because the creature itself also shall be delivered from the bondage of corruption into the glorious liberty of the children of God" (8:20-1).

However, it is not the sins of the creation that concerns us here, but rather the first sinner, Satan, and his subsequent affect upon the crown of God's creation, mankind. Although the scriptures do not give a clear chronology of events concerning when Satan rebelled against God, it is clear that Satan was already in opposition to God while Adam and Eve were in a state of innocence in the Garden of Eden. As the first recorded sin and sinner, Lucifer was the anointed cherub, yet he was not content to serve, but wanted to be exalted even above the Father of Creation. Lucifer was so enamored with his own created perfection that he envied the creator himself. Having forgotten the source of his beauty, his pride and envy torn his from the heights of the heaven and cast him into the depths of hell: "Thou wast perfect in thy ways from the day that thou wast created, till iniquity was found in thee" (Ezekiel 28:15).

In Isaiah 14, we find all the great markers for sin: "How art thou fallen from heaven, O Lucifer, son of the morning! how art thou cut down to the ground, which didst weaken the nations! for thou hast said in thine heart, I will ascend into heaven, I will exalt my throne above the stars of God: I will sit also upon the mount of the congregation, in the sides of the north: I will ascend above the heights of the clouds; I will be like the most High. Yet thou shalt be brought down to hell, to the sides of the pit" (14:12-15). In essence sin is placing, "I" before God, and this Satan did in abundance. Satan, however, was not alone in rebellion; a third of the host of heaven followed in his sin. Yet, it is this same tendency in man to place our wills and desires above God's that make us the children of our father the devil, rather than in the sons of light.

With regards to the context of the fall of man, Adam and Eve were created in the image and likeness of God, and God saw all that He had created, and it was very good. Man was created without sin, but with a choice, to follow the commands of God or too break them. God only imposed one prohibition on Adam, "and the Lord God commanded the man, saying, Of every tree of the garden thou mayest freely eat: but of the tree of the knowledge of good and evil, thou shalt not eat of it: for in the day that thou eatest thereof thou shalt surely die" (Genesis 2:16-17).

The tragic fall of mankind is recorded in Genesis 3. Woman, being beguiled by the serpent, took and ate of the forbidden fruit, and Adam, hearkened unto the voice of his wife rather than unto the voice of God, does the same. It is fascinating to note, however, that the fall of mankind is attributed to the man and not the woman, for Adam was the corporate head of the human race and it was his action that condemned all of his descendants (Romans 5:12-7). Regardless if we hold to a federal or seminal view of Adam's headship (the federal view sees Adam as a representative of the human race appointed by God, so we fall with him, or the seminal view sees Adam like the first apple tree, in him was every human to follow, thus every human as progenies are tainted, just as every apple could be traced by to the first apple tree), mankind is charged as sinners regardless of our perceptions our behavior.

It is from such passages as mentioned above that Saint Augustine and others developed the *doctrine of original sin*. Many people claim that this is unjust. Why should we suffer for the sins of Adam? Yet, Paul makes it quite clear in Romans 1-3 that "all have sinned and come short of the Glory of God" (3:23). Mankind has sinned both corporately and individually, and the penalty of sin is death: "For the wages of sin is death; but the gift of God is eternal life through Jesus Christ our Lord" (Romans 6:23). Fortunately, that is not the end of the story for God has made glorious provision through His Son, but this will be discussed in the next section on salvation.

For further additional explanation see the following video(s)
"Theodicy for 'the problem of evil.'" *YouTube,* recorded and uploaded by Fred Blackburn. 7 April 2020, https://www.youtube.com/watch?v=fGK-lOtQppr8&feature=youtu.be

For additional biblical references and resources
MATTHEW 21:19 - "And when he saw a fig tree in the way, he came to it, and found nothing thereon, but leaves only, and said unto it, Let no fruit grow on thee henceforward for ever, And presently the fig tree withered away."
LUKE 13:6-9 - "He spake also this parable; A certain man had a fig tree planted in his vineyard; and he came and sought fruit thereon, and found none. Then said he unto the dresser of his vineyard, Behold, these three years I come seeking fruit on this fig tree, and find none: cut it down; why cumbereth it the ground? And he answering said unto him, Lord, let it alone this year also, till I shall dig about it, and dung it: And if it bear fruit, well: and if not, then after that thou shalt cut it down."
ROMANS 5:12-7 - "Wherefore, as by one man sin entered into the world, and death by sin; and so death passed upon all men, for that all have sinned: [...] For if by one man's offence death reigned by one; much more they which receive abundance of grace and of the gift of righteousness shall reign in life by one, Jesus Christ."
1 CORINTHIANS 15:22 - "For as in Adam all die, even so in Christ shall all be made alive."

List of Figures

WHAT IS A CHRISTIAN?

THE DOCTRINE OF SALVATION / HOW A PERSON BECOMES A
CHRISTIAN

The following section has been heavily influenced and transcribed in accordance with the commentary of Ryre's KJV Study Bible (see citation for further information). The doctrine of salvation is of upmost importance. In a sense, it is the history of mankind and was foreknown by God before the foundation of the earth. God built the plan of salvation into the entire creation process. Sin and rebellion, although not created by God, are used by Him to magnify His Glory.

The doctrine of salvation is rooted in the prehistory of the world. Because of the eternal and omniscient nature of God, He already foreknew and predestined those who would be saved from before the foundation of the world. 2 Timothy 1:9-10, Ephesians 1:4-5, and Romans 9 provide biblical support for the doctrine of predestination which could be further discussed in detail through extensive biblical study, yet this discussion shall be saved for another time.

It is incredible to think that God already knew all of human history before it was even physically created. Yet, God already knew the heart of man and the long and painful path which we would trod, until we were made joint heirs of Christ in his glorious salvation. God did not pre-ordain the fall of man. Yet, God did know of it. And with such knowledge, He prepared a way for mankind to be forgiven and reconciled unto himself. Romans 8:28-30 is significant since it details that God not only calls us to repentance but he provides a way of calling, justification, and glorification that has been in place from beginning to end; "And we know that all things work together for good to them that love God, to them who are the called according to his purpose. For whom he did foreknow, he also did predestinate to be conformed to the image of his Son, that he might be the firstborn among many brethren. Moreover, whom he did predestinate, them he also called: and whom he called, them he also justified: and whom he justified, them he also glorified" (Romans 8:28-30).

III.B.1.a WHAT IS SALVATION, OR WHAT IS IT THAT WE ARE SAVED FROM?

Salvation is rescue from death. The penalty for disobedience to God was and is death and Adam in his disobedience condemned all mankind to this fate. Romans 6:23 states, "For the wages of sin is death; but the gift of God is eternal life through Jesus Christ our Lord." We are saved from the wrath of God. Yet on a personal level, I think that God sent His son and saved me from myself.

III.B.1.b WHO NEEDS TO BE SAVED?

All of us need saving. Romans 3:23 articulates this clearly: "For all have sinned, and come short of the glory or God" (Romans 3:23). Because of Adam's headship of the human race, sin has passed to us all—both corporally through Adam's actions and individually through our own rebellion; "Wherefore, as by one man sin entered into the world, and death by sin; and so death passed upon all men, for that all have sinned" (Romans 5:12).

III.B.1.c ATONEMENT THROUGH CHRIST

Even before God cursed Adam and Eve for their disobedience, He already had made a way of reconciliation. The provision of salvation is foreshadowed in the Old Testament. God sent prophets and the law, but all pointed towards the future coming of Christ. Christ, himself, is the perfect and Holy Lamb of God. Atonement means to reconcile. The process of atonement is one of covering over and was administered by the sacrifice of animals throughout the Old Testament. But this reconciliation was ultimately completed by the blood sacrifice of Christ on the cross. In Leviticus 16, we see the Old Testament practice of the High Priest making atonement for the children of Israel. This occurred once a year; the High Priest would enter into the Holy of Holies and sprinkle blood on the Mercy Seat. This practice was the great foreshadowing of the sprinkling of Christ's blood in the heavenly Holy of Holies which only needed to be done once for the eternal reconciliation of mankind to God.

CHRIST ALONE IS THE MEANS OF SALVATION

Acts 4:10-2 articulates that salvation only occurs through Christ; "Be it known unto you all, and to all the people of Israel, that by the name of Jesus Christ of Nazareth, whom ye crucified, whom God raised from the dead, even by him doth this man stand here before you whole. This is the stone which was set at naught of you builders which is become the head of the corner. Neither is there salvation in any other: for there is none other name under heaven given among men, whereby we must be saved." It is only the person and work of Christ that satisfies God's standard of holiness. Jesus echos this in John 14 when he says, "I am the way, the truth, and the life: no man cometh unto the Father, but by me" (14:6).

For further additional explanation see the following video(s)
"Ethics Part 3: What is a Christian?" *YouTube,* recorded and uploaded by Fred Blackburn. 29 Jan. 2020, https://www.youtube.com/watch?v=nsM-w69RO8UY&feature=youtu.be

For additional biblical references and resources
2 TIMOTHY 1:9-10 - "Who hath saved us, and called us with an holy calling, not according to our works, but according to his own purpose and grace, which was given us in Christ Jesus before the world began, but is now made manifest by the appearing of our Savior Jesus Christ, who hath abolished death, and hath brought life and immortality to light through the gospel."
EPHESIANS 1:4-5 – "According as he hath chosen us in him before the foundation of the world, that we should be holy and without blame before him in love: Having predestinated us unto the adoption of children by Jesus Christ to himself, according to the good pleasure of his will,"
ROMANS 9 – see full chapter
GENESIS 2:15-6 – "And the Lord God commanded the man, saying, Of every tree of the garden thou mayest freely eat: but of the tree of the knowledge of good and evil, thou shalt not eat of it: for in the day that thou eatest thereof thou shalt surely die."
JOHN 1:29 – "The next day John seeth Jesus coming unto him, and saith, Behold the Lamb of God, which taketh away the sin of the world."
1 PETER 1:18-21 – "Forasmuch as ye know that ye were not redeemed with corruptible things, as silver and gold, from your vain conversation received by tradition from your fathers; but with the precious blood of Christ, as of a

lamb without blemish and without spot; who verily was foreordained before the foundation of the world, but was manifest in these last times for you, who by him do believe in God, that raised him up from the dead, and gave him glory; that your faith and hope might be in God."

GENESIS 3:15 – "And I will put enmity between thee and the woman, and between thy seed and her seed; it shall bruise thy head, and thou shalt bruise his heel."

ROMANS 5:8-11 – "But God commendeth his love toward us, in that, while we were yet sinners, Christ died for us. Much more then, being now justified by his blood, we shall be saved from wrath through him. For if, when we were enemies, we were reconciled to God by the death of his Son, much more, being reconciled, we shall be saved by his life. and not only so, but we also joy in God through our Lord Jesus Christ, by whom we have now received the atonement."

HEBREWS 5:9 – "And being made perfect, he became the author of eternal salvation unto all them that obey him."

HEBREWS 7:25 – "Wherefore he is able also to save them to the uttermost that come unto God by him, seeing he ever liveth to make intercession for them"

1 TIMOTHY 1:15 - "Christ Jesus came into the world to save sinners; of whom I am chief."

JOHN 3:14-6 - "And as Moses lifted up the serpent in the wilderness, even so must the Son of man be lifted up: That whosoever believeth in him should not perish, but have eternal life. For God so loved the world, that he gave his only begotten Son, that whosoever believeth in him should not perish, but have everlasting life."

Works cited

C. C. Ryrie. *The Ryrie Study Bible: King James Version.* Chicago: Moody Press. 1976.

III.B.2 GOD IS RESPONSIBLE FOR OUR SALVATION

God purposed and provided for our salvation before the world began. 2 Timothy 1:9 speaks to God's role and timing in our salvation; "Who hath saved us, and called us with an holy calling, not according to our works, but according to his own purpose and grace, which was given us in Christ Jesus before the world began."

God chose us. The following verses show how God predestined those he called to salvation. Romans 8:29 states, "For whom he did foreknow, he also did predestinate to be conformed to the image of his Son, that he might be the firstborn among many brethren" and Ephesians 1:3-5 adds that "Blessed be the God and Father of our Lord Jesus Christ, who hath blessed us with all spiritual blessings in heavenly places in Christ: According as he hath chosen us in him before the foundation of the world, that we should be holy and without blame before him in love: Having predestinated us unto the adoption of children by Jesus Christ to himself, according to the good pleasure of his will."

God is the one who draws us unto Himself: "Jesus therefore answered and said unto them, 'Murmur not among yourselves. No man can come to me, except the Father which hath sent me draw him: and I will raise him up at the last day'" (John 6:43-4). Just as a dead man cannot reach for help, so too, we who are dead in Adam are fully dependent on God for our salvation. From a human perspective, it certainly appears that we play a part in our salvation even if that part is simply limited to accepting God's gift. However, I believe that without the quickening of the Holy Spirit we are not even able to realize the existence of God--let alone that He has offered us reconciliation unto Himself. There is nothing in man by which we can love God. It is only by God dwelling within us that we can participate on some level of God within us loving God outside us. But such wonder and mystery are ineffable.

WHAT IS THE END RESULT OF SALVATION? *III.B.2.a*

Death of the old man: *III.B.2.a.i*
Who we once were in Adam is now reckoned dead. "For ye are dead, and your life is hid with Christ in God" (Colossians 3:3).

New Life in Christ: *III.B.2.a.ii*
Even though we are dead to our old selves, we have been quickened to newness of life by the Holy Spirit. This is clear in 2 Corinthians 5:17, "Therefore if any man be in Christ, he is a new creature: old things are passed away; behold, all things are become new."

III.B.2.a.iii **We shall be with Christ:**

Christ promised to come again for those who believe in him; "In my Father's house are many mansions: if it were not so, I would have told you. I go to prepare a place for you. And if I go and prepare a place for you, I will come again, and receive you unto myself; that where I am, there ye may be also" (John 14:2-3).

III.B.2.a.iv **We shall be one with Christ and the Father and all other believers:**

With the indwelling of the Holy Spirit we are not only reconciled to God, but also have an ontoligcal (theory of being/essence) unity with other believers. John 17:21-3 states, "That they all may be one; as thou, Father, art in me, and I in thee, that they also may be one in us: that the world may believe that thou hast sent me. And the glory which thou gavest me I have given them; that they may be one, even as we are one: I in them, and thou in me, that they may be made perfect in one; and that the world may know that thou hast sent me, and hast loved them, as thou hast loved me."

III.B.2.a.v **We become partakers of the divine nature:**

In our reconciliation to God, we actually get to be joined to his very spirit; "Whereby are given unto us exceeding great and precious promises: that by these ye might be partakers of the divine nature, having escaped the corruption that is in the world through lust" (2 Peter 1:4). 1 Corinthians 6:17 echoes this saying, "But he that is joined unto the Lord is one spirit."

III.B.2.a.vi **Glorification:**

God manifests his glory through his creation especially those who have been transformed into the image of his son: "And the glory which thou gavest me I have given them; that they may be one, even as we are one:" (John 17:22). Additionally, in John 15:8, Jesus says, "Herein is my Father glorified, that ye bear much fruit; so shall ye be my disciples."

III.B.2.b **HOW IS ONE SAVED?**

The main element of salvation is centered on *belief*. This belief is given by God to man as a free gift. James warns us, however, in his Epistle: "Thou believest that there is one God; thou doest well: the devils also believe, and tremble. But wilt thou know, O vain man, that faith without works is dead?" (James 2:19-20). Salvation is not merely an intellectual assent to a belief in God or the life and work of Jesus. Rather it is a belief in the sense of total commitment and a death to self. We do not accomplish our own deaths, but we have been crucified with Christ, we are no longer our own. Old things are passed away, and all things have become new. The life that we now live is in Christ Jesus our Lord. This type of belief is experiential and life giving.

FAITH

III.B.3

We often use the words *faith* and *belief* as synonyms, but I would like to be clear on what I mean by "saving faith." In Greek, as well as, English, *faith* and *belief* can have a wide array of meaning. We can have faith in our significant other that they will be faithful, meaning "true." We can have faith in our leaders or socio-political causes. We can have faith that our sports team will be victorious. Yet, all these types of faith are self-generated, or perhaps based on our past experiences. But all of the above types of faith are self-generated and can also be described as "wishful thinking". We can even have inherited faith where we take on the beliefs of our family or community, but neither inherited faith nor wishful thinking will save us. "Saving faith" is a gift from God and is given by measure; Ephesians 2:8-9 states, "For by grace are ye saved through faith; and that not of yourselves: it is the gift of God: Not of works, lest any man should boast." Also, Romans 12:3 says, "For I say, through the grace given unto me, to every man that is among you, not to think of himself more highly than he ought to think; but to think soberly, according as God hath dealt to every man the measure of faith." Faith that is based on inheritance, reason, wishful thinking or experience is not "saving faith." The faith that saves does not come from us, but is a gift from God and transcends what we could generate from our own knowledge or experience. Hebrews 11:1 defines faith, saying, "Now faith is the substance of things hoped for, the evidence of things not seen."

III.B.3.a **THE APOSTLE'S CREED**

> I believe in God, the Father Almighty,
> Creator of heaven and earth;
> and in Jesus Christ, His only Son, Our Lord;
> Who was conceived by the Holy Ghost,
> born of the Virgin Mary, suffered under Pontius Pilate,
> was crucified, died, and was buried.
> He descended into Hell;
> the third day He arose again from the dead;
> He ascended into heaven,
> sitteth at the right hand of God, the Father Almighty;
> from thence He shall come to judge the living and the dead.
> I believe in the Holy Ghost,
> the Holy Catholic Church,
> the communion of saints,
> the forgiveness of sins,
> the resurrection of the godly,
> and life everlasting.
> Amen.
>
> (Thurston 1)

The Apostle's Creed is an accepted statement of orthodoxy within the Christian community. Unfortunately, one could recite and even believe in the Apostle's Creed and still not be a Christian. Being a Christian is not just an intellectual accent to a list of propositional truths. You can know what a Christian is or what a Christian believes without personally being a Christian. Christianity is a new ontological orientation. The former state of being has been crucified with Christ and has been replaced by a new creation (Romans 6:6). So, in conclusion, to define what a Christian is in the truest sense of the word, is a person who has died to self and is indwelt by the very Spirit of God.

For further additional explanation see the following video(s)
"Ethics Part 3: What is a Christian?" *YouTube,* recorded and uploaded by Fred Blackburn. 29 Jan. 2020, https://www.youtube.com/watch?v=nsMw69RO8UY&feature=youtu.be

For additional biblical references and resources

1 THESSALONIANS 5:9 - "For God hath not appointed us to wrath, but to obtain salvation by our Lord Jesus Christ."

2 TIMOTHY 2:4 - "No man that warreth entangleth himself with the affairs of this life; that he may please him who hath chosen him to be a soldier."

1 THESSALONIANS 5:9 - "For God hath not appointed us to wrath, but to obtain salvation by our Lord Jesus Christ."

ROMANS 9 – see full chapter

JERIMIAH 31:3 – "The Lord hath appeared of old unto me, saying, Yea, I have loved thee with an everlasting love: therefore with lovingkindness have I drawn thee."

ROMANS 6:2 – "God forbid. How shall we, that are dead to sin, live any longer therein?"

ROMANS 6:11 – "Likewise reckon ye also yourselves to be dead indeed unto sin, but alive unto God through Jesus Christ our Lord."

JOHN 17:24 – "Father, I will that they also, whom thou hast given me, be with me where I am; that they may behold my glory, which thou hast given me: for thou lovedst me before the foundation of the world."

ACTS 16:31 – "And they said, Believe on the Lord Jesus Christ, and thou shalt be saved, and thy house."

MARK 16:16 – "He that believeth and is baptized shall be saved; but he that believeth not shall be damned."

JOHN 3:16 – "For God so loved the world, that he gave his only begotten Son, that whosoever believeth in him should not perish, but have everlasting life."

JOHN 11:25-6 – "Jesus said unto her, I am the resurrection, and the life: he that believeth on me, though he were dead, yet shall he live: and whosoever liveth and believeth in me shall never die. Believest thou this?"

ROMANS 10:9 - "That if thou shalt confess with thy mouth the Lord Jesus, and shalt believe in thine heart that God hath raised him from the dead, thou shalt be saved."

MATTHEW 10:32 – "Whosoever therefore shall confess me before men, him will I confess also before my Father which is in heaven."

Works cited

C. C. Ryrie. *The Ryrie study Bible: King James Version*. Chicago: Moody Press. 1976.

Thurston, Herbert. "Apostles' Creed." *The Catholic Encyclopedia*. vol. 1. New York: Robert Appleton Company, 1907. 30 May 2020, https://www.newadvent.org/cathen/01629a.htm

III.C WHAT IS A CHRISTIAN ETHIC?

If a Christian is one who has died to self and is indwelt by the very Spirit of God, and if ethics are the theory of right conduct, a Christian ethic would seem to be a God-directed-way of living. In this sense, Christian ethics would fall nicely under the broader category of Divine Command Theory Ethics with an emphasis placed on Christ to distinguish it from other non-Christian theistic ethical theories. The advantage of a Christian ethic over other types of more tradition Divine Command Theory propositions is that not only do we have God's commands as revealed through general and special revelation (through creation and scripture), but we also have the Holy Spirit at work in our very being, thus providing an internal, as well as, an external moral compass. The disadvantage of this type of ethic is that not only do we need to externally measure up to the commands of God, but we also must do it with right internal intention.

Christian ethics are often presented as a type of new and improved Judaism, or Islamic type ethics with a grace safety net in case we mess up. Biblical Ethicists treat the Bible as a guide to moral behavior, and it becomes a type of rule book for how to avoid what God hates, and to do what God loves. Christian ethics must still deal with objections such as, how do we know God exists? Or, if there is a God, how do we know we are serving the right one? If you have the Spirit of God living inside you, then these objections probably bear little weight in your ethical reasoning process. A more poignant question would be: how do we know the will of God? If it is determined that the Bible is God's revealed truth towards man and the standard by which men should live, no easy task, then how do we know which Bible to use, or do we need to learn the original languages in which the Bible was written to understand it correctly? Even if we can agree that God exists, we are following the True God, and He has revealed His will to us in the Bible, assuming we have the "right" Bible, how do we know we are interpreting it correctly?

Even Christians who believe that the Bible is the authoritative word of God have wildly diverse views on how we should then live. Many Christians only feel compelled to follow the teachings found in the New Testament whereas others will "cherry pick" through the Old Testament, keeping the laws they want to impose on others and excusing themselves from the laws they do not wish to keep themselves. Yet, even this is not the major problem of a Biblically based Christian ethic. Even if we believe in the TRUE God, and even if we believe that God has revealed His will to us in the Bible, and even if we believe we can interpret the Bible correctly, there is still a huge problem. No one can perfectly live out a divine standard of ethics besides God!

Christian ethics are an ideal but impossible ethical theory to uphold. Let me put it to you this way: if God is an infinite, holy, and perfect being, then how are you as a finite, foul, and fallible being going to live up to the standard of God? I am not saying Christian ethics are wrong or lacking, I'm saying they are too good and holy. Many Christians feel compelled to try and live a life in accordance with the Bible and the Christian ethical theory that it produces. They are sincere in their desire to love and obey God. If God sent His only begotten son to die for us, then the least we can do is to try and live for Him. Unfortunately, we can no more sanctify, live a life of holiness, ourselves than we can save ourselves. I used to believe in Christian ethics until I realized that I am no longer trying to live up to some impossible standard. Not only do I no longer believe in Christian ethics, but I no longer believe in ethics at all—at least not for myself yet, I still want others, who are outside of Christ, to have at least some code of conduct to which they try to live. Having completed the prologue, thus providing an in-depth background of vital terms and concepts, this text shall now go on a journey through a list of ethical theories. Watch and read carefully as I show why each and every one of them cannot produce true morality. following this deconstruction of ethics, I will show you why the title of this book rings true: *The Dead Have No Need of Ethics.*

For further additional explanation see the following video(s)
"Christian Ethics Part 1" *YouTube,* recorded and uploaded by Fred Blackburn. 2010, https://www.youtube.com/watch?v=Jo4LYCggzL0&feature=youtu.be
"Christian Ethics Part 2" *YouTube,* recorded and uploaded by Fred Blackburn. 2010, https://www.youtube.com/watch?v=Z-7QxucvBrI&feature=youtu.be

PART 1

A Critique of Ethics and Morality

§

ETHICS: THEORY OF RIGHT CONDUCT

ETHICS AND MORALITY DEFINED

The words *ethics* and *morality* are commonly used in our society; yet, many people would be hard pressed to define what these words mean. You will often hear people exclaim, usually with disdain in their voice, "oh, he is so unethical" or "she is so immoral." What people are generally expressing in these types of statements is that the person does not share their views on right conduct or is not living up to their ethical standards. The reality is that the "unethical" male or the "immoral" person may be acting perfectly ethical and moral within their own ethical framework. Ethics is the field of philosophy which deals with the theory of right conduct. Many people will use the words *ethics* and *morality* as synonyms, but I will try to use *ethics* when talking about the theoretical basis for right conduct and *morality* when talking about *applied ethics*. Let me give you an example from another field: an aesthetician is one who studies the nature of art, form, and composition while an artist is one who actively applies these principles. An aesthetician can also be an artist, but they are not the same thing, and so it is with *ethics* and *morality*. *Ethics* deals with questions of value, right and wrong, good and evil, good, better, best. *Morality* deals with how well one is able to apply and live up to one's ethical theory. It is from these questions that ethical theories have developed and been applied to a vast array of human endeavors.

For further additional explanation see the following video(s)
"Ethics introduction." *YouTube,* recorded and uploaded by Fred Blackburn.

4 June 2010, https://www.youtube.com/watch?v=04l_alH43AM&feature=youtu.be

"Objective Evaluation of Ethical Theories Part 1." *YouTube,* recorded and uploaded by Fred Blackburn. 8 June 2010, https://www.youtube.com/watch?v=UbEJ8EMf43I&feature=youtu.be

"Objective Evaluation of Ethical Theories Part 2." *YouTube,* recorded and uploaded by Fred Blackburn. 8 June 2010, https://www.youtube.com/watch?v=-eY9aW-R028&feature=youtu.be

II MAJOR DIVISIONS IN ETHICAL THEORIES

In the current study of ethics, it is often customary to divide the topic into three major categories since they deal with different aspects of ethical theory. The major divisions of study are *metaethics, normative ethics,* and *applied ethics.*

II.A METAETHICS

Metaethics deals with the overarching questions related to the study of ethics. Metaethics deals mainly with abstract concepts and presuppositions, using questions such as: are ethics absolute or relative? Is there a universal standard for ethics or is it a matter of taste? Is there any foundation for ethics in the natural world or do ethics have a supernatural source? Are there any foundations for ethics at all or are they just products of various cultures in different times and different places? Metaethics also deals with is/ought distinctions, the is deals with how things are and the ought with how things should be. Can we take the way things are in the world and use them to determine how things should be? Or do we have a standard of how things ought to be and should this determine how things ought to be in the world? Questions also arise about the nature of human beings and the issue of freedom. Some ethicists would see freedom as a prerequisite for ethics. If we are not free to make moral choices, how can we be held accountable for moral actions? This final question of freedom raises the question of, "are ethics even humanly possible?" These presuppositions along with issues such as metaphysics (that which is beyond the physical), ontology (the theory of Being), logic (the theory of right reasoning), and epistemology (theory of knowledge) must be addressed before normative theories of ethics can be developed and evaluated. The following formatting of this topic has been heavily influenced and transcribed in accordance with the *Stanford Encyclopedia of Philosophy* section on metaethics (see citation for further information).

Metaphysical questions—questions dealing with the nature of reality and things that are outside of the physical realm (such as ideas, thoughts, values, souls, spirits, etc.)—are foundational to ethical theories. If one subscribes to philosophical naturalism, the belief that all phenomena can be explained through natural processes, then one will have a very materialistic, meaning that only the material world exists, approach to ethics. If one believes in the supernatural and that we are more than just physical beings, then one's ethical foundations will have a very different starting point. Aristotelian realism will produce very different results as compared to platonic idealism, and philosophic naturalists will come to radically different conclusions than those who believe in a God or gods as a supreme law giver. A pantheist, an individual who believes that all is one, thus spirit is reality, will have a very different ethic than a naturalist, a person who holds to the belief in only the physical world, thus the physical is reality, and from a theist, an individual that believes in a God who is immanent and transcendent, and that there is both a physical and spiritual world and a physical and spiritual side to man, who believes humans are made in the image of God. A pantheist has a very different ethic from a naturalist or a theist. Individuals' presuppositions, regarding the nature of reality, will have major implications regarding their view of right conduct.

Metaethics also deals with the philosophic discipline called ontology which is a subcategory of Metaphysics and deals with questions concerning the nature of being:

"Why am I here?"

"Why is there something rather than nothing?"

"What is a human being?"

"How are human beings different from other types of beings?"

"How should I live?"

"What is the purpose and meaning of life?"

There are also anthropological, psychological, and sociological factors to be considered when studying metaethics which deals with emotion, reason, the will, self, others, culture, class, caste, sexual orientation, and gender. Depending on how one answers the previous questions, their answers will have a major impact on how a person determines right conduct and what one considers to be good.

Logic is the theory of right reasoning or thinking. Even though it is a philosophic discipline in its own right, it plays a role when discussing the nature of ethics. Certain ethical theories rely heavily on the use of logic, so the ability to reason correctly is crucial for these types of theories. If one subscribes to a more Aristotelian approach to logic through the correspondence theory of truth or the law of non-contradiction or the excluded middle (perceiving the world as either/or or black/white), the results (what is true or considered rational) will be quite different from those who subscribe to a more existential type of truth or an inclusive coherence theory of truth as is found in Hegel and his dialectic. Hegel took Aristotle's traditional either/or thesis and anti-thesis and looked for a synthesis between the two. Hegel did not believe that the synthesis was more true than the antithesis or thesis, but rather the thesis, antithesis, and synthesis should be taken as a whole; thus his dialectic is "the truth is the whole" (Redding, Paul, "Georg Wilhelm Friedrich Hegel"). Unlike Aristole, Kierkegaard states that truth is subjectivity, only what we have personally experienced is true for us (Kiekegaard 189-300). Kierkegaard was not denying absolute TRUTH, he simply believes that humans are limited to truth. Heidegger emphasizes in his "Being and Time" the unveiling of truth; for him a lie is that which covers something up and a truth is a form of unveiling; by this definition, God alone would have completely unveiled TRUTH, whereas humans can only see truth as slightly unveiled. Right reasoning does seem to be an important element in determining that which is true, certainly in what is reasonable. But the final philosophic discipline I want to discuss asks the question: is knowledge even possible, is truth even know-able and are we able to appy such knowledge to the way in which we live?

Epistemology is the philosophic discipline that deals with the theory of knowledge. It asks questions like: "is knowledge possible?" "What types of things can we know?" "How do we know things?" It is this final question that leads to an interesting exercise I enjoy discussing with my students. First, I ask the students how they know things and generate a list based off of their suggestions. The list usually ends up looking something like Figure 3 (for reference sake, the bolded worlds in the chart are what is written on the board and the definitions/explanations are what is verbally said in conjunction to further convey the concept):

HOW DO WE KNOW THINGS?	
Sense Perception	This includes empirical knowledge (that which we can know through our five senses and observations of the world), tactile knowledge (that which can be felt, tasted, smelled, heard, seen, weighed or measure) and any tangible type of knowledge (such as the scientific method with its emphasis on observation, experimentation and repeatability).
Experience	This can have much in common with empirical knowledge, but it could also include internal states and feelings which cannot be weighed or measured like physical material objects.
Reason	The use of logic and our ability to deduce or infer knowledge from our past observations or experiences or previously held beliefs on what is *true*.
Intuition	This is direct knowledge not based on observations or experiences.
Enculturation	This refers to knowledge handed down to us by our culture and society.
Authority	Similar to enculturation, authoritative knowledge comes from someone held in esteem or high regard. This could be anyone from your mother, to a priest, to a government official or expert in any given field of inquiry. This type of knowledge can be acquired directly or by learning through books, articles, or other types of dissemination of the authority's teachings.
Revelation	Revelation refers to knowledge that is beyond a person's reason, experience or sense perception. Usually revelatory knowledge is seen within a religious or spiritual context where the knowledge being gained is coming from an external source. This contributes to **signs, dreams, omens, visions, illumination, mystical states** and even **faith** can all be seen as various subcategories or knowledge through revelation.

Figure 3. Class discussion of *epistemology.*

After our list of is generated, I then begin the process of critically analyzing the various ways of knowing. Similar to the deconstruction done by Rene Descartes (in his quest to see if there was anything we could know with absolute certainty) I evaluate all the various types of knowledge and see if students can withstand radical doubt. Like Descartes did in his "Meditations," we look at the various ways that we think we can know things and see if there are any flaws.

Most of us use our sense perceptions as a major source of knowledge about ourselves and the world in which we live, but have your senses ever deceived you? If so, why do you trust them as a means of knowledge? Such thinking is based on the presupposition that there is an actual and external world that we take in through our senses and then we use *reason* to make sense of those impressions.

Experiences are another means by which we know ourselves and the world around us. But by their very nature, they are subjective and while they may seem true to us, experiences have no external or objective authority which can be applied to others. Also, we will often use a past experience to project ideas onto future events, but no two events are the same and our projections could be wrong. Even memories become suspect because we are interpreting them through our present point of view. This makes personal experiences appear to be a fickle guide for true knowledge.

Reason is seen by many to be the only means by which we can truly know things. With the use of *reason*, we can evaluate our sense percep-tions and evaluate our past experiences. Unfortunately, even the greatest intellectuals or logitians like Emmanuel Kant are not immune to misusing reason. *Reason* can perhaps tell us what is reasonable, but reasonable is not always synonymous with what is true. Saint Augustine once quipped, *fallor ergo sum,* meaning "I err, therefore I am" (*City of God* XIX). *Reason* seeks to tell us if something is *logical*, yet it cannot tell us is something is *true*.

Intuition is the ability to have direct knowledge or insight that does not come through reason or observation. Intuition may simply be the subcon-scious piecing together evidences that the conscious mind was not able to put together previously. Whether it is the subconscious being manifested, an apparent revelation, or the invocation of a muse like that which is found in poetic history, the problem with intuition is that sometimes one "just knows" something to be true but the assumption turns out to not be *true*. How can we distinguish between *true* intuitions and those that seem *true* while having no basis in *reality*? *Intuition* is a direct knowing, unfortunately that direct knowing is not always factual.

Enculturation is indoctrination where one's culture tells what is *the Good, the True*, and *the Beautiful* and how we then should live. We are taught the norms, values and ideals of our cultures, and these concepts are usually presented as "givens," truths not based on other types of knowledge. In many ways, this is like an inherited type of knowledge that we receive from those who came before us. This could also include religious knowledge, and enculturation is based on some type of authority. This knowledge is helpful for teaching us how to live within a given culture. However, the knowledge is relative to time and place and is not based off of any universal truth. If knowledge based on culture or authority is never questioned or challenged, no progress can be made. This also brings into question the type of cultural knowledge and where it came from in the first place before there was a society or culture. This is also the problem with knowledge based on authority. Such thinking leads to the following questions: "Why do some people, books, or systems have authority while others do not?" "Where did this authority come from, and how does one know if those in authority are accurately disseminating knowledge, or if they are using authority for their own purposes and gain?"

Revelation is the final source of knowledge that I want to discuss. Revelation type knowledge is that knowledge which cannot be gained through personal experience, observation or reason. It is knowledge beyond us and must be given. This is usually explained through some sort of prophetic vision or transmission of knowledge through a higher, usually divine source. This would include anything from the Oracle at Delphi to God speaking with the prophets of Judaism, Christianity, or Islam. The problem with this type of knowledge is that it is hard to accept outside of one's own religious context. If one does not believe in God or gods, then the very notion of divine revelation seems preposterous. Even if one believes in divine revelation, on is not likely to believe in any revelations outside of one's own religious tradition. Even if people share a belief that divine knowledge has been revealed through various prophets or scriptures, there is often a huge debate, regarding the meaning of these divine revelations. The critiques regarding revelation as a way of knowing would equally apply to all the various subcategories of revelation, whether we are talking about signs, dreams, visions, illumination, omens, personal mystical experiences or even faith. These may be authoritative to the people having them, but they are certainly not authoritative for those who do not share in receiving personal revelation.

Due to the above critiques of knowledge, it is easy to see why one might embrace skepticism as the only legitimate form of knowledge. This could be like David Hume, who did not believe knowledge was possible, or like Socrates, who believed knowledge was possible but he acknowledged that he did not know anything (besides the fact that he knew that he did not know anything). Or like Descartes who came to the conclusion that at least one thing he could truly know without a doubt was that he himself existed. This was the result of critiquing all the various types of knowing of which all could foster doubt, besides the idea of self-knowledge with Descartes's famous maxim, "*cogito ergo sum,*" meaning "I think therefore I am" (*Meditations of First Philosophy*). Descartes proceeded from his self-knowledge as a being that thinks to believe that he was not a self-existing thing, and that his very thoughts indicated he was the creation of a higher being, such as God. This higher being, because of His perfect nature, would be *good* and would not allow our senses to deceive us or our reason to mislead us if they were used correctly. This is an interesting conclusion, but it is based on certain presuppositions concerning the nature of God and man.

The point of this epistemic exercise is to show how important our theory of knowledge is with regards to our formulation of ethical theories. If you believe knowledge is not possible, it will lead to nihilism (the belief in nothing). If you believe we can only know ourselves, it will lead to egoism or solipsism (you are the only one that exists). If you believe reason can be trusted, it will produce a rationalistic ethic (an ethic based on logical analysis). And if you believe your personal experiences are the only thing you can truly know, then existential ethics (the belief that personal experience is the highest source of knowledge) will be your particular choice. Those who believe in revelation will probably have some sort of divine command theory (the stance that God's commands are *good,* and His prohibitions are *evil*) as their ethical compass. So, not only will metaphysical presuppositions influence personal ethic, but epistemology will shape an ethical paradigm as well.

For additional resources and biblical references
René Descartes: Meditations on First Philosophy, edited by John Cottingham, Cambridge University Press, 2013.
Augustine, Saint. *The City of God, Books XVII-XXII,* Catholic University of America Press, 1954.
Kierkegaard, Søren. *Concluding Unscientific Postscript to Philosophical Fragments.* Princeton University Press, 1992.
Heidegger, Martin. *Being and Time.* HarperPerennial/Modern Thought, 2008.

List of Figures
Fig. 3. Class discussion of *epistemology.*

Works cited
Descartes René, and Mike Moriarty. *Meditations on First Philosophy: With Selections from the Objections and Replies.* Oxford U P, 2008.
Sayre-McCord, Geoff. "Metaethics." *The Stanford Encyclopedia of Philosophy.* Spring 2012 ed., edited by Edward N. Zalta, www.plato.stanford.edu/ar-chives/spr2012/entries/metaethics/
Redding, Paul, "Georg Wilhelm Friedrich Hegel." *The Stanford Encyclopedia of Philosophy.* Spring 2020 ed., edited by Edward N. Zalta, www.plato.stanford.edu/archives/spr2020/entries/hegel/

NORMATIVE ETHICS   *II.B*

Ethics is a subcategory of philosophy and being a philosophic discipline, definitions are very important. Take for example the word *good.* This is another exercise I like to do the first day of my Ethics class. I simply ask my students, "How would you define the word *good*?" At first the students are usually taken back on how difficult it is to define such a common word. We use the word *good* all the time in our daily conversations, but it is rare that someone asks us to actually define what *good* means. What is interesting about the word *good* is that depending on how you define it, it becomes predictive of the type of ethical theory you will embrace. Let me give some common examples of how my students will often try and define the word *good:*

Good = pleasure
Good = self interest
Good = what your momma says (or the norms, values and ideals of your culture)
Good = God's will
Good = aligns with God's order and reason
Good = the most happiness for most people
Good = what is in accordance with reason
Good = well balanced or proportioned
Good = what is caring or loving
Good = positive experiences
Good = following the way of nature
Good = social harmony

Figure 4. Good equals ___.

Personally, I believe *Good,* not only referring to the objective construct, but also the absolute ideal, is synonymous with "the *True* and the *Beautiful*," referring to that which is the perception of ideals that is only held by God. But if I had to define it separately, I would probably say, that *good* is that which is complete, perfect, whole without blemish, without limit, or in other words God. Yet, even the word *Good* as I have defined it seems to fall short of what I mean by God, but that is the topic for another study. Let's go back to the above list that my students have generated over the years and see how it corresponds to some of the major ethical theories that have been developed by some of the brightest philosophic minds in history:

Student's description of Good	Major Ethical Theories
Good = pleasure	Hedonism
Good = self-interest	Egoism
Good = what culture says, or your momma says	Ethical Relativism
Good = God's will	Divine Command Theory
Good = aligns with God's order and reason	Natural Law Theory
Good = the most happiness for most people	Utilitarianism
Good = what is in accordance with reason	Kantian Ethics
Good = well balanced or proportioned	Aristotle's Virtue Ethics
Good = what is caring or loving	Ethics of Care
Good = positive experiences	Existential Ethics
Good = following the Way of nature	Taoist Ethics
Good = social harmony	Confucian Ethics

Figure 5. Good corresponding to various ethical theories.

Normative ethics are formed by taking one's beliefs on *metaethics* and formulating them into theories of right conduct. The above list is an adequate example of the variety of ethical theories that have been produced as a result of different presuppositions on the nature of ethics in general. Normative ethics can be divided into three broad categories: Teleological (consequential or end based) Ethics, Deontological (duty and intention based) Ethics, and Virtue (character based) Ethics. These categories will be further addressed and discussed in detail later. There are also theories that combine character, intention, and outcomes. And these will also be looked at under hybrid or post-modern ethical theories.

II.C APPLIED ETHICS

Applied ethics—which when used personally, we will call morality—is the pragmatic and practical use of ethics. Applied ethics can be coupled with other disciplines and produce a variety of sub-topics and specific issues where one evaluates right and wrong actions based on their ethical theory. For example, we could study applied ethics in all human endeavors: business ethics, medical ethics, counseling ethics, ecological ethics, bio-tech ethics, sports ethics, social and political ethics, and academic ethics. Then in each of these disciplines you could discuss even more specific topics. For example, under medical ethics topics such as abortion, euthanasia, stem cell research, and a vast array of bio-medical issues can be addressed. Social and political ethics could deal with topics such as war, capital punishment, civil disobedience, equality, and freedom. Applied ethics could also be used in determining what would be right conduct in a wide variety of worldviews, occupations, organizations and creeds. For example, we could have Christian ethics, secular humanist ethics, Native American ethics, Boy Scout ethics, forestry ethics, mining ethics, and parenting ethics.

Hopefully, by seeing what ethics are and how they can be applied across the entire spectrum of human endeavors, we can see the importance of studying ethics. Not as just an abstract ivory tower discipline, but also as a real-life tool to help us navigate the various conflicts and dilemmas that face us on our human journeys. Perhaps studying this text will encourage us to each evaluate our own ethical beliefs and to know what we believe and why. Many people around us go through life with a type of inherited ethic that they receive from their parents, schools, church, or society without evaluating such beliefs.

As we embark on this journey, my encouragement to each of you would be to think about how you determine right and wrong behavior, how would you define the word *good*, and how will you apply what you believe to be right to your daily life. In many ways, this is one of the most difficult, but also one of the most important of human endeavors. It will require you to do a great deal of honest introspection, but also to be able to observe yourself in the context of your place and time as well as the many outside influences that have affected your thought process. I do not expect everyone to arrive at the same ethical conclusions since living out personal ethics is a whole different battle. Yet, this study and opportunity for introspection will at least let you know why you believe what you believe and hopefully, have a greater understanding of others who happen to have a different ethic than you.

NORMATIVE ETHICAL THEORIES *III*

Normative ethical theories can usually be placed within two broad categories. These are known as teleological or consequentialist theories as opposed to deontological theories. There is also a branch of ethics that deals primarily with virtue—or character development—which can have elements of both teleological and deontological type theories. This hybridization is also one of the earmarks of many postmodern types of ethics which reject the "either/or" approach to right conduct. As we saw under *metaethics*, ethical theories can also be categorized as absolute, or relative which in many ways correspond to the deontological and teleological type theories. Absolute or universal type ethical theories believe that there is an objective and authoritative standard for right conduct which is universal in that it applies to all people in all places at all times. Relativistic type theories believe right and wrong conduct is largely determined by place, time, and circumstance. It is more subjective and leaves room for different people or cultures to have different values in different places and times. There are also many gradations or hybridizations between these major approaches to ethics and these will be discussed under "Hybrid and/or Existential Postmodern Ethics."

TELEOLOGICAL ETHICS (RELATIVISTIC AND CONSEQUENTIAL BASED) *III.A*

Teleological ethics is based in relativistic and consequential values. Teleological ethics—the term *teleological* comes from the Greek words: *telos* (end) and *logos* (science); this theory of ethics is based on outcomes and end results rather than intention. Teleological ethics are also known as consequentialism because it is the consequences of your actions which determine whether or not your action was good or bad. This is an ends-based category of ethical theories since it looks at the net results of one's actions to determine moral worth, rather than the actions themselves. The most well-known consequential ethical theory is Utilitarianism which will be further examined when we address the ethical theories in detail.

III.B DEONTOLOGICAL ETHICS (INTENTION AND DUTY BASED)

Deontological ethics are based on intention and duty values. Deontological ethics and the study of deontology is from the Greek words: *deon* (duty) and *logos* (science). This means there are absolute standards of conduct, regardless of the situation. Intention takes primacy over outcomes. It is typical to see commands and prohibitions in deontological theories which prescribe specific behaviors for specific activities. Of the various deontological ethical theories, Kantian ethics is one of the paramount examples and will also be further discussed later.

For additional resources and biblical references
Alexander, Larry and Moore, Michael, "Deontological Ethics", *The Stanford Encyclopedia of Philosophy*. Winter 2012 ed., edited by Edward N. Zalta, www. plato.stanford.edu/archives/win2012/entries/ethics-deontological.

III.C VIRTUE ETHICS (CHARACTER BASED)

Virtue ethics are based on character values. Unlike deontology which is concerned with intention and teleological which is concerned with consequences, virtue ethics are derived from one's character. The focus is on developing a strong character. It is similar to the analogy that "a good tree brings forth good fruit, and a corrupt tree brings forth corrupt fruit;" so, the goal is to produce good trees. It is not that virtue ethics are not concerned with intentions or outcomes, but the primary concern is with the individual. Aristotle is the major proponent of virtue ethics which will also be further discussed in the section on ethical theories.

For additional resources and biblical references
Hursthouse, Rosalind, "Virtue Ethics." *The Stanford Encyclopedia of Philosophy*. Summer 2012 ed., edited by Edward N. Zalta, www.plato.stanford.edu/ archives/sum2012/entries/ethics-virtue/.

HYBRID ETHICS (EXISTENTIAL POSTMODERN ETHICS)

Hybrid, or postmodern ethics as I prefer to call them, are not to be found in any traditional study of ethics, but I think is important to include this category here. Over the course of my teaching career, I have noticed an interesting trend regarding my students and their view of ethics. When I first began teaching, my students were almost uniformly Divine Command Theorists to one degree or another. This uniformity was not surprising due to the fact that I teach at a Christian college which requires a statement of faith and agreement to a community doctrinal statement in order to be enrolled—some of the major tenants of this doctrinal statement regard the person and nature of God, as well as the inerrancy, inspiration, and authority of the Bible as God's Word. Over the past couple of decades, I have noticed a rejection of systems and dogmatic points of view. This has corresponded to the general trend in late twentieth and early twenty-first century America in which postmodern critiques of metanarratives have extended to a critique of *metaethics*. I suppose what did surprise me was that this trend was also happening at my private college and not just in American society at large. Yet, the thorough discussion of postmodernism and existentialism will be discussed later.

MAJOR WESTERN NORMATIVE ETHICAL THEORIES

EGOISM, HEDONISM, AND ASCETICISM

Egoism is one of the most basic of all ethical theories. It is centered on the idea of self-interest and that the good of the self is its overriding guideline: "What's good for me is good, and what's bad for me is bad." Selfishness and self-interest are synonyms. Altruism, doing good without ulterior motive, is a myth.

There are two main divisions of egoism. The first is psychological egoism which claims that all humans operate out of a sense of self-interest; this spans from self-preservation to self-realization with self at every step in-between. Maslow's Hierarchy of Needs is based on this premise (see *Figure 6*). Additionally, Freud talked about the difference between the id, the ego, and the superego. From this perspective, ego attempts to rule between the impulses from the depths while values and expectations are imposed from the outside. We see the world through our own perspectives—the self, the me, the mine, the I is the center of our universe.

Maslow's Hierarchy of Needs

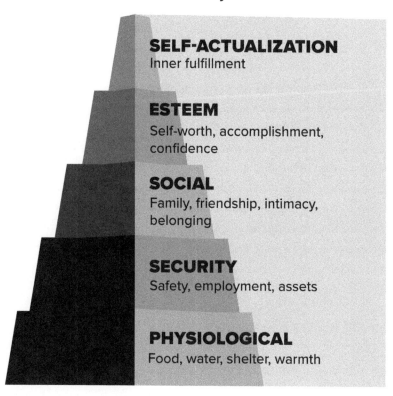

SELF-ACTUALIZATION
Inner fulfillment

ESTEEM
Self-worth, accomplishment, confidence

SOCIAL
Family, friendship, intimacy, belonging

SECURITY
Safety, employment, assets

PHYSIOLOGICAL
Food, water, shelter, warmth

Figure 6. Maslow's Hierarchy of Needs.

Ethical egoism was developed out of these psychological foundations. If this is how we are psychologically wired, then we shouldn't feel guilt or shame in acting on these impulses. This does not mean that we cannot be concerned and aid in the interest of others, but that the final result must be some benefit for oneself.

Egoism also has degrees of severity. The universal egoist believes that everyone is out for their own best interests. It's a "dog eat dog" world with the "survival of the fittest." In a world where it is "eat or be eaten," we must always be on our guard against others. This does not mean we cannot help or collaborate, but each should realize that everyone is doing what they think is best for themselves. In private personal egoism, the egoist pretends to be an altruist on the outside while practicing egoism internally. Through this mindset, the personal private egoist can encourage others to engage in giving behavior while they reap all the rewards of others helping them without the obligation of reciprocation. The final degree of egoism is megalomania, also known as an egomaniac. These people do not only believe in looking out for their own best interests, but they believe everyone else should be looking out for their best interests as well. This type of egoism is usually found in adolescent teens, petty tyrants and dictators. Philosophical support for this theory can be found in Plato's "Myth of Gyges" and in the writings of Ayn Rand. Egoism boils down to "what is good for me is good and what is bad for me is bad."

HEDONISM

Hedonism, also known as Epicureanism, was developed by the Greek philosopher Epicurus in the third and fourth century BCE. Epicurus was a philosophic materialist (believes only matter exists), so his philosophy was centered on the here and now. He had no hopes or fears regarding an afterlife, so no promise of rewards or fear of punishment effected his judgement regarding ethics and morality. He believed ethics could be evaluated solely on the criteria of pleasure. For Epicurus, the absence of pain, both physical and mental, was the right way to live. In other words, for the hedonist, pleasure equals good and pain equals evil.

Epicurus divided pleasures up into two main categories, natural and unnatural pleasure.

Natural pleasure would include things like food, clothing, shelter, sex, and rest. Unnatural pleasure would be things like fast cars, big screen televisions, or any non-natural object or activity. He also divided natural pleasures into two categories: natural necessary and natural unnecessary pleasures. Natural necessary pleasures would include food, drink, and rest but not sex. Now one may argue that sex is natural and necessary for the perpetuation of humanity and it certainly can be pleasurable. Epicurus, however, believed that there were plenty of people who would continue to have sexual relations even though in the end it would bring them more pain than pleasure. For example, as pleasurable as sexual congress may be, those fleeting moments of orgasmic pleasure usually require another human which means their basic other natural necessary pleasures must be met. In addition, we also now know how babies are made, and a few moments of pleasure could result in a lifetime of obligation and responsibility.

Even natural necessary pleasures, like food, clothing/shelter, and rest must be done in moderation if one wishes to maximize their pleasure. For example, if one keeps their food simple, both in cost and nutritional value, one would have to work very little to provide for their dietary needs. If, on the other hand one wants rich sauces, prime cuts of meat, or decadent desserts, there is both an economic, and health cost associated with these desires and tastes. Another example could be clothing, if one is content with secondhand clothes, one could outfit themselves quite cheaply. If, on the other hand, one needs name brands and the latest fashions, it will cost them in time of labor, and upkeep and cleaning of their fancy threads. The last example is shelter. For a relatively low cost, one could by a sleeping bag, fifty feet of cord and a twelve-foot by fifteen-foot tarp. In temperate climes this would be enough to protect one from the elements; however, if one owns or rents a home, the monthly cost could be tremendous and much of one's labor would go towards simply keeping a roof over one's head. Keep it natural, necessary, simple, and moderate; according to Epicurus this will allow time and energy for the greatest natural necessary pleasure of them all, repose.

Repose is almost unheard of in contemporary American society. In fact, many of us have either internal or external prompters to keep us from reposing. Repose in an Epicurean sense means to simply be; it is the mind and body at rest, not a rest due to tiredness or fatigue, but rather a being at rest. It is in such a disposition, that one can come up with great ethical theories, like hedonism. I do believe it is important to note that Epicurus lived for all intents and purposes a very frugal and almost ascetic life. Tradition claims that he died of malnutrition, so he might have overdone the simplicity part regarding food.

Now you may be thinking to yourself, "wait a second, I thought epicureanism hedonism was like, 'eat, drink, and be merry, for tomorrow we die?'" Well, that is because of the Romans. When Rome conquered Greece, they were impressed by many of the Greek philosophers including Epicurus. Some Romans reasoned if pleasure is good, then a lot of pleasure must be great. They didn't understand that too much pleasure could bring about a whole other set of pains. The Romans changed Epicurus' ethic from one of moderation and simplicity to one of excess and debauchery.

A CRITIQUE OF EGOISM - WHY SELF-INTEREST AND PLEASURE *IV.A.1* DO NOT PROVIDE TRUE MORALITY

While it may appear to be easy to be an Egoistic Hedonist, since all you have to worry about is what is in your own self-interest, seeking what is pleasurable and avoiding that which brings pain, this ethical theory is not without its flaws. Unfortunately, the egoist does not have the foresight or knowledge to know what that *good* is even when it only concerns themselves. Because you cannot see the future, you cannot always know what will be in your best interests. Since choices are made off of limited data or incorrect interpretations of perceptions, you often end up harming yourself through your choices even though such decisions were motivated by the self-seeking of pleasure. Humans do not know the future, and even though it seems like we are choosing what will produce pleasure and benefit to ourselves, we can easily achieve the opposite of our intentions.

It may be easy for you to think that according to Egoism, at least I know what pleasure is and it is easy to tell when something is bringing me enjoyment or causing me discomfort. This is true, but pleasure is a "fickle mistress" for it is subject to the law of diminishing returns. That which brings you pleasure today may not seem so pleasurable tomorrow, and that which once brought you excitement, wonder, and passion now is nothing but dust and ashes to your senses and your taste. The ultimate problem with pleasure being your guide is that pleasure always requires more to get the same pay off. The drug that got you high yesterday may only maintain normalcy tomorrow. Those images or actions that once aroused you sexually are now bland and unalluring. The thrill you received from walking the slackline in your backyard may one day require you to cable walk across a canyon to get the same adrenaline rush. Pleasure does not satisfy, but rather it becomes the tyrant that always demands more.

Perhaps you are not a crass hedonist, but rather are searching for the higher pleasures of the mind. You love to repose and think about the wonders and mysteries of life. You enjoy good literature, music, and drama. You are a connoisseur of the arts and nurture that which nourishes your soul rather than indulging in that which merely titillates your body. Yet, even these high-end type pleasures are not free from diminishing returns Even the highest and brightest thoughts will one day be brought low and find themselves shrouded in darkness. When the evil days come, you find no more pleasure in them and you return to the dust from whence you were taken. This is why Ecclesiastes declares that you are to "Remember your Creator in the days of your youth, before the days of trouble come and the years approach when you will say, 'I find no pleasure in them'" (12:1).

You who seek to find happiness and fulfillment by only seeking that which brings self-satisfaction will have limited pleasure indeed. For in light of the cosmos, you are but a speck. If all your ambitions, hopes, fears, and dreams are focused on the speck of yourselves, you are a miserable and isolated creature. Because you are only concerned about yourself, you will never know true love or friendship. You will be suspicious and cynical of others because you will project your own selfish motives and intentions onto others. You will be paranoid that others will find out your true motivations or become indifferent to the thoughts, cares, and concerns of those around you. Solitude will be your abode and loneliness your only companion. You will serve a petty god, whose name is self, and it will not be able to deliver you from your own self-created hell. This is why Egoism does not provide *true morality*.

IV.A.2 THE YANG TO THE YIN OF EGOISM: ASCETICISM - WHY SELF-DENIAL AND ASCETICISM DO NOT PROVIDE TRUE MORALITY

While the egoist seeks self-interest and pleasure to achieve the good life, the ascetic practices self-denial and mortification of the flesh. Although union with God is often the stated goal of the ascetic, it is easy for self-control and self-discipline to become their highest *good*. This confusion can arise because of the severity of their practice through which they hope to achieve freedom from carnal desires and egoistic ideas of self-worth or self-importance. Taste not, touch not, handle not become the mantra of the ascetic. The spirit is *good*, and the flesh is *evil*. By starving the flesh and beating it into submission, a person can release the spirit within. The physical world is a distraction to our true selves and will tempt us through our senses to get lost in the false promises that the world of transitory things has to offer.

The flesh is at war with the spirit, and the ascetic brings the focus of his will to tip the balance towards the spiritual. There are many practical practices the ascetic can incorporate into his struggle against the flesh— fasting, exposure to the elements, wearing coarse clothing if clothing is worn at all, hair shirts and a celise (device worn to discourages sexual urges) —can all help keep the flesh agitated and from feeling pleasure. Simple foods are eaten for sustenance not for pleasure; bland and bitter foods aid against the seduction of the sweet, salty, and spicy. Dry and lean wards off the richness of fat and flavor, and herbs and grains are preferred to meat, sauces and pastries. If it is pleasing to the touch, do not touch it. If it is pleasing to the eye, do not look at it. And if it is pleasing to the ear, do not listen to it—especially if it makes you tap your feet or move your body. If it is pleasing to the nostrils do not smell it, and if it is pleasing to the taste, do not eat it. In a nutshell, this mindset holds that if it feels good do not do it.

If the ascetic has stumbled and given into the flesh, various forms of penance can be performed to get him back on track. Self-flagellation is perhaps one of the most direct and impressionable tools at the ascetic's disposal. By physically beating the very flesh that betrayed the bearer through the urges, it brings a quick causal connection to body and soul of the consequences of sin. Some ascetics become masters of psychological flagellation where they beat themselves up emotionally and spiritually in psychic bouts of internal bloodletting. They will beat themselves raw in an attempt to show true contrition and to show that they are serious about dealing with their sins as a person would deal with a rabid dog in the yard.

In some cases, even amputation or castration may be reasonable. Such thinking stems from the biblical direction of Jesus in Matthew 5:29-30: "And if thy right eye offend thee, pluck it out, and cast it from thee: for it is profitable for thee that one of thy members should perish, and not that thy whole body should be cast into hell. And if thy right hand offend thee, cut it off, and cast it from thee: for it is profitable for thee that one of thy members should perish, and not that thy whole body should be cast into hell." Thus, these words were taken literally and seriously.

However, the problem with this type of self-denying morality is that the denial of the physical body is very appealing to our "soulish flesh." What I mean by soul is the mind, will, and emotions. It is the non-physical part of humans that makes even identical twins different from their genetically identical sibling. The soul is the seat of the temperament and personality; it is where the ego lives and what we are referring to when we say me, myself, or I. The reason asceticism is appealing to the ego is that it exalts it above the physical frame. All acts of self-control, discipline, and restraint serve to embolden and empower the ego within. What externally may appear as humility, contrition, and even self-abuse is really a mask for pride, self-sufficiency, and self-exaltation. Even if the ascetic succeeds in subduing his carnal desires and mortal frame by one's very success, one will have lost oneself to oneself.

It is an odd paradox indeed when that which looks like the antithesis to egotistical hedonism turns out to be its mirror image and twin. By denying the self, even when the intention was to be united with God, the self ends up being more its own god than it was in the beginning. Perhaps the worst thing possible for the ascetic is if he succeeds in his attempts at self-mortification and control. If it is the self that is the means of controlling the self, then it is the self that is the ultimate authority and power in a person's life. Egoism and asceticism are simply two names for the same path and this path leads to self-righteousness, the worst kind of moral failure.

Questions for further practice and understanding of this theory:
respond to the following scenarios as an Egoist or Hedonist
1. There is a life raft with seating for six people, but seven people need to be rescued, what do you do and why?

3. What are three strengths and three weakness of this theory?

4. Summarize and define this theory in a single phrase.

5. What is the difference between self-denial and denial of self?

For further additional explanation see the following video(s)

"Ethics Part 4: Egoism." *YouTube,* recorded and uploaded by Fred Blackburn. 15 Feb. 2020, https://youtu.be/MpmFISwG6o0

"Metaphysics and Philosophy of Origins Part 3: The Stoics, Epicureans, and Neoplatonists." *YouTube,* recorded and uploaded by Fred Blackburn. 5 Feb. 2020, https://youtu.be/ZQDer_oH964

For additional resources and biblical references

ECCLESIASTES 12 – see full chapter

Notes

The egoist convolutes self-interest with selfishness. These are not the same thing.

Pleasure = good, pain = evil.

Possessing natural, necessary pleasures such as food, shelter, and rest in moderation will produce less pain in one's life, resulting in more pleasure.

As a hedonism, long term pleasure must be considered and favored over short-term gratification.

While it may appear opposite of egoism or even hedonism, asceticism can actually be a cloaked form of both.

List of Figures

Fig 6. Maslow's Hierarchy of Needs.

Works cited

Timmons, Mark. "Conduct and Character: Readings in Moral Theory." *Cengage Learning,* 6th ed., 2011.

DIVINE COMMAND THEORY   *IV.B*

Divine command theory states that what God commands is *good* and what God prohibits is evil. This ethical theory can be found primarily among the Western religious traditions of Judaism, Christianity, and Islam, but also apply to polytheistic or pantheist religions where a person believes in a god or gods that gave instruction in right conduct. Divine command theory is based on the presuppositions that there is a God, God has revealed God's will, this will can be understood, and this will can be obeyed. Divine command theory is a very legalistic system: an eye for an eye, a blow for a blow, a life for a life. It is not about grace or mercy, but rather obedience and reaping what you have sown.

Divine command theorists will argue that if there is a God, then who better to make the rules governing human behavior than the one who actually created humans. Not only does God know best, but also knows the purpose and end result of humanity. God not only has the right and authority to determine ethical behavior, but God also has the power to enforce it, either in this life or in the next. Divine command theory is very good at answering the questions: "Why are we here?" "What is the meaning of life?" "What happens to us when we die?" Divine command theory is also very good at determining right conduct and giving explanations as to why the wicked may appear to prosper for a season, but it is the righteous who will ultimately be rewarded.

IV.B.1 A CRITIQUE OF DIVINE COMMAND THEORY - WHY ETHICS DERIVED FROM DIVINE COMMAND THEORY AND/OR LAW AND AUTHORITY DO NOT PROVIDE TRUE MORALITY

Divine Command Theory only works and is relevant if God is real. This theory is based on the assumption that God exists, and we can know his commands. Not only do we need to know that God exists, but also, we need to know which God is the true God. We must believe this God has revealed His will to humans and that we can interpret His will correctly. The greatest problem, however, is that even if there is a God and He had revealed His will and we have interpreted His will correctly: no one can live up to the perfect will of God. This leaves all people condemned, regardless of good intentions.

In practice, this theory seeks to use an authority to justify actions and behaviors. The inclination to use foundational authority (the God role in Divine Command Theory) to fix humanity and support ideas is a common underlying motive in American culture. The problem is that when one tries to impose an external authority, whether that be God or government, you are not producing morality, rather behavior modification through fear of punishment or hope of reward.

In the latter part of the twentieth century, many social and political organizations were formed in an attempt to stem the tide of moral decline in America. Such organizations sought to return the United States of America to what they believed were original, neglected biblical principles and Christian values. Many Christian organizations, which out of respect I shall not name, tried to revert a perceived moral degradation by glorifying and transforming religious practices and communities. Similarly, political figures, various Presidents and judicial courts especially, attempted to bring out change in society through the development of new programs and legislation, such as that which concerns abortion, euthanasia, stem cell research, biomedical issues, education, the LGBTQ+ community, marriage equality, gender roles and other issues religious practices. Yet morality cannot be legislated. Conflicting worldviews cannot become the same through authoritative direction. While these actions and organizations had good intentions and perhaps changed many people's lives, they are unable to actually change the heart of humanity within its brokenness.

Whether a person is progressive or traditional—a Biblical Christian or a secular humanist—every person has distinct beliefs. For example, one might believe in personhood rights for the unborn or the right of a woman to have control over her own reproduction. One may believe in heterosexual monogamous marriage or marriage equality, in creation or evolution, a class hierarchy or socialism, civil rights or slavery. Individuals will always possess unique views. Laws will come and go, but they will not change the human condition. One can externally impose all sorts of behavior modification upon people whether through punishment or reward. But once the positive or negative reinforcements are removed, so will be the behavior unless it is internalized. Additionally, in some cases people will comply with the laws of the land but will actively work to change them or choose not to follow them in their personal thoughts or actions. There have been many laws and institutionalized attempts to regulate, promote, or educate the populous to a particular point of view were ineffective, and numerous laws and social influences try to bring about change. Society cannot enact laws and expect people to internally conform to what is now the legal point of view.

Even though Divine Command Theory and Ethical Relativism (a theory to be discussed later), believe that ethics can be dictated by law, compliance or disregard of the law is not what provides *true* ethics or morality. Blind obedience to authority does not make a person a free moral agent, but rather a moral automaton who only acts within prescribed moral perimeters. Compliance with unjust laws is still participating in injustice, and obedience for the sake of hope of reward or fear of punishment makes a person a little more than a moral mercenary. When someone presents a better offer, such a person will change their ethic like a chameleon changes its color. Do we give moral accent to something because it is the law of the land, or because someone in authority told us it is the right thing to do? Or is there some other standard and guideline we use to evaluate the laws of the land or the commands of those in authority over us?

For example, in the Genesis account, Adam and Even lived without the law in freedom and innocence. They were, however, under the ultimate authority in the universe: The Creator. Because Adam and Even did not have the knowledge of good and evil, they had no code of ethics or standards for morality. In many ways, they were like the beasts of the field. However, they were under God's authority just as God had placed creation under the authority of man. Even with the ultimate authority in their lives, it still did not guarantee that Adam and Eve would comply with God's divine command. In fact, by God giving Adam and Eve a prohibition, it implies that they had the choice to disobey God's command. God's authority did not provide morality for Adam and Eve, because it was external to them. And with the prohibition, it awoke the temptation to disobey. The problem with authority-based ethics is that it can show the standard of right conduct whilst not enabling humanity to live up to it, so Divine Command Theory cannot provide *true* morality.

The Bible itself makes it apparent that Divine Command Theory falls short of offering righteousness before God. In Romans 4:13, Paul begins his talk about the law saying, "Because the law worketh wrath: for where no law is, there is no transgression." Additionally, in Romans 5:13, he says that sin was in the world, but without the law, sin is not imputed; also in verse 20, he adds that the law existed so that our shortcomings could be exposed, but where the offenses abounded, grace abounds more. In Galatians 3, Paul tells us why the law was given; the law showed humanity God's standard which is perfection. It also exposes our inability to live up to God's standard.

The law cannot justify us before God; not because the law is not just or holy, but because no man can keep the law. If the law could have provided life and justification, then Jesus would not have needed to suffer and die on the cross. The law was our teacher to show us that we could never live up to the standard of God's righteousness. What the law could not do, Christ would accomplish. The Law of Moses was never meant to save anyone, but rather to show the impossibility of keeping God's standard. It is strange that the law rather than making us good, rather provokes us to evil. Paul tells us in Romans 7 that the law is holy and *good*; it is us that are the problem. So, it is foolish to think that by keeping most of the law, we will be reconciled for God requires perfection.

Many people are looking for better laws or a better set of rules. Unfortunately, even if we had the perfect law, given by God almighty Himself, it would still not enable us to be righteous people. It seems to be a basic part of human nature, or perhaps it is our own ego. Either the law provokes us to rebellion and disobedience, or we think we can keep the law and it leads us to legalism and self-righteousness. Both reactions miss the mark and either show us our own depravity, or we delude ourselves into thinking we are actually good people and can keep the law. If we have a holy, perfect, righteous, infinite God, creating the standards for morality, we cannot keep it as fallen, imperfect, unrighteous, finite, creatures. Even though, Divine Command Theory theoretically could be the most superior of all the ethical theories, it's glaring weakness is that it is impossible to live in accordance with it. Therefore, Divine Command Theory cannot provide *true morality*.

Questions for further practice and understanding of this theory:
respond to the following scenarios as a Divine Command Theorist
1. There is a life raft with seating for six people, but seven people need to be

rescued, what do you do and why?

3. What are three strengths and three weakness of this theory?

4. Summarize and define this theory in a single phrase.

5. How do you know God's commands? And how do you know that your understanding is accurate?

<u>For further additional explanation see the following video(s)</u>
"Ethics Part 5: Divine Command Theory." YouTube, recorded and uploaded by Fred Blackburn. 7 Mar. 2020, https://youtu.be/GT6JICABGhQ

<u>For additional resources and biblical references</u>
GALATIANS 3:10-26

ROMANS 7:7-14 – "What shall we say then? Is the law sin? God forbid. Nay, I had not known sin, but by the law: for I had not known lust, except the law had said, Thou shalt not covet. But sin, taking occasion by the commandment, wrought in me all manner of concupiscence. For without the law sin was dead. For I was alive without the law once: but when the commandment came, sin revived, and I died. And the commandment, which was ordained to life, I found to be unto death. For sin, taking occasion by the commandment, deceived me, and by it slew me. Wherefore the law is holy, and the commandment holy, and just, and good. Was then that which is good made death unto me? God forbid. But sin, that it might appear sin, working death in me by that which is good; that sin by the commandment might become exceeding sinful. For we know that the law is spiritual: but I am carnal, sold under sin."
The Euthyphro dilemma – Plato poses the question: are things good because God declares them good? Or are things good in and of themselves apart from God and that is why he commands them? If the concept of good is separate from God, he is not absolute authority because He is conforming to a standard outside of Himself. On the other hand, if good is what God declares it to be, good and evil become arbitrary based on the commands of God. For example, in the Ten Commandments, we are told "Thou shalt not kill," but when Israel came into the promised land, they were commanded to not only kill the inhabitance but sometimes do worse to various peoples (Exodus 20:13, Numbers 39).

<u>Notes</u>
God's commands are good. God's prohibitions are evil.
How do you know that God exists?
How do you know which God/gods to obey?
How do you keep God's will?

Works cited

Timmons, Mark. "Conduct and Character: Readings in Moral Theory."
Cengage Learning, 6th ed., 2011.

VIRTUE ETHICS   *IV.C*

Aristotle developed his ethic based on the concept of an individual's character development. Ethics could be seen as a habituation or education in
right-thinking that would lead to right conduct. Rather than just looking
at duty and what is right like the deontologists or merely focusing on the
outcomes like the consequentialists, Aristotle incorporated both aspects
into his theory. According to his line of thought, a good person will do
good things, because those are the types of things good people do. How
do you make a person good? Aristotle believed that this could be done
through education. Aristotle like many of his Greek contemporaries believed knowledge was good and ignorance was evil. People only do evil
when they are ignorant of what they are actually doing.

In addition to education and placing a high value on knowledge,
Aristotle advocated *arete* which means *excellence* in Greek. In other words,
be excellent in all that you do. This attitude and standard would apply to
everything from scrubbing toilets to being the President. Be excellent in
little things and you will be excellent in big things. Aristotle's second principle was *eudaimonia;* this was the Greek word for happiness or wellbeing. It
literally means to be indwelt by a *good* spirit and is probably best translated
as deep contentment or human flourishing. For Aristotle, the end of man
was happiness; however, it is not a "yuppie" type of circumstantial happiness, but rather a deep-seated joy and wellbeing that could be achieved by
having a well-balanced or well-proportioned life.

How does one have a well-balanced or well-proportioned life?
Through avoiding the extremes of excess or deficiency one could hope
to achieve what is called the "golden mean." The Greeks discovered the
beauty of the golden mean and applied it to architecture and art. It was
observed that asymmetry was actually more beautiful than symmetry in

many instances since it provided a dynamic rather than a static element to art. If a rectangle is divided into thirds and then into thirds again and so on, we can chart out the golden mean and see the pattern emerge of the Fibonacci Sequence which is based on the number *Phi* (1.618 and so on).

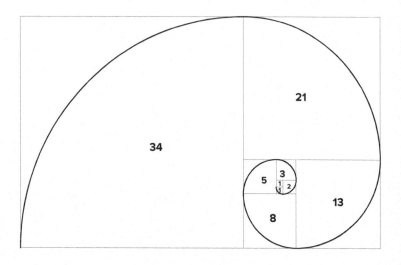

Figure 7. Aristotle's Golden Mean as seen in the Fibonacci Sequence.

Aristotle used this principle to plot out a well-balanced mean between two extreme positions. This does not mean that he was looking for the center or half-way point, but rather a well-proportioned balance (see *Figure 8*). For example, excess of fear would be called cowardice whereas a

Action or Feeling	Deficiency	Mean	Excess
Fear & Confidence	Cowardice	Courage	Rashness
Pleasure & Pain	Insensibility	Temperance	Licentiousness
Anger	Lack of Spirit	Patience	Irascibility
Shame	Shamelessness	Modesty	Shyness
Justice	Injustice	Fairness	Undiscerning

Figure 8. Application of the Golden Mean.

deficiency of fear would be called foolhardy. A balance between cowardice and foolhardiness would be courage; a courageous life is a life of balance between two extremes.

A CRITIQUE OF ARISTOTLE'S ETHIC – WHY VIRTUE, KNOWLEDGE, EXCELLENCE AND A WELL-BALANCED LIFE DO NOT PROVIDE TRUE MORALITY

IV.C.1

The philosopher Aristotle had one of the keenest intellects known to man, and although he wrote on many topics, it was his view of ethics that impresses me the most. Aristotle developed what is known as Virtue Ethics. Unlike deontological ethical theories that are concerned with duty, honor, "doing what is right because it is right," or even teleological ethical theories which are more concerned with outcomes, Virtue Ethics are primarily concerned with the character of the individual involved in the decision-making process. Aristotle believed that knowledge was *good*, and ignorance was *evil*. Morality for Aristotle was a habituation of practice, and people could be taught how to think and act correctly. Aristotle put a premium on education and the mentoring of youth. Unlike the other ethical theories, Virtue Ethics is not so concerned about systems, rules, regulations, or projections on what the outcome may be. Instead it is about training a virtuous person, and just like a good tree will bear good fruit—a virtuous person will perform good deeds, regardless of the situation or moral dilemmas in which they may find themselves. Aristotle begins with knowledge but then adds to it *arête* (excellence). In other words, be excellent in all that you do. The end of ethics is to provide *eudemonia*, a happy well-balanced life that comes from avoiding extremes (see *Figure 8*).

While Aristotle's Virtue Ethics provides a strong basis for making informed, well-reasoned and well-balanced ethical decisions. Yet, for all its benefits it still does not escape the critique that comes with all reason-based forms of ethics (reason-based ethics will be critiqued later). Aristotle speaks of knowledge being *good* and ignorance being *evil*, yet he maintains that no one knowingly commits an evil act, but rather their act is done out of ignorance. If they really would have reasoned out their decision, then they would not have chosen poorly. This is a strong argument, but it reaches the level of the philosophical fallacy of non-falsifiability. For no matter what counter example, we give of someone willfully choosing an evil act, Aristotle could respond with, "well if they really, really knew all the facts, they would not have done this." On the one hand, this makes *good* synonymous with *knowledge* by definition. On the other hand, it implies that one can know all the facts before making a correct judgment. While there is not a severe problem with equating knowledge with *the good*, there are no humans with all knowledge of all things, so correct judgment cannot be made.

The idea of the end of ethics being a life of happiness or wellbeing is very appealing. Yet, this is dependent not only on having correct knowledge, but on being able to balance our choices between extremes. What is well balanced for one person could be quite extreme for another—this seems to make this theory rather relative in its application. If we apply the golden mean to practical moral dilemmas like, "what is a well-balanced use of the truth," or "what would be a well-balanced view on abortion, capital punishment, or civil disobedience. We can see that the outcomes might not be as generally agreed upon or practical as one would wish. If we are to be moderate in all things, wouldn't this apply to moderation itself? Someone with a strong intellect could easily reason a justification for just about any action, claiming it was done lacking knowledge and overall balance. If the action chosen indeed turns out to be an excess or deficient act, it can be claimed it was done out of ignorance and that our now corrected reason will do better next time. Unfortunately, some errors in judgment cannot be undone and what is accomplished under the guise of a well-proportioned life and a commitment to excellence, could in reality be the mechanizations of an evil genius. Aristotle would object on the grounds that an evil genius is an oxymoron, but I have already objected to Aristotle's objection, and it is for this reason that virtue, knowledge, excellence, and a well-proportioned life do not provide true morality.

Questions for further practice and understanding of this theory:
respond to the following scenarios in alignment with Virtue Ethics
1. There is a life raft with seating for six people, but seven people need to be rescued, what do you do and why?

3. What are three strengths and three weakness of this theory?

4. Summarize and define this theory in a single phrase.

5. Would Aristotle require us to be moderate even in moderation?

For further additional explanation see the following video(s)

"Ethics Part 11: Virtue Ethics Aristotle's Perfectionism." YouTube, recorded and uploaded by Fred Blackburn. 12 Sept. 2019, https://youtu.be/R8g-nuPTBRng

For additional resources and biblical references

Aristotle, et al. The Nicomachean Ethics. Oxford U P, 2009.

Notes

Knowledge is good. Ignorance is evil.

A well-balanced life is a happy life.

List of Figures

Fig. 7. Aristotle's Golden Mean as seen in the Fibonacci Sequence.

Fig. 8. Application of the Golden Mean.

Works cited

Timmons, Mark. "Conduct and Character: Readings in Moral Theory." Cengage Learning, 6th ed., 2011.

NATURAL LAW THEORY   *IV.D*

Saint Thomas Aquinas developed Natural Law Theory. It is based on the belief that there are "universal laws" given by God, under which we can discover natural laws through the use of human reason. Humans in turn will make civil laws to best live out the natural laws which have been established by God. The natural laws which Thomas Aquinas is talking about are not laws of nature, like the first and second Laws of Thermodynamics or principles like gravity or magnetism. In fact, these laws do not refer to how things are, but rather how things ought to be. He lists these natural laws as four rights or duties which are held by all human beings. These are followed by two qualifiers for when there arises a situation when these rights may come into conflict with one another:

Four Rights	
1.	The Right to self-preservation
2.	The Right to procreation
3.	The Right to education
4.	The Right to socialization
Two Qualifiers	
1.	Forfeiture - When a person's rights are threatened or violated, the offender forfeits their own right that they are threatening or violating in another.
2.	Double Effect - If in order to good, an unintended evil is also accomplished, you may proceed if it is of a serious enough situation.

Figure 9. Thomas Aquinas's Natural Law Theory.

The key to the double effect principle is that sometimes unintended bad actions accompany good actions. According to this theory, one cannot intentionally commit an evil action in the hopes of accomplishing good.

The four rights and two qualifiers of Thomas Aquinas are a result of tapping into the scholastic philosophical idea of *synderesis*. *Synderesis* is the idea that part of what it means to be human is to be made in the image of God, and part of this divine image is to be created with reason. The highest aspects of reason can access *a priori* types of truth. Examples would include such ideas as *the law of non-contradiction* (something cannot be one thing and another at the same time) and "the whole is greater than its parts" and even the concept of *the Good*. Aquinas based much of his reasoning on this topic from a Christian interpretation of Aristotle's Nicomachean ethic.

It is incredible to think that intelligent beings such as this did not recognize the limitations of their own reason and intelligence. Natural Law Theory has all the strengths and weaknesses of Divine Command Theory as well as the strengths and weaknesses that accompany reason-based ethics. The critique of this theory will be discussed at length within the other critiques on Divine Command Theory and reason-based ethical theories such as Kantian Ethics, thus exposing how Natural Law Theory cannot provide true morality.

Questions for further practice and understanding of this theory:
respond to the following scenarios as a Natural Law Theorist
1. There is a life raft with seating for six people, but seven people need to be rescued, what do you do and why?
3. What are three strengths and three weakness of this theory?
4. Summarize and define this theory in a single phrase.
5. What are the four natural rights and two qualifiers of Natural Law Theory?

For further additional explanation see the following video(s)
"Ethics Part 7: Natural Law Theory." YouTube, recorded and uploaded by Fred Blackburn. 10 Sept. 2019, https://youtu.be/9tVlRxd7JTQ

Notes
God's commands plus human reason determines right conduct.
Natural Law theory has all the strengths and weaknesses of Divine Command Theory along with all the strengths and weakness of reason-based theories.

List of Figures
Fig. 9. Thomas Aquinas's Natural Law Theory.

Works cited
Timmons, Mark. "Conduct and Character: Readings in Moral Theory." Cengage Learning, 6th ed., 2011.

KANTIAN ETHICS   *IV.E*

Emmanuel Kant was seeking for a universal ethic that would transcend religious dogma, opinion, external rules, and cultural dictates. His solution was his ethical theory on pure reason: the only thing that Kant saw as *good* was a good will. In Kantian terminology, *good* will equals *pure practical reason*. This foundation led to his categorical imperative which states: "to will that your maxim be made a universal law." In other words, is it logical to have all people in all places at all times do what you are about to do? If the answer is yes, then you may proceed with your action in accord with reason. If the answer is no, then one must not proceed. In addition to this reason based ethical foundation, Kant added, "the Kingdom of Ends." The Kingdom of Ends states that all sentient beings should be treated as an end unto themselves never as merely a means to an end. In other words, do not use people; treat them as subjects with inherent worth, never as mere objects to be used.

IV.E.1 A CRITIQUE OF KANTIAN ETHICS (AS WELL AS NATURAL LAW THEORY) - WHY REASON DOES NOT PROVIDE TRUE MORALITY

Reason-based ethical theories have many advantages over theories based on self-interest, cultural norms, pleasure, or authority. Human reason is one of the major components that separates us from animals, and the application of human reason to the field of ethics has produced some of the greatest ethical theories known to man. Natural Law Theory combines human reason with Divine Command Theory, Utilitarianism combines human reason with pragmatism and usefulness, Aristotle's "golden mean" uses reason to find a well-balanced life, and Kantian ethics applies reason as a stand-alone guide for right conduct. Reason has been applied to teleological, deontological, and virtue ethics. Yet, all of these ethical theories encounter the same problem, the problem being, "how do we know if we are reasoning correctly?"

Saint Thomas Aquinas in his Natural Law Theory believed that there are universal laws given by God under which we can discover natural laws through the use of human reason. Humans in turn make civil laws to best live out the natural laws which have been established by God. The natural laws which Thomas Aquinas is talking about are not laws of nature, like the first and second Laws of Thermodynamics, or principles like gravity or magnetism, in fact these laws do not refer to how things are, but rather how things ought to be. He lists these natural laws as four rights or duties, which are held by all human beings, and these are followed by two qualifiers if there arises a situation when these rights may come into conflict with one another (see *Figure 7*).

Reason-based ethics come in both secular and sacred forms. Aquinas blends the sacred with the secular in his reason-based interpretation and application of Aristotle's ethic. Aristotle along with other Greeks such as Plato, Anaxagoras, Heraclitus, and Zeno of Citium, the founder of Stoicism, saw different aspects of reason within human beings. *Nous* (often translated as mind or intuition) was the highest type of reason and could allow us to think in terms of first principles or in the case of Plato to be able to conceptualize ideal forms and ideas such as *the Good*. The *logos* (often translated as reason, or practical thinking) was the use of logic and the practical application of knowledge. *Synderesis* was the bridge between these two types of knowing or reasoning. Aquinas and Aristotle both attempted to apply a universal standard for the correct conceptualization and application of reason, yet both of them came from very monistic (one or singular) type cultures. The lack of plurality, cultural blindness, or religious presuppositions would affect the way that Aristotle and Aquinas would both render reason. This critique applies to the monoculturalism and intellectual rarefication of Immanuel Kant.

Kant was seeking for a universal ethic that would transcend religious dogma, personal taste or opinion, external rules and cultural dictates. His solution was to build his ethical theory on pure reason, and the only thing that Kant saw as *good*, in and of itself, was a "good will." In Kantian terminology, good will equates pure practical reason. This foundation led to his categorical imperative, which states: "act as if the maxim of your action were to become by your will a universal law of nature;" I often abbreviate it as: to will that your maxim be made a universal law (Kant 31). In other words, "is it logical to have all people, in all places, at all times, to do, what you are about to do?" If the answer is yes, then one may proceed with one's actions in accord with reason. If the answer is no, then one must not proceed. This in conjunction with the Kingdom of Ends, the prohibition against using others like objects, forms Kant's ethic.

Kant, like Aristotle and Aquinas before him, put a huge amount of stock into the development of correct thinking and the proper application of reason to the topic of ethics and morality. Yet, these great thinkers did not always come to the same conclusions on how reason should be correctly applied to specific ethical dilemmas. "Why would these great thinkers come to different conclusions regarding right conduct, if they all claimed that reason was their guide?" One could argue that Aquinas' reason was tainted by his medieval presuppositions, concerning God and the Catholic Faith, or that Aristotle's reason was skewed by his ethnocentrism and classism. While claiming to have a purely reason-based ethic, Kant comes curiously close to mimicking the same conclusions of his Christian pietistic upbringing even though he does not invoke the belief or will of God into his ethical system.

Jeremy Bentham and John Stuart Mill also attempted a reason-based ethic, founded on pragmatism and utility. They wanted an ethic that was not prejudiced by time, place, politics, or religion. These thinkers were looking for a well-reasoned projection of what actions would provide the greatest *good* (pleasure), to the greatest number of people. Efficiency and efficacy became qualifiers, as well as the extent, duration, and quality of the pleasure that could be achieved through calculations of potential outcomes. This reason-based theory later became associated with consequentialism which will be discussed and critiqued later in this book in the section on Utilitarian ethics.

In contrast to the efforts to control one's reason, the Stoics sought to bring their emotions under the self-control and discipline of reason. It is this philosophy that is modeled by the fictitious race of Vulcans in the science fiction series, Star Trek. Spock was the half human half Vulcan who struggled to have logic and reason be his supreme guides for all of his behaviors. Unfortunately, for us mere humans our emotions are rapid and raw and often are in full effect before our reason has a chance to catch up and calm things down. Perhaps persons with a more introspective temperament and have well-disciplined minds can keep the majority of their emotions in check and can carefully craft their decisions based on pure reason. This, however, does not seem to be the case for most mere mortals, and it is often after the initial emotional response that we have time to consider what we have done. Yet, even if we were the ideal Stoic or the perfect Kantian, even if we claimed to be able to see the universal law of God, and even if our reasoning was pure and our logic was flawless, it still would not guarantee that we arrived at true conclusions. Reason and logic are limited to the truth of their a priori presuppositions. In other words, the premises we start with, such as *the Good*, cause and effect, freewill, sovereignty, non-contradiction, eternality, or perfection must be true in order for our conclusions to be true. If we have a flawed understanding of these foundational ideas and concepts, it taints the outcome of even the greatest reason or the most diligent logic. This is later be discussed in the critique on why conscience does not provide true morality. Because our *nous* (mind) has been darkened, our premises are flawed. And the conclusions we come to will be relative to our epistemic point of view. This results in subjective judgments rather than a universal apprehension of truth.

Rationalization (the misuse of reason) is the great flaw and weakness of all reason based ethical theories. Individuals given to an analytical mindset can literally justify anything if given enough time and motivation to massage any given issue. Emotions at least are honest even though they may seem raw or out of control. They appear and dissipate as quickly as a summer thunderstorm. Reason, on the other hand, is much steadier and plodding. Even when our reason may initially recoil or sound a warning to our wandering desire, it can all too easily be impressed into the very service of that desire. What may begin as an obvious black or white issue can over time be muddied into whatever shade of gray is needed to justify one's actions and to keep the conscience at bay. The reason of the Stoics permitted slavery and suicide. The reason of Aristotle allowed for the subjection of non-Greeks, promoted classism over equality, and opted for political stratification over democracy. The reason of Aquinas allowed for maiming or killing if it was an unintended consequence of seeking something of consequence in accordance with natural law. The reason of Kant, while almost unassailable in the "Ivory Tower of Platonic Ideals," breaks down when it is applied to practical situations where one's personal honor and integrity take precedence over the preservation of human life or human suffering. The reason of the utilitarian and consequentialist allows for torture and the mass extermination of civilian populations if the end results produce more pleasure than pain. Human reason is broken because of sin; even our loftiest thoughts are debased before God "Because the foolishness of God is wiser than men; and the weakness of God is stronger than men" (1 Corinthians 1:25). Each and every one of us is susceptible to the same twisting of reason to provide a justification for our own desires—a rationalization to allow us to live with the poor conduct we chose for our lives. This is why reason and reason-based ethical theories do not provide true morality.

<u>Questions for further practice and understanding of this theory:</u>
respond to the following scenarios in alignment with Kantian Ethics
1. There is a life raft with seating for six people, but seven people need to be rescued, what do you do and why?
3. What are three strengths and three weakness of this theory?
4. Summarize and define this theory in a single phrase.
5. How does Kant know he is reasoning correctly?

<u>For further additional explanation see the following video(s)</u>
"Ethics Part 9: Kantian Ethics." YouTube, recorded and uploaded by Fred Blackburn. 11 Sept. 2019, https://youtu.be/luC321Gcfsc

<u>For additional references and biblical references</u>
1 CORINTHIANS 1:18-31 – "For the preaching of the cross is to them that perish foolishness; but unto us which are saved it is the power of God. For it is written, I will destroy the wisdom of the wise, and will bring to nothing the understanding of the prudent. Where [is] the wise? where [is] the scribe? where [is] the disputer of this world? hath not God made foolish the wisdom of this world? For after that in the wisdom of God the world by wisdom knew not God, it pleased God by the foolishness of preaching to save them that believe. For the Jews require a sign, and the Greeks seek after wisdom: But we preach Christ crucified, unto the Jews a stumblingblock, and unto the Greeks foolishness; But unto them which are called, both Jews and Greeks, Christ the power of God, and the wisdom of God. Because the foolishness of God is wiser than men; and the weakness of God is stronger than men. For ye see your calling, brethren, how that not many wise men after the flesh, not many mighty, not many noble, [are called]: But God hath chosen the foolish things of the world to confound the wise; and God hath chosen the weak things of the world to confound the things which are mighty; And base things of the world, and things which are despised, hath God chosen, [yea], and things which are not, to bring to nought things that are: That no flesh should glory in his presence. But of him are ye in Christ Jesus, who of God is made unto us wisdom, and righteousness, and sanctification, and redemption: That, according as it is written, He that glorieth, let him glory in the Lord."

<u>Notes</u>
Good is that which is in accord with reason. Evil results from ignorance.
What is the Kingdom of Ends?
Kant's theory is appealing to many for his lack of culture or religion-based value system, but his own ethnocentricity blinded him to the way in which

others thought, so it falls short in its own efforts to establish universal reason. Why did Kant think all the previous moral theories failed?

Works cited

Kant, Immanuel. *Groundwork of Metaphysics of Morals.* Cambridge U P, 1998., https://cpb-us-w2.wpmucdn.com/blog.nus.edu.sg/dist/c/1868/files/2012/12/Kant-Groundwork-ng0pby.pdf

Timmons, Mark. "Conduct and Character: Readings in Moral Theory." Cengage Learning, 6th ed., 2011.

UTILITARIANISM AND CONSEQUENTIALISM   *IV.F*

Teleological Ethical Theories determine what is *good* based on the outcomes, consequences, or results of actions. *Good* is defined by these types of theories as that which maximizes usefulness, happiness, and pleasure. Two of the major theories in this category are Utilitarianism with its emphasis on utility or usefulness and Consequentialism with its emphasis on end results. Teleological slogans would include statements such as "the greatest *good* for the greatest number," "the ends justify the means," "actions speak louder than words," and "the road to hell is paved with good intentions." Teleological theories are also highly pragmatic, applicable, and adaptable. Efficacy and efficiency weigh heavily when making moral choices; for example, "what works best, costs cheapest, and lasts longest," would hold great weight for this type of ethic.

One of the most well-known teleological theories is called Utilitarianism and was developed by Jeremy Bentham and John Stuart Mill. It was an attempt to come up with an ethical theory based on reason rather than on culture, tradition, authority, or some type of mystical instruction. Jeremy Bentham presented a hedonic form of Utilitarianism; in other words, he was looking for an ethic that would provide the greatest amount of pleasure for the greatest amount of people. Bentham even developed what he called *hedonic calculus* to try and determine which actions would maximize pleasure and minimize pain. It is often called *social hedonism* for unlike the egoistic hedonist who is simply looking out for their own pleasure, Utilitarianism is looking out for the pleasure of the many.

John Stuart Mill contributed to the theory of Utilitarianism by addressing its critics. He addressed the criticism that an ethic based on pleasure was perhaps suitable for beasts but not for man. Mill responded that utilitarianism seeks higher pleasures rather than base pleasures, so it was perfectly suited for human beings. Another critique argued that the variables in determining what were in humans' bests interests were beyond the ability of humans to predict. The final critique was that we often must make quick moral decisions and do not have the time to work through all the variables involved in conducting a hedonic calculation. For the last two critiques, Mill believed the detractors did not fully understand how the principles of utility work. There are also major divisions in a utilitarian approach to ethics, and these can be divided into act-based and rule-based Utilitarianism.

In act-based Utilitarianism, a person simply chooses the action—which they believe based on calculations—will produce the greatest pleasure and avoid the greatest amount of pain. In rule-based utilitarianism, certain rules are put into place based on the principle of utility—to help avoid situational actions which may seem to produce greater happiness, but reason and prior actions have taught us that certain actions must be avoided because they generally produce more pain than pleasure. For example, one could reason that to murder, rape, or torture could produce good in certain circumstances, yet based on the overall effect of murder, rape, and torture, these actions would be prohibited under rule-based Utilitarianism. Not because they are wrong in and of themselves, but because the consequences of these actions have been demonstrated to bring about more suffering and pain than pleasure and happiness.

IV.F.1 A CRITIQUE OF UTILITARIANISM - WHY ETHICS DERIVED FROM PRAGMATISM, UTILITY OR CONSEQUENTIALISM DO NOT PROVIDE TRUE MORALITY

Teleological arguments by their very nature are pragmatic, this is part of why utilitarianism is so popular, is because it works. When something no longer works, we change our approach; unfortunately, some actions and decisions cannot be undone or the trajectory amended. With consequentialist type theories, we do not know whether an action is good or evil until all the results are examined. Throughout our society, there are numerous instances in which humanity applies and practices Utilitarianism where it appears advantageous.

The development of utilitarian ethics followed the development of "Democratic Political Philosophies." In many ways, utilitarianism is the perfect ethical companion for a democracy. If right conduct is determined by that which produces the greatest good or happiness for the greatest number, then a democracy—in which individuals get to cast their vote for what they believe will provide them the greatest good or happiness— seems to ensure that the majority of the people will be happy with the outcome. The United States tries to mitigate the potential tyranny of the majority over the minority by providing a basic set of individual rules or rights which could not be trampled on by the majority decision. Many of these rights and rules were taken from the political philosophy of John Locke who preceded Bentham by a little over a hundred years. Americans are enamored by utilitarian thinking, and for much of the population, it is a national norm and value compatible with their democratic ideals. This utilitarian-type thinking is very pragmatic and applicable to a host of social, political, environmental, economic, and ethical issues. The use of utilitarian-type ethical thinking crosses ethnic, racial, class, political, and religious lines and has become the default ethical system for many Americans.

One public utilitarian justification that I found striking was in regard to the atomic bombing of Hiroshima and Nagasaki. I was in my seventh grade U.S. history class, and the class was discussing World War II. My history teacher explained to us, students, that the dropping of the atomic bombs on Japanese cities was justifiable because it brought a quick end to the war. If the war had continued and the U.S. was forced to mount a conventional invasion of Japan, it would have cost thousands more American and even Japanese lives. While the dropping of atomic bombs is horrific, but it was justified because the good it produced was greater than the evil. In retrospect, it was shocking how reasonable this explanation seemed; So much so, that I did not really give it another thought until I was studying history again in college and gained a more precise understanding of what atomic bombs were and the affect they have on human beings. There was far more to the story of Japan's surrender than I was told about in high school, and the atomic bombs were meant as a message to the Soviets as much as to the Japanese in command. I realized how since Japanese were people too and they had a completely different perspective on the atomic bombs and about World War II in general.

The world will never know what would have happened if the U.S. would not have dropped the atomic bombs on civilian population centers in Japan. We do know, however, that the atomic bombs killed between 160,000 to over 180,000 people in addition to the long-term effects of radiation on humans and nature for years to come. Japan actually offered to surrender before the dropping of the atomic bombs with the condition that it could keep its emperor. The United States rejected the terms and would only accept an unconditional surrender by Japan. It is odd that when the United States did accept Japan's surrender especially since after the dropping of the atomic bombs, they allowed Japan to keep their emperor. It is hard to imagine anyone would claim the wholesale slaughter of hundreds of thousands of people would be anything but a horrifically monstrous act. Yet with Utilitarianism or Consequentialism even the most horrific acts can be justified since the ends justify the means.

Utilitarianism and Consequentialism with its pragmatism are not restricted to secular humanists or war-time politics. It can be seen across a vast social, ethnic, and religious spectrum. Even among more conservative evangelical groups that are often strong proponents of right to life issues like the life of the unborn and human dignity, they often fall prey to utilitarian justifications when it holds the promise of great good even at the expense of some questionable means. An example of utilitarian justifications for what would normally be deemed immoral by most Evangelicals is the use of embryonic stem cells for research in the hopes of finding a cure for a host of genetic and degenerative diseases, spinal cord injuries, and even the growing of replacement organs which could be more viable than donor organs. The vast majority of Evangelicals are opposed to abortion on the grounds that it is murder, the taking of an innocent life. This argument is based on the Scriptures and what is taught in regard to the sanctity of life.

And it rests on the ontological belief that all humans are made in the image of God. It is rather disturbing to find that almost half those who hold such a view on abortion also permit and advocate the use of cells taken from destroyed embryos in the hopes of accomplishing some good. Here the argument is perhaps a little subtler, but it still comes down to an ends-based justification. Although most Evangelicals and even former President Bush believes that the making of new embryonic stem cell strains needs to be prohibited, the argument claims that destroying the existing embryonic stem cell lines we already have would be a double tragedy. A life was taken to acquire these stem cells for research, but the life cannot be brought back so why not use the existing cells for good? Another argument is that the zygotes used for embryonic stem cell research were never implanted in the womb and were therefore never intended to become human so their cells can be used. When utility becomes one's guide, one may find one's self building monuments and medical wonders into the heavens; yet, at least in this case, one's foundation rests on the desecration of the dead and the slaughter of the innocent.

The final example is the utilitarian justification for the use of torture. I have taught "Christian Ethics" for the past fifteen years, and this is the first semester I actually had to set aside time to explain to my class why torture is categorically wrong. After all, Americans do not torture others--and certainly not Christians—yet, 90% of my students believed torture was an acceptable means of acquiring information if that information could save lives. When presented with the "ticking bomb scenario" (which is stated at lengths at the end of this section), the consensus was that we must do whatever it takes to save lives. In fact, students went so far as to say that if they did not torture the terrorist subject, they were culpable and responsible for any lives lost due to their lack of zealous interrogation. And unfortunately, my students are not alone in their beliefs. In a survey by Pew Research Center, 62% of white evangelical protestants believe that torture is often or at least sometimes justifiable under certain conditions as opposed to only 40% of the unaffiliated public thought torture is may be justifiable (see *Figure 10*).

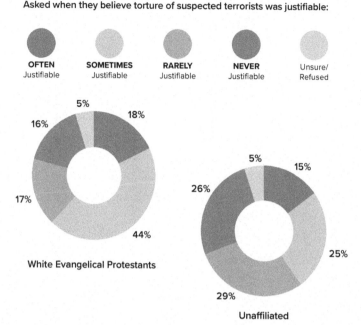

Asked when they believe torture of suspected terrorists was justifiable:

OFFEN
Justifiable

SOMETIMES
Justifiable

RARELY
Justifiable

NEVER
Justifiable

Unsure/
Refused

White Evangelical Protestants

Unaffiliated

Figure 10. Survey of Torture.

However, in every instance in which I have read the justifications for the use of torture, it becomes an argument of utility—meaning that while torture is wrong, but it would be a greater wrong not to do all within one's power to save innocent lives. Torture is the lesser of two evils when compared with the massacre of thousands of innocents. When clear biblical mandates are violated in the hopes of achieving some greater good or preventing some greater evil, the winds of Utilitarianism deviate Evangelicals from their ethical moorings.

The use of Utilitarianism and Consequentialism can be applied on various thing like deciding what kind of shoes or car to buy, picking which size bag of chips gives the best value, deciding who should receive health care or government bailouts. The reason why this ethic can never provide true morality is not because it is unlivable, but rather since it is untenable. It is one of the most pragmatic ethical theories ever conceived by the mind of man, yet it is also limited by the same frailties that affect all men.

If we accept act-based utilitarianism as an ethical standard, it becomes a standard with no standard; for literally any action is potentially possible if it can be presented as a viable means of producing more benefit than harm. Lying, assassinations, theft, murder, fraud, infidelity, tyranny, human medical experimentation, organ farming, child or slave labor, acts of terror or counter terrorism and numerous other options are reasonable if they can be rationally demonstrated to have a chance of producing more happiness for more people than it brings misery.

If for this reason we advocate a rule-based utilitarian ethic, we invalidate utilitarian ideals for the rules generated must come from some other ethical system. If we claim the rules come from observation of what experientially has been most expedient in the past. This allows for radical conflict if those making future decisions have had different past experiences. If after years of field experience an interrogation officer claims that he has determined torture is counterproductive, how will this persuade someone who has always gotten whatever information they wanted to know every time they practiced torture? Who gets to make the rules in rule-based Utilitarianism? What are the rules based on? Reason? Experience? Certain presupposed core values, human values, or obligation?

Utilitarianists will often claim that it is not farfetched to make projections into the future of likely outcomes. The better data we have, the better predictions we can make. Utilitarianism and consequential based ethical theories in general often site how good intentions can bring unintended, but none the less, horrific consequences. Yet, could not the same be said about utilitarian based ethics? No matter how well thought out or researched, no matter what our past experience or expertise predicts, the future is beyond the scope of human insight and speculation. When our ethical theory cannot tell if we acted correctly or incorrectly until the consequences of our actions have been revealed, this seems like a poor map and guide for living a moral life.

Certainly, utilitarianists can claim that one of the advantages of this type of ethical approach is that it is flexible and can adapt to different needs, environments, and criteria. Increased knowledge can help increase accurate predictions of outcomes, and the more one practices an ends-based ethic, the more proficient one will become at choosing the best-case scenarios and means of action. This certainly is true for a vast array of ethical dilemmas and real-life quandaries. If we interact with undesirable consequences, we are allowed to make adjustments and corrections within a utilitarian framework. A deontological ethical theorist must press on through hell or high water; he is bound by duty or a code of conduct which is not based on circumstances or unforeseen unpleasant outcomes. Even for the consequentialist, who can theoretically make adjustments, some moral choices cannot be undone, and like the deontologist, the best of intentions do not mitigate against unforeseen unpleasant consequences. We cannot take back certain actions, and often the consequences of many well thought out, good intended acts cannot be known for generations to come.

For example, DDT (dichloro-diphenyl-trichloroethane), a famous pesticide commonly used in the '40s, was thought to be a wonder of modern chemical science and allowed for an unprecedented control of insects with the results of major improvements in crop yields. Yet, the side effects of DDT poisoned the water table and contributed to incalculable negative side effects on the health of migratory foul, fish, and even human populations. When actions affect the life and wellbeing of others, there are no "take backs" or "do overs." It is true that some mistakes, like use of DDT, we can learn from and make appropriate adjustments for future actions, but some mistakes may not allow for a future in which learning can take place.

Even if humans possessed the knowledge of what would produce the most good for the most people, this does not alleviate the consequences of this type of thinking on the minority of the population or the violation of individual choice by the will and actions of the majority. Utilitarianism and Consequentialism, coupled with American consumerism and a culture of instant gratification, created an exceptionally toxic combination with regards to morals. We see firsthand the devastating socio-economic consequences of trying to please the masses in the present without concern for the consequences of the present pragmatic choices on future generations. It will be of little consolation for those who come after us if we admit that the sum total of our current choices brought increased misery to the majority.

In conclusion, Utilitarianism, Consequentialism, pragmatism, teleological ethical theories and whatever else we want to call such concepts cannot provide true morality. Without the knowledge of how our choices will turn out in the future, we are not in an epistemic position as humans to determine which actions will produce the best consequences. Yet, even if we somehow gained this type of insight, it would still not justify the suffering of the few in exchange for the pleasure of the majority especially if one happens to be in the minority. An ethical system which has no boundaries for that which is an ethical act is a poor guideline by which to make ethical decisions and is therefore not able to provide true morality.

Questions for further practice and understanding of this theory:
respond to the following scenarios as a Utilitarianist
1. There is a life raft with seating for six people, but seven people need to be rescued, what do you do and why?
3. What are three strengths and three weakness of this theory?
4. Summarize and define this theory in a single phrase.
5. How would one determine which actions will produce the most good?

For further additional explanation see the following video(s)
"Ethics Part 8: Utilitarianism Consequentialism." YouTube, recorded and uploaded by Fred Blackburn. 11 Sept. 2019, https://youtu.be/hGaYpJ4yKH8

Notes
The greatest good for the greatest number.
"What works best, costs cheapest, lasts longest."
Lesser of two evils.
How would one protect the rights of the individual against the utility of the group?

List of Figures
Fig. 10. Survey of Torture

Works cited
Pew Research Center, "The Religious Dimensions of the Torture Debate." Religion and public Life. 7 May 2009, https://www.pewforum.org/2009/04/29/the-religious-dimensions-of-the-torture-debate/
Timmons, Mark. "Conduct and Character: Readings in Moral Theory." Cengage Learning, 6th ed., 2011.

IV.G ETHICAL RELATIVISM

Ethical Relativism is the belief that culture determines what right conduct is for its members. "When in Rome do as the Romans" is a way of thinking that aligns with ethical relativism. Because of the word *relativism* in the name of this theory, many people mistakenly believe that the theory itself is relative with regards to right conduct. Ethics may be relative to time and place since there are no universal ethical standards. But ethics are absolute in their cultural context. Society and culture determine if we are living in accordance with right conduct. Ethical Relativism is prescriptive and tells us how we ought to behave in the society in which we live or are visiting.

Ethical Relativism was based on the understanding that came out of Cultural Relativism. Cultural Relativism was championed by people such as Franz Boas and Margaret Mead. They challenged the unilineal anthropology views of their day and addressed that the Eurocentric bias had been placed on cultural studies. They believed that evaluating others based on European values and history produced ethnocentrism rather than seeing the value and historical particularism that each culture had in itself. After years of fieldwork and seeing the vast diversity of cultural norms, it was concluded that humans formed ethical values from a wide arrange of sources and came to a wide range of conclusions on what was the right way to live. Cultural Relativism is descriptive and simply describes how things are, without placing a value judgment on how things ought to be.

Based on vast field work studies and seeing the diversity of human norms, values, ethics and laws, ethicists developed the idea that each culture determined its own standard of right conduct. Ethical Relativism became the practical application of cultural relativism's observations. Ethical Relativism, while being an absolute standard locally, also believed that other cultures could only be judged and evaluated within their own cultural and historical context. "To each their own," but know the norms of where you intend to live, because this is the ethical standard to which you will be held accountable.

A CRITIQUE OF ETHICAL RELATIVISM – WHY ETHICS DERIVED *IV.G.1* FROM CULTURE OR SOCIETY DO NOT PROVIDE TRUE MORALITY

Many people derive their view of ethics from the enculturation that they receive in their upbringing. Formally, this is called Ethical Relativism which is a confusing term because although it is relative in a universal sense, it is quite absolute in its regional manifestations. Simply put, Ethical Relativism claims that the standards of right and wrong are dictated by your culture. "When in Rome, do as the Romans, when in Southern California; do as the Southern Californians, etc." This theory was developed after tomes of field work were produced by cultural anthropologists who documented the wide array of ethical systems throughout time and place. When certain ethicists looked at the data, they came to the conclusion that there were no universal moral guidelines; rather each culture formulated an ethic that suited their particular needs. Franz Boaz and his student Margaret Meade were pioneers of a field work approach in which a person becomes a participant observer in a culture and then formulated theories of human behavior based on observations. This practice is contrary to what had been common in the past (formulating theories and then going out to find data to corroborate previously held views). This approach made cultural anthropology a much more viable social science in which data was observed, hypotheses were formulated, and then tests were conducted to verify or refute the hypothesis.

This also led to looking for cultural universals which accounted for the entire range of human experience in different locations and different times. Previously cultural anthropology has been very *ethnocentric*, and other cultures were judged and evaluated based on the cultural norms of the cultures from which the researchers came. Even though some universals were discovered across geography and time, many more unique variations were found than similarities which brought into question the very notion of a "universal Ethic."

Some of the universals that cultural anthropologists discovered include gender and age roles, language, art, music, religion or beliefs about origins and the meaning of life, modesty, marriage, tools, and good and evil (or at least right and wrong). While many universals exist in human cultures, how they are actualized is where the relativism occurs. Although every society has gender and age roles, what those roles are vary widely depending on time and place. Language, although a universal human trait, has thousands of variant forms and different rules of grammar and intonation. Art and music are as equally diverse as the forms of religious belief and practice. Modesty is universal but can range from complete bodily coverage to simply wearing a piece of string, a bead, feather or paint, yet feeling completely covered. Marriage is found in almost every culture, but its variations are so vast that it is almost impossible to define what marriage is. Tools can be as simple as a digging stick or as complex as an atom smasher, but all cultures use specialized tools. All cultures also have a sense of *the Good, the Right,* what is *Fair* and *Just.* From these universals, norms (what is considered normal behavior), values (the ideals of that culture), and laws (enforced norms or values) develop. The range of what is considered normal, however, is what led ethicists to come to the conclusion that morals and values are culturally constructed. So, we must use our cultural guidelines to determine right and wrong behavior within the culture in which we live or are visiting. Ethical Relativists hold that each culture must be evaluated in its own light and not by the norms, values, laws and ethics of other cultures.

The enculturation of ethical values usually begins in the home by immediate family. Parents train their children as to know what acceptable and unacceptable behavior is. For many behaviors there may be sound reasons whereas others are simply a result of tradition, habit, or because the parent says so. This ethical and cultural training is then continued by the extended family, community, clan, or tribe. In more urban societies, the training of values is often carried out in schools or in agrarian or pastoral cultures moral training takes place while working with others. Religious institutions re-enforce ethical guidelines and are often quite successful at gaining compliance, especially if there is a strong belief in supernatural consequences for adhering to or rebelling against the social mores. The state, or whatever form of government is culturally in place, also re-enforces the socially accepted customs in the forms of laws and penalizes or removes those who violate convention.

This type of ethical theory has many advantages. This theory seems so natural. We simply behave in a way that seems normal and appropriate to us because that is how we were raised, and everyone around us was raised with the same ideas of right and wrong. Our norms, values and laws are in sync with our culture's worldview and religious beliefs. The government, or powers that be, enforce the laws of our culture and society. Abhorrent behavior is obvious and draws attention to itself and can be easily seen as out of tune with the rest of society. Other societies are free to pursue their own values as long as their practice does not infringe on the wellbeing of our culture and society. This perspective helps prevent ethnocentrism and promotes toleration of those who have different views and values than our own. In fact, if people don't like the norms, values, or laws of their own culture, they may have the option to immigrate to a culture whose mores are more compatible with their personal taste. Ultimately, we could set up our own culture if we could find an uninhabited island and set up our own standards of what was ethical and what was not.

Yet, if ethics are really nothing more than social norms and cultural conventions, then why should we have to adhere to them? Social norms and mores change generationally and geographically, so why should we have to wait for social change or move to a place that agrees with how we want to live? Ethical Relativism does not allow for individuals to critique the norms or mores of other cultures or, for that matter, even their own. Since culture and society are the standard for right and wrong behavior, the standards produced by it cannot be questioned by members of that society. Even practices which might seem morally repugnant to us cannot be judged as being immoral in another culture that finds them acceptable. The subjugation of women, child abuse, slavery, torture, or even genocide may be acceptable among certain culture groups. If we judge them by our own cultural values, we are being ethnocentric and intolerant. Even seeking social change in our own culture puts us in the category of the immoral, rebellious, and fomenters of social unrest. The only justification for rebellion is if rebellion is successful and one overthrows the old order and sets up a new standard of what is moral, normal, and legal. If we are successful, we will be hailed as liberating heroes against oppression: freedom fighters, and perhaps even founding fathers of a new cultural or national identity. If we lose, however, we will be branded as outlaws and traitors, terrorists and fanatics, malcontents and criminals. The key to rebellion is to win, but, ironically, we become the new standard that others will one day rebel against and we have already set the precedent on how social change takes place.

Ethical Relativism can be especially problematic in pluralistic societies like the United States of America. The laws apply to all people and are absolute, but because there are so many sub-cultures and even counter cultures in America, the norms and values of the American people cover a wide range of behaviors and beliefs. Various subcultures will attempt to get their norms and values passed into laws and are opposed by those with competing value systems. This results in social unrest and culture wars, often leaving both sides dissatisfied or for minority groups, being disenfranchised. Often our social identity and rules for conduct find greater loyalty in our subculture than in our national identity. This could apply to gangs, various ethnic, religious or political groups. The subcultures' ethics and values are in conflict with other subcultures and rather than not judging other groups by their own standards and promoting toleration, these subgroups often try to impose their standards on the whole of society.

Ethical Relativists do not have to give reasons or justifications for their ethic. It really just comes down to, that's the way it is, we've always done it this way, and do we think we know better than those who came before us? Perhaps if we knew the history and background of certain norms, it might make more sense to us, or could give us grounds of why social mores should be changed or enforced. But Ethical Relativism is an absolute ethical system based on the standards of the culture from which it comes. To challenge Ethical Relativism is challenging the very culture that gave citizens life, language, a worldview, and values. This culture reared us, protected us, and provides a mate for us. Who are we to question the values of our culture? It would be like a child telling the parent they were not parenting right.

The development of Ethical Relativism as a social theory coincided with the rise of the counter-culture movement in the '60s. Many American youth rejected the values, norms, laws and religious beliefs of their parent's generation and even went beyond ethical relativism into moral relativism. If there are no ethical absolutes except those mandated by our culture, and if our culture just arbitrarily made standards up because there are no universal standards, then why can we not just make up our own standards—especially if ethical standards are based off of a relativistic non-foundation? With the rise of moral relativism, everyone did that which was right in their own eyes. Peace and love seemed more valid to most youth rather than the values of the military industrial complex of their elders. The norms of the protestant work ethic and Judeo-Christian values were seen to be the values of another time and place and were easily replaced with sex, drugs, and rock and roll. Many people chose to drop out, turn on, and seek a less totalitarian form of economics and religion.

Socialism challenged the assumptions of capitalism; experimental economic and family systems were explored—everything from co-ops and communes to group marriages. Western dogmatism was replaced by Eastern mysticism, and everyone did that which was right in their own eyes. Moral relativism opened the possibility of situational ethics, in which right and wrong is dependent on each particular instance and each particular moral agent. Ethics were no longer a dictate from on high or a list of rules and calculations; there could be a plurality of morally acceptable choices, so things weren't so black and white anymore. No more absolutes. Besides there being no absolutes, toleration of everything besides intolerance, and being open and accepting of all types of expression ultimately leave us "hating nothing except hatred."

This progression from ethics, derived from culture or society, to moral relativism and situational ethics really just leads us back to egoism. The same reasons ethical egoism does not provide true morality applies to relativism as well. When everything is ethical and moral, nothing is ethical and moral. The toleration espoused by Ethical Relativism causes it to label any universal ethic as being ethnocentric, judgmental and bigoted. The moral relativists see any check on their personal moral choices as oppressive, bigoted, and hateful. And the situational ethicists basically do whatever they want since they are not accountable to anyone but themselves. Relativism in any of its forms does not satisfy man's quest for ethics or morality. What has the appearance of normalcy, toleration, and freedom turns into a morass of conflicting values and judgments. It is the oppression of toleration—a toleration which has now been transformed to mean acceptance—for if someone does not agree with us, they are being intolerant. Toleration used to mean putting up with and being respectful of other people or other views that a person does not agree with; but in a relativistic world, I suppose toleration can mean whatever people want. Therefore, Ethical Relativism cannot provide *true* morality.

Questions for further practice and understanding of this theory:
respond to the following scenarios as an Ethical Relativist
1. There is a life raft with seating for six people, but seven people need to be rescued, what do you do and why?
2. What are three strengths and three weakness of this theory?
3. Summarize and define this theory in a single phrase.
4. How is Ethical Relativism different from moral relativism?

For further additional explanation see the following video(s)
"Ethics Part 6: Ethical Relativism." YouTube, recorded and uploaded by Fred Blackburn. 17 Sept. 2019, https://youtu.be/AYQT_no38AE

For additional resources and biblical references
Judges 21:25 – "In those days there was no king in Israel: every man did that which was right in his own eyes."
Bob Dylan – "It's Alright Ma, I'm Only Bleeding"

Notes
Culture determines right and wrong behavior.
In order to be a good person, one must know the norms, values, and laws of their culture and adhere to them.

Works cited
Timmons, Mark. "Conduct and Character: Readings in Moral Theory." Cengage Learning, 6th ed., 2011.

ETHICS OF CARE

Carol Gilligan, who is credited with developing an Ethic of Care, looked into how men and women approach ethical theories from different perspectives. In her book, "In a Different Voice," she argued against Kohlberg, her fellow instructor at Harvard, and his stages of moral development in children. Kohlberg's studies led him to postulate that girls did not reach the same levels of moral development that could be found in boys. Gilligan sought to challenge this. Part of her critique focused on the way moral development was scored. She pointed out that there was a bias towards reason-based judgments as opposed to moral processing done through relationship. Most ethical theories were created by men and focus on virtues that are associated with masculine qualities. Gilligan pointed out that woman often have a different set of virtues that are associated with feminine qualities. Gilligan points out the benefits of incorporating feminine values into future discussions of ethics. This critique holds great weight since half of the population is female. If women are expected to also live moral lives, leaving out what they have to contribute would be a great disservice to the study of ethics.

A CRITIQUE OF THE ETHICS OF CARE - WHY EMOTION DOES
NOT PROVIDE TRUE MORALITY

Human beings are constituted in such a way that some are ruled by their reason whereas others are ruled by their emotions. In the previous section it was shown why reason cannot be trusted to be our moral guide, but what about emotion and the host of feelings under its domain? Love, fear, joy, sorrow, peace, anxiety, compassion, condemnation, contentment, and jealousy are just a few of the colors on the palate of emotional possibility. Emotions can be both positive and negative aspects of the human condition. If we could manage to construct an ethic built on the more positive aspects of our human nature, could this perhaps provide us with a more caring and nurturing ethic—an ethic that is not merely based on justice and retribution, but one that considers the value of mercy and relationship? Thus far in the book, most of the critiques against various forms of ethical outlooks have been based upon masculine virtues or dispositions, what about an ethic that was more feminine in nature? Could such an ethic succeed where others have failed?

It could be argued that there are no such things as male and female virtues, but rather these are cultural constructs and learned behaviors. A case could be made for associating different types of moral interaction with temperament as well as sex. Yet, based on culture, certain virtues and even temperaments are seen as being more masculine or feminine by nature. Male and female are biological traits and are determined by chromosomes; we could also include an entire section on middle-sex values (individuals who have both male and female biology), but this will have to be a future project. Biology determines one's sex, whereas culture determines one's gender.

In other words, culture and society has norms which are considered masculine or feminine which are associated with maleness and femaleness. There are cultural norms associated with being masculine or feminine; a male who exhibits feminine attributes is often labeled effeminate, and a female who exhibits masculine traits is often labeled a "tomboy." We can imagine the difficulty for those who identify as transgender or queer when it comes to these socially constructed or biological norms. Temperaments are not sex-specific, culturally certain temperaments are viewed as being more masculine whereas others are seen as being more feminine. A choleric or phlegmatic female could be judged as being un-lady like, whereas a melancholy or sanguine male could be viewed as unmanly. When a man or woman does not identify with the corresponding traits associated with masculinity or femininity, it can lead to what is called *gender dysphoria*. So, what are masculine and feminine virtues and how does this relate back to the topic of emotions being a guide to ethical behavior? In twenty-first century America, many efforts have been made at producing a more egalitarian society; yet, man social stereotypes remain, especially in the realm of masculine and feminine virtues (see *Figure 11*).

Masculine	Feminine
Justice	Mercy
Protection	Care
Provision	Nurture
Individualistic	Relational
Single Minded	Multitasking
Self-Reliant	Communal Support
Analytic/Rational	Emotive/Feeling

Figure 11. Masculine and Feminine Virtues.

It is easy to see by looking at this list why an ethical evaluation developed and evaluated by men would give a masculine-based rating on a person's ethic. If we had a feminine-based ethical evaluation, woman would score considerably higher than their male counterparts. Gilligan was not suggesting that traditional, male virtues should be replaced with female virtues, but rather feminine virtues should be evaluated and applied to the formulation of ethical theories. This re-evaluation could produce a more balanced and applicable ethic since humans are comprised of both male and female members. It is interesting to note as a Christian that Jesus Christ embodies both masculine and feminine virtues. With regards to the masculine, Jesus spoke out boldly in rebuke of those in the temple; Luke 19:45-6 records, "And he went into the temple, and began to cast out them that sold therein, and them that bought; Saying unto them, 'It is written, My house is the house of prayer: but ye have made it a den of thieves.'" In contrast, Jesus welcomes children to himself in a very warm and welcoming manner after his disciples initially intended to turn them away; "But Jesus said, 'Suffer little children, and forbid them not, to come unto me: for of such is the kingdom of heaven'" (Matthew 19:14). There are many more verses from both the Old and New Testaments in which the messiah appears masculine and feminine. Jesus exhibits both the strength of masculinity with the gentleness of femininity throughout scriptures.

There are benefits and limitations of feminine and masculine virtues. For years, I worked as a line staff counselor at a boys' group home. In many ways, it was like a house jail with very strict guidelines imposed on the young men who were sent to us by the courts. I was amazed at the diversity of staff and their varying philosophical approaches to working with these young men. On one extreme, we had male counselors who saw themselves as jailers, and they believed the young men had been sent to us to be punished for their actions. They were authoritarian and tyrannical in their interaction with our wards, demanded unquestioning obedience to their directives, and they were punitive towards any that would disobey their authority. On the other end of the spectrum, we had what I referred to as the "earth mother" types. These women believed that those sent to us needed love and nurturing. These young men who had perpetrated heinous crimes, were sick and in need of healing, and it was through compassion and relationship that they could be best served. For those on the punitive end of the spectrum, they had no relationship with the young men in their charge. When I would challenge the authoritative men on their style of management, they would respond by saying the young men respected them. I tried to explain to them that what they were interpreting as respect was actually fear, and it produced resentment and anxiety in the home. On the other end of the spectrum, I saw manipulation and disrespect, towards the workers who tried to manage by being compassionate, merciful and giving. When I would confront these workers on their management style, they would acknowledge feeling betrayed and manipulated. And although their normal interaction was caring, these women would often lash out in retaliation and emotional outbursts when their efforts were not appreciated. Personally, I believed a balance between these two approaches is the key to success, but this in itself is complicated to discuss, much less achieve.

There is tension between traits like respect and relationship, justice and mercy, protection and compassion, fairness and grace played out in many scenarios. Let us examine at the ditch of those virtues we associate with the feminine for this part of the critique. Feeling is immediate and encompassing, and it can allow us to connect in ways that our well thought out rational responses never can. For all the problems that emotions can potentially bring to pass, we can at least credit our emotions with being true and honest down to the very core of our being. Analytical thinking can be aloof and detached, and it is easy to perceive a person who is governed more by their head than their heart as being cold and disingenuous. An emotional response of love or hate, if nothing else, is honest; it conveys a passion and connection to other humans that abstract thinking can never achieve.

Having emotions is part of the human condition. How people express their emotions will vary due to a wide array of factors, but an emotionless human is a human who has fallen outside of the normal range of human behavior. For all of the philosophers and their ivory tower configurations when push comes to shove, it is rarely our rules or reason that govern our behavior. People act on impulse and passion; often, they do not intend to feel a certain way, but rather find themselves caught up in a feeling that seems to well up from within. Emotions are rapid and conflicting feelings of love or hate, happiness or sadness, hope or fear seem to be on us long before our reason has a chance to evaluate and engage the situation. A moment of rage or a consent to passion can dismantle years of meticulous well-reasoned ordering of a person's life.

The ancient Greeks were not only the progenitors of philosophy, but they were also the masters of psychological observation. The Greeks understood the appeal of reason, order, consistency, stability and self-control; these virtues were all seen personified in the god Apollo who was represented by the sun. He was the god of order, illumination, self-reflection and the patron of architecture, painting, and sculpture. Durability, symmetry, composition, and form in the arts corresponded with reason, self-discipline, and self-control in the lives of his adherents. Yet, the Greeks also understood the appeal of passion, chaos, spontaneity, and being fully immersed in the moment. These traits were personified in the god Dionysius, who was the god of wine, women, and song. Dance, poetry, and music were the realm of this deity. For those given over to the Dionysian mysteries, they lived in the moment and were fully engaged in the wild and ecstatic carnival of life. The Greeks gave homage to both and could see these diverse principles at war within their own being. Apollo was safe—yet sterile—whereas Dionysius was dangerous—but full of life. These are both dynamic ways in which to engage life, yet for some people the best solution is to withdrawal.

Such indifference provides a type of psychological protection, but it is also a backing away from life. Alfred Lord Tennyson is famously quoted "tis better to have loved and lost, than to never have loved at all."Yet the pain of loss and joy of love are hardly to be addressed mildly due to the great influence emotions hard on our beings. Even with the powerful emotion of hatred, emotions like it at least show that someone cared for we do not hate those for whom we have no concern. Emotions connect us to others and our own humanity. Emotions are honest and true. Emotions can convey to others our unguarded feelings in an instant; a laugh can deconstruct the soundest argument, and a single tear can negate a well-reasoned disputation. Yet, for all that emotions may grant us, they can also blind our judgments and enslave ourselves and others.

Emotions themselves may be honest and real, but they may be based on false information or be twisted by distorted interpretations of the facts. Showing people compassion and mercy may bring healing and salvation, but it can also stunt a person's development and give them a false impression on the nature of cause and effect. Forgiveness and forbearance can lead to a lack of understanding, concerning the consequences of one's actions. Nurturing can turn to enabling, and comfort can lead to dependency and a victim mentality. Love is powerful, but it is the seedbed of hate, resentment, and bitterness. For all of the good feelings and ecstasy that emotions may bring us, such emotions travel in pairs. Their negative counterparts often take up abode where their pleasant twin once dwelled. I am not saying that emotions are bad or that they should be suppressed, but they are fickle and can change like the weather.

If one tries to base their personal ethic on how they feel, their ethic will change direction in accordance with their passions. Passions can be life giving or life taking. Love can make the world come alive, but can bring with it suffocating jealousy, anxiety, and fear. The scriptures tell us that "perfect love casts out fear," but this is not the type of love that I am talking about here (1 John 4:18). When it comes to our feelings and our emotions being our guide, Jerimiah 17:9 states, "The heart *is* deceitful above all *things*, and desperately wicked: who can know it?" Since emotions can be so deceitful, and despite the Ethics of Care's good intentions of focusing on the loving and kind virtues, ultimately, it cannot provide *true* morality.

Questions for further practice and understanding of this theory:
respond to the following scenarios in alignment with the Ethics of Care:
1. There is a life raft with seating for six people, but seven people need to be rescued, what do you do and why?
3. What are three strengths and three weakness of this theory?
4. Summarize and define this theory in a single phrase.
5. What could possibly be wrong with having a more loving, and gracious personal ethic?

For further additional explanation see the following video(s)
"Ethics Part 10: Ethics of Care." YouTube, recorded and uploaded by Fred Blackburn. 12 Sept. 2019, https://youtu.be/lI50Cg8Zk_g

Notes
A feminine supplement to masculine-dominated ethical theories.
Is a balanced approach to ethical guidelines what is needed to correct the excesses of being too rigid or too flexible?
Could we have an ethic of love, care and compassion? The benefits seem self-evident, but what might be some of the potential flaws?
If one had to choose between justice and mercy, why wouldn't mercy always be the obvious choice?

Works cited
Timmons, Mark. "Conduct and Character: Readings in Moral Theory." Cengage Learning, 6th ed., 2011.

EXISTENTIAL/POSTMODERN ETHICS   *IV.I*

It is not really possible to define what Existential or postmodern ethics are, and this is because they are often based on individualism and a rejection of labels and formulas. However, Existentialism does often share certain themes. Postmodernism is often viewed as a rejection of modernism in its emphasis on objective truth as well as the disciplines of science and logic to help uncover the nature of reality. Postmodernists generally reject metanarratives (big stories like religion, science, or philosophy) that try and explain everything. Postmodernists are more given to perspectival truths rather than objective *truth*. The philosophical foundations of Postmodernism are found in existential philosophy. Existential philosophy, like Postmodernism, is impossible to define, but below I will give you a list of themes that many existentialists may embrace (*Figure 12*).

Existential Themes	
Individualism	You are unique and one of a kind.
Alienation	Because you are such a unique individual no-one else can possibly understand you which leaves you all alone in the world.
Angst	This includes fear, anxiety, and dread, of you know not what.
Radical Freedom	You have real choices with real consequences. You may not be able to choose your circumstances, but you can choose your responses.
Authenticity	Find out who you actually are, not what other people want or expect you to be and then be true to yourself.
Truth is Subjective	We can only know things through our own perspective. Even if there was absolute or objective truth, once we heard it, we would subjectify it.
Experiential Knowledge	We can only truly know what we have personally experienced; all other type of knowledge is either hearsay or head knowledge.

Figure 12. Existential Themes.

As can be seen from the above list, this type of thinking leads to a pursuit of individual personal truth over absolute, objective, universal *truth*. This tends to make truth relative not only to time and place, but also to each individual. Interestingly enough, this theory was actually created by a Christian by the name of Soren Kierkegaard; he emphasized the importance of not only knowing about Jesus, but also having a personal relationship with Jesus. Most people who practice or claim existential beliefs today are usually quite hostile to Christianity and are more atheistic or gnostic in their core beliefs. This later type of existentialism often leads to anarchy-- where everyone does what is right in their own eyes--or eventually to nihilism in which a person does not believe in anything.

A CRITIQUE OF EXISTENTIALISM - WHY PERSONAL   *IV.I.1*
EXPERIENCE DOES NOT PROVIDE TRUE MORALITY

Existentialism is one of the most liberating and dynamic philosophical constructs known to man. It places great emphasis on the individual and puts a premium on personal freedom. True knowledge is experience-based and truth, ultimately, is also a subjective experience. Being true to oneself and living an authentic life are lofty goals, but they often come at great cost, especially when a person is no longer willing to live under the expectations, guidelines, or goals that others have placed on them. However, this philosophy has its drawbacks, like alienation from others since no-one else can truly know you or that overarching feeling of angst (fear, anxiety, and dread) all rolled into one. There are many different versions of existentialism from the Christian perspective of Soren Kierkegaard to the Anti-Christian sentiments of Nietzsche. Sartre, Camus, and Heidegger provide various agnostic versions, but in the end, they all suffer from some of the same shortcomings.

Subjective truth and experiential knowledge may be very honest and helpful guides for our personal conduct, but how do we navigate this type of radical relativism when trying to construct an ethic for not just ourselves but for a society at large. We can use mantras like "to each his own," "tolerate everything besides intolerance," or "do no harm" but are these catchy sayings even possible to live out? Who gets to arbitrate when two people's diverse perspectives on that which is true come into conflict? Perhaps if we could all live as hermits the problem would be limited. But since the vast majority live their lives among their fellow human beings, how are we supposed to all live with our own personal codes of conduct? Toleration sounds great but toleration ends when one person's personal beliefs contain absolute truth claims. "Do no harm" is a lovely sentiment, but many of our actions cause great harm to ourselves, others, and the environment which in turn causes harm to everyone. Even if we had the knowledge to know how our actions affected others, would we have the ability or even the desire to change our habits?

It has been said that experience is the greatest teacher, and in many ways this is true. Yet, experience is also a harsh schoolmaster—many are the marks and scars left under its cruel tutelage. There are some lessons that are so severe that they cost us our very lives or bring about irreparable harm. Even though we now have the experiential knowledge of our mistake, we do not have the means to make it right. Experience is also very much marked by space and time, and even though it may provide true knowledge, that knowledge is limited to an event or condition that has already passed. Perhaps we got a case of food poisoning after eating a particular brand of snack or from dinning at a certain restaurant; our connection between our illness and what or where we ate are indeed true for us, but it does not mean that this truth will apply to future snacks or future visits to the same restaurant. A person may have had a positive or negative experience with a medical practitioner, mechanic, or contractor, but this experiential knowledge will not necessarily be repeated by this person or by others who seek or avoid similar services based upon personal experience. The problem is that they are not us and what may have been a life enriching encounter for one person, may be one of heartbreak and ruin for others.

Personal experiences are also just that, personal, so when we seek to guide, warn, or council others based on our own experiences, our advice might be counterproductive, since the person we are advising is not us. Authenticity, freedom, and subjective truth are an alluring combination. Yet, if our true selves are not "such a great thing to be," our freedom brings bondage, or our disregard of the truth of others leads to anarchy. In the end, experiential knowledge is found wanting, and the logical conclusion is a world of anarchy where everyone does that which is right in their own eyes or according on their own experience. It is for these reasons that experience cannot provide true morality.

Questions for further practice and understanding of this theory:
respond to the following scenarios as an Existentialist
1. There is a life raft with seating for six people, but seven people need to be rescued, what do you do and why?

2. What are three strengths and three weakness of this theory?
3. Summarize and define this theory in a single phrase.
4. What is the basis of knowledge?

For further additional explanation see the following video(s)
"Ethics Part 12a: Existential/Postmodern Ethics (Pluralism and Particularism)." YouTube, recorded and uploaded by Fred Blackburn. 12 Sept. 2019, https://youtu.be/vDJpCcvfzsI
"Ethics Part 12b: Existential/Postmodern Ethics (Pluralism and Particularism)." YouTube, recorded and uploaded by Fred Blackburn. 12 Sept. 2019, https://youtu.be/_-35SZTF2NM

For additional resources and biblical references
Kierkegaard, Søren. Concluding Unscientific Postscript to Philosophical Fragments. vol. 1, Princeton U P, 1992.

Notes
Existential ethics, due to its individual nature, has as many variations as there are people.
Truth is subjective.
One only knows what they have personally experienced.
You have to know who you are before you can know how to live.

Works cited
Timmons, Mark. "Conduct and Character: Readings in Moral Theory." Cengage Learning, 6th ed., 2011.

IV.J ADDITIONAL NOTES RELEVANT TO ALL ETHICAL THEORIES

IV.J.1 A NOTE ON CONSCIENCE - WHY CONSCIENCE, INTUITION
OR A "GUT FEELING," DOES NOT PROVIDE TRUE MORALITY

"Preacher was a talkin', there's a sermon he gave
He said every man's conscience is vile and depraved
You cannot depend on it to be your guide
When it's you who must keep it satisfied."

- Bob Dylan

The idea of conscience being a moral guide is a widespread belief and
has religious, philosophic, and secular proponents. The benefits of having
conscience be a guide are numerous. It provides a law unto itself which
can either condemn or excuse the user. It is an internal compass that can
give us moral direction, and it can stand against external pressures and
manipulation. A clear conscience provides internal peace and an ability to
act boldly in the face of opposition.

This section will attempt to show the various beliefs regarding the
origin and function of the conscience. It will show the various strengths of
a conscience-based morality along with its corresponding weaknesses. In
the end, however, a conscience in and of itself is not enough to provide true
discernment on ethical issues and that guilt and shame are not sufficient
guides or pressures to keep us from moral failure.

In both eastern and western religious traditions, conscience is seen as
a type of inner spark or light that illumines the reason and allows humans
to discern between right and wrong. In Hinduism, this can be seen as
knowledge gained over the course of various incarnations. In Buddhism,
this is seen as a reflection of universal mind; the Pali Scriptures say: "when
the mind is face to face with the Truth, a self-luminous spark of thought is
revealed at the inner core of ourselves and, by analogy, all reality." In Taoism,
conscience is the internal measure to inform if a person is in harmony or
discord with the Way. Confucianism focuses more on the internal measure
of an individual's relationship to others. Zoroastrians focus on discerning
between their higher nonphysical spiritual desires, associated with light,

and their lower base fleshly desires, associated with darkness. These types of internal dualism can be seen in various Gnostic sects, who as children of light seek that which leads back to the Father of Lights and suppress that which feeds the lower carnal cravings that keep one bound in the darkness. The western religious traditions of Judaism, Islam, and Christianity also share in the view that humans have an internal moral compass. This view is based largely on the belief that humans were created in the image of God. However, this simplistic overview is only intended to show that the religiously universal idea of conscience and each tradition has a broad spectrum of teaching and understanding on this topic. The following will deal mostly with the Christian tradition and the biblical teachings on conscience after briefly summarizing some of the leading evolutionary, sociological, neuro-psychological, and philosophical views.

From an evolutionary perspective, human conscience is seen as an inheritable survival trait in which members of a community, who show care and concern for one another, aid to the survival of the group and in turn to themselves. This adaptive trait has obvious benefits over individuals who are only self-centered or self-seeking in their attempt to survive. From a sociological or cultural anthropological perspective, conscience is enculturated by a person's society or ethnic group. The young would be taught what is acceptable and unacceptable behavior, norms, values, and laws of their culture. When a person violates these learned traits, there would be feelings of violation of conscience which is really just a learned social construct. In modern naturalistic neuro-biological thinking, the conscience is genetically inherited just like eye or skin color or any other inheritable biological trait.

From a philosophical perspective, there are many views on conscience; some of these mentalities are intertwined with religious explanations. This is especially noticeable in medieval philosophy and has been related to the term *synderesis*. The term *synderesis* can be traced all the way back to Saint Jerome's commentary on Ezekiel chapter one where he describes the appearance of four mysterious creatures who had the appearance of men, but they had four wings and four faces. The four faces where that of a man, a lion, an ox, and an eagle. Jerome goes on to allegorically explain this vision and the various faces as different aspects of man. The human face represents reason and the intellect (which is related to the *logos*), the lion represented the passions and emotions (as in the heart or *kardia)*, the ox represented man's more base and fleshly desires, whereas the eagle represented *synderesis*, or the part of man which soared above all these other qualities.

Synderesis relates to the part of man called the *nous*, usually translated as "mind." *Nous* is Greek for mind or intellect and refers to first principles, akin to platonic forms. For example, the objective concepts of *the Good, the True,* and *the Beautiful* along with the ability to make value judgments and critiques.

IV.J.2 A NOTE ON NOUS – WHAT LOGIC, FEELING, AND FIRST PRINCIPLES HAVE TO DO WITH A STANDARD OF MORALITY

The pre-Socratic philosopher, Anaxagoras, was one of the first people to use the word *nous* and he described it as the underlying foundational principle which directed everything else. The philosopher, Anaxagoras describes *nous*:

All other things partake in a portion of everything, while nous is infinite and self-ruled, and is mixed with nothing, but is alone, itself by itself. For if it were not by itself, but were mixed with anything else, it would partake in all things if it were mixed with any; for in everything there is a portion of everything, as has been said by me in what goes before, and the things mixed with it would hinder it, so that it would have power over nothing in the same way that it has now being alone by itself. For it is the thinnest of all things and the purest, and it has all knowledge about everything and the greatest strength; and nous has power over all things, both greater and smaller, that have soul [psuchê]. (Anaxagoras, DK B 12, trans. by J. Burnet)

Anaxagoras was a materialist, but he understood *nous* as the finest and purest of all material things which was the cohesive substance which held everything together.

In Platonic and later neo-Platonic terminology, *nous* was the place or personal of the archetypal forms; this realm of ideal forms was eternal and the template from which all things came. *Nous* had both a cosmic form and one that also indwelt humans, and it was through this faculty that we could know foundational principles and ideal forms, although our knowledge would be slightly skewed or distorted because of our temporal state of being.

The classical Greeks, namely Aristotle, identified the soul as having various distinct qualities. They saw the soul as being made up of three components that are simply defined in our language as mind (*nous*), reason (*logos*), and passion (*kardia*). For example, *logos* is analytic reason such as mathematics or formal logic, whereas the *kardia* is the seat of the passions such as love or anger. The *nous* however deals with first principles such as *the Good, the True, and the Beautiful*. Within Aristotle's Nicomachean Ethics, intellect and feeling are perceived as limited, having a beginning and an end, whereas *nous* extends beyond, correlating to intuitive understanding. In this tri-partite concept of the soul, one sees the tension between reason and passion, between the head and the heart. Plato illustrated this in his allegory of the chariot. Aristotle saw the *nous* as the highest part of the soul. This aspect transcends analytic reason and emotion because it is based on first principles; these would equate to the ideal forms in Plato's understanding.

What does *nous* have to do with morality? Such a question causes me to wonder: what does it mean to be a human being? What is it that separates human beings from other types of beings such as angelic beings, animal beings and plant beings? From a Christian perspective, humans are made in the image of God. Yet, what does it mean to be made in the image of God? If God is a spirit, it is not physical attributes that make mankind in His image. There must be traits that are unique to God and man but not to any other created being for in the Genesis creation account only humans are made in the image and likeness of God. I believe it is in the *nous*. Both angels and animals can reason, have memory, can problem-solve, and show emotion. Yet, if God is the cosmic *Nous* which holds together and directs all things, and if humans are imparted with *nous*, humans possess a template of first principles and causes. Perhaps this is the key to understanding why humans are unique types of beings. The first principles that humans contemplate include things such as perfection, infinity, holiness, eternality, and even *the Good*.

According to the Genesis account, Eve had a concept of *good* even before eating of the tree of knowledge of good and evil: "And when the woman saw that the tree was good for food, and that it was pleasant to the eyes, and a tree to be desired to make one wise, she took of the fruit thereof, and did eat, and gave also unto her husband with her; and he did eat" (Genesis 3:6). Unfortunately, the Hebrew word for *good*, is very similar to the English word for *good* and can have an incredible spectrum of meaning from "that which brings pleasure" to "that which is ethically right." Regardless, it seems that the type of *good* Eve perceived before she ate of the tree of knowledge of good and evil, and her understanding of *the Good* afterwards changed dramatically. Whatever type of knowledge of good and evil was obtained by eating of the forbidden fruit, the consequences were devastating. The Bible says their eyes were opened, and they knew they were naked. Something dramatically changed for Adam and Eve, and when God confronted them on their newfound knowledge, Adam subtly blamed God and openly blamed Eve, Eve blamed the serpent, and the serpent had no one to blame. God told Adam and Even in Genesis 2:17 that on the day that they ate of the forbidden fruit they would die. This is interesting for Adam and Eve went on to live for hundreds of years after their disobedience, so what did God mean that they would die? I believe Adam and Eve *spiritually* died that day. And although I do not believe they lost their knowledge of the *nous* completely, their understanding had become darkened and there was a veil placed over their minds. This is what is called the "noetic effects of sin," not only were Adam and Eve cut off from God spiritually, but their minds (*nous*) corrupted, reason fallen, and knowledge of good and evil stolen and crippled by their limited perspectives, resulting in a type of egocentrism and moral relativism.

So, from a Biblical perspective it seems as though we could equate *conscience*, or "higher reasoning" to the *nous*. I am still working through the Biblical dynamic and interplay with being made in the image of God and the effects on that divine image with the knowledge gained by eating of the forbidden fruit. Whether humans had a conscience before their disobedience or as a result of their disobedience I do not know, but neither the tree of knowledge of good and evil, nor the *nous* in a post fallen human

race could provide a true moral compass. This compass had been broken
and could no longer provide an accurate moral course.

The human perspective depends on a template of *nous*; the word
nous appears many times within the Bible. In John 1, light can be seen as a
metaphor for spiritual enlightenment and illumination. Jesus was the light
and the provider of life, yet, man who had been made as children of light,
now walked in darkness. Humanity was created with the light of God in
us, but our disobedience darkened our understanding. So, in this context,
the light is the *Nous,* the foundation of human values and judgments. Jesus
states this clearly, "If therefore the light that is in thee be darkness, how great
is that darkness!" (Matthew 6:23b). There are many more verses throughout
the Bible that contain the word *nous* (see the end of the section for details).

The reason why conscience, intuition, or a "gut feeling" does not
provide true morality, is because we are a broken people. Our understanding has been darkened and our minds (*nous*) have been broken, blinded
and deceived. Our knowledge of good and evil is limited to our own
natural reason, intelligence, and experience and can be easily swayed by
base appetites, passions, or emotions. We often confuse right judgment
with enculturation or instinct. Often, we think we are doing what is right
because we have conformed our behaviors to the norms, values, or laws
of those around us. All of these internal promptings are tainted and flawed.
Perhaps some people's moral compasses are more flawed than others, but if
the standard of good and righteousness is perfection, then even the slightest
flaw will land us far off course. The *nous* offers no guarantee that we are
conforming our actions to "right conduct." Although following our inner
conscience may help us sleep at night, because the *nous* is broken, it cannot
provide true ethics and morality.

A NOTE ON THE NOETIC EFFECTS OF SIN   *IV.J.3*

When we talk about the *noetic effect* of something, we are referring to the
application of consequences to day-to-day activities; this includes an effect
upon our ability to reason correctly. Because of sin, our reason has been
blinded and our hearts have been darkened. According to tradition, towards
the end of his life, the great thinker Aquinas stopped writing. When asked

why, he replied to the effect that the things the saw rendered all his works "as nothing more than straw." I believe Aquinas was given a glimpse of the glory of God and an inkling of God's mind—by contrast, his own works appeared to be little more than shadows in the darkness. Not only has the highest realm of our mind (*nous*) been compromised, but our reasoning capacities (*logos*) have also become tainted by our Adamic fallen nature.

Rather than bringing the light of truth to illuminate our souls, our reason now becomes subservient to our carnal mind, our flesh (*sarx*). Reason no longer makes clear and unbiased judgments, but is affected by ego, desire, class, caste, gender, ethnicity, philosophy, politics, and religion. Kant believed that pure reason could transcend these baser filters, but even Kant with his conscious desire to find a more rational approach than the charismatic emotionalism of his upbringing, ended up coming to rational conclusions in line with the spiritual teachings of his youth. Untainted reason would be a powerful tool in apprehending a true ethic and a legitimate guide for right conduct. Yet, because we are broken and separated from the mind of God, reason becomes the servant of our desires rather than its master and its intuited propositional foundations. Instead of providing sound logical conclusions, reason has been twisted to provide rationalizations to justify our imperfect conduct. Due to the noetic effects of sin, we are incapable of untainted reasoning; therefore, any reason-based approach to morality falls short.

Figure 13. All attempts at perfection fall short

For additional resources and biblical references

Bob Dylan – "Man in the Long Black Coat"

JOHN 1 – see full chapter

JOHN 14:6 – "Jesus saith unto him, I am the way, the truth, and the life: no man cometh unto the Father, but by me. Jesus came from the light, and was the light of the world."

JOHN 3:19 – "And this is the condemnation, that light is come into the world, and men loved darkness rather than light, because their deeds were evil. So you may be asking, what does this have to do with nous or with conscience?"

ROMANS 1:18-28

ROMANS 7:23 – "But I see another law in my members, warring against the law of my mind [nous], and bringing me into captivity to the law of sin which is in my members."

1 TIMOTHY 6:5 – "Perverse disputings of men of corrupt minds [nous], and destitute of the truth, supposing that gain is godliness: from such withdraw thyself."

TITUS 1:15 – "Unto the pure all things are pure: but unto them that are defiled and unbelieving is nothing pure; but even their mind [nous] and conscience is defiled."

EPHESIANS 4:17-24 – "This I say therefore, and testify in the Lord, that ye henceforth walk not as other Gentiles walk, in the vanity of their mind [nous], Having the understanding darkened, being alienated from the life of God through the ignorance that is in them, because of the blindness of their heart: Who being past feeling have given themselves over unto lasciviousness, to work all uncleanness with greediness. But ye have not so learned Christ; If so be that ye have heard him, and have been taught by him, as the truth is in Jesus: That ye put off concerning the former conversation the old man, which is corrupt according to the deceitful lusts; And be renewed in the spirit of your mind [nous]; And that ye put on the new man, which after God is created in righteousness and true holiness.

PHILIPPIANS 4:7 – "And the peace of God, which passeth all understanding, shall keep your hearts and minds [nous] through Christ Jesus."

ROMANS 11:34 – "For who hath known the mind [nous] of the Lord? or who hath been his counsellor?"

1 CORINTHIANS 2:16 – "For who hath known the mind [nous] of the Lord, that he may instruct him? But we have the mind [nous] of Christ."

ROMANS 12:2 – "And be not conformed to this world: but be ye transformed by the renewing of your mind [nous], that ye may prove what is that good, and acceptable, and perfect, will of God."

COLOSSIANS 3:10 – "And have put on the new man, which is renewed in knowledge after the image of him that created him."

Notes

Where does the conscience come from? And how do we know it is a reliable guide for correct behavior?

Is it possible to do evil, but have a clear conscience, or is it possible to even do what is right, but still have feelings of guilt, shame, and moral failure?

How does nous relate to one's standard of morality?

What does the noetic effect of sin have to do with reason-based ethical theories?

List of Figures

Fig. 13. All attempts at perfection fall short

Works Cited

Anaxagoras, and Patricia Curd, "Anaxagoras." *The Stanford Encyclopedia of Philosophy.* Winter 2019 ed., edited by Edward N. Zalta, www.plato.stanford. edu/archives/win2019/entries/anaxagoras/

V ALL ETHICAL THEORIES FAIL AND ANY ATTEMPT AT MORALITY IS DAMNED

V.1 MORAL FAILURE - A UNIVERSAL PRINCIPLE

Now that you have been introduced to a wide array of ethical theories and moral applications, you can see the enormous difficulties resolving the age-old-question, "how should we then live?" You now have at least an overview of the major ethical systems and how they are applied to various ethical dilemmas. But with the possible exception of egoism, even the best intentioned among you would be hard pressed to live out any of the ethical theories without making errors in judgment or practice. You may be thinking to yourself: "sure I may make some mistakes, but I'm doing the best I can," or you might be thinking, "at least my good deeds outweigh my bad deeds at the end of the day." Or perhaps you are thinking, "sure I mess up, but overall I'm generally a good person." It is at this point that I want to give you another perspective on ethics and morality, one that is not based on human insight and wisdom, but rather one that comes through divine revelation. In other words, now we shall study what the Bible says, concerning God's perspective on ethics and morality (this is not to be confused with Divine Command Theory).

For those of you who do not believe in God or that the Bible has any more authority or insight on ethics than any other book, I encourage you to continue reading. Perhaps it will merely inform you on how Divine Command Theorists think, and why they come to many of the conclusions they do. It is also possible that some of what you read may resonate with you, challenge you or possibly even convict you, helping you recognize the ways in which the following conclusions of Christian ethics land far from Divine Command Theory. Formalities aside, the Bible has many things to say about "right living."

For those of you unfamiliar with Biblical terminology, *righteousness* is that which hits the mark or reaches the standard which is perfection, and *sin* is that which misses the mark or falls short of perfection. Romans 1:16-22 tells us that not only has God given a divine law, but also all humans have a law within their *nous*. Unfortunately, because our *nous* is broken, it must be resored by an act of God. This restoration is accomplished through God-given faith and a renewal of our *nous*. God's righteousness is revealed from faith. The type of faith being talked about in Romans 1 is not wishful thinking or a set of beliefs, but rather it is the gift of God. This type of faith is a divine gift that brings absolute certainty in spite of personal doubt or understanding. This type of faith brings substance to hope and evidence for that which cannot be seen. Hebrews 11:1 says, "Now faith is the substance of things hoped for, the evidence of things not seen." Romans 1 tells us that God has manifested Himself throughout all of creation, so no one has an excuse to say, "I didn't know." This applies to the Jews and the Greeks, the bond and free, the high and low, the educated as well as the illiterate, for this message of God's existence and power is proclaimed through creation itself and can be encountered by any who can perceive the world in which they live. Unfortunately, Romans 1 goes on to say that they rejected the knowledge of God revealed in creation and became darkened in their minds and gave themselves over to their own imaginations, some even chose to worship the creation rather than the Creator.

Then Romans 2:11–15 discusses the moral failure of those with and without the law. In this passage the law is referring to the Law of Moses, given by God. The Jews had the Law and were expected to live by it, if they could keep the law they would be justified and counted righteous. Yet, even those who were not given a written law by God still had a law in their own hearts. Their own conscience set up a standard of right and wrong behavior by which they were to live. If one could live up to their own conscience, they too would be justified and considered righteous even though they did not receive the written law of God. Yet, no one lives up to the standard of God because God's standard is perfection (see *Figure 14*).

Figure 14. The chasm of perfection that separates us from God.

Unfortunately, Paul goes on to tell us in Romans 3 that no one hits the mark, no one does *good*. Those with the written law of God cannot keep God's standards and those who are only trying to live up to their own conscience and the law within their hearts cannot even live up to their own standards. Now you may be thinking to yourself, "I know lots of good people." If you remember earlier when we talked about what the word *good* means, I showed you a wide variety of definitions. God's definition of *Good* in this passage is that which is perfect, without spot, stain or blemish. No human, except one, has or ever will achieve that level of goodness and God does not judge on a sliding scale, a person either reaches the standard of perfection or does not. I often find the analogy of a lantern to be a good illustration of this point. When a lantern is lit, it lights up the night and can be seen for miles around. But when day dawns, it is often difficult to discern if the lantern is still burning or not because the light of the sun is so much greater. In many ways, this is how I see the goodness of people and things. I am not denying people are capable of goodness from a human perspective or context, but when viewed through God's standard of goodness, human goodness is not even in the same category. It is this inability to achieve God's standard of goodness that the above passage is referring to, "for all have sinned and come short of the glory of God" (Romans 3:23). Therefore, all attempts at human ethics and morality fail.

Notes

Contrary to what many Christians assume, Divine Command Theory is not the same as a Christian ethic.

No one can live up to the standard of God because God's standard is perfection.

All attempts at developing a standard of morality or right conduct are flawed.

List of Figures

PART 2

Personal Journey & a Mystical Approach to Ethics and Morality

§

PREFACE

At this point you may be thinking to yourself, "Well, I can see why none of the ethical theories developed by man can provide true morality, but does that mean we should give up hope and despair of ever living an ethical life?" I understand the part about our old selves being dead, and we are new creations in Christ. But are you saying the Holy Spirit is now our only moral compass? If this is the case, doesn't this make ethics and morality completely subjective and relative to each individual and how they are perceiving the voice of God within themselves? If worldview, culture, location, language, gender, intelligence, education, class, caste, personality, and temperament all affect the way we perceive the world and are influential in how we form ethical constructs, how can we hope to distinguish these things from our own mind, let alone the mind of Christ? I believe there are ways we can know the answers to these questions, and I will be discussing these in the section below. I do want to make it quite clear, however, that I am not offering a new and improved ethical theory. I am not advocating some new law or a more Christ-like set of rules. The law never saved anyone. I got off that train a long time ago; I am now riding comfortably and safely on the Grace train; being given the ticket of faith, my passage has been paid for and is secure. If there is a law on the grace train, it is the Law of the Spirit, and if there are any rules, it is the rule of Love. Furthermore, this grace, faith, Spirit, and love are not self-generated and do not come from myself but are the gift and outworking of God.

II PERSONAL TESTIMONY

It has been a long strange journey for me—from the legalism of my childhood, the antinomianism (lawlessness) of my youth, the neonomianism (new law) of my young adulthood, to the liberating pneumanianism (beyond the law) that I found through death around my twenty-sixth year of age. In many ways, I may have actually been a religious Jew in my childhood even though I was raised in a Fundamentalist Christian household. I loved the law of God and the rules and traditions of men. Intellectually, I understood the idea of atonement, and that Christ was sent to be the ultimate and final sacrifice for my sins. But for all intents and purposes, I was working out my own salvation by accruing good deeds and trying to personally atone for my deeds that were evil (see *Figure 15*). I was like an ancient Zoroastrian or Manichean, who believed that God had a great cosmic scale on which he would weigh my good deeds against the evil. If my good deeds outweighed the evil, I would enter into the place of the blessed; however, if my evil deeds outweighed the good, I would be given over to eternal damnation (*Figure 16*). I was highly motivated to keep short balances with God, lest at any time I should be found wanting. I loved God, but didn't really give much thought about Jesus, let alone the Holy Spirit; yet, in reality the person I really loved with my heart, mind, and strength was myself.

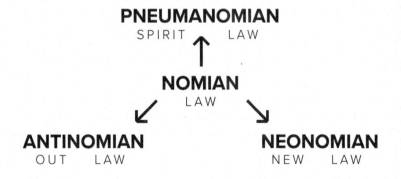

Figure 15. Iterations of the Law.

Figure 16. Cosmic Scales – Each sin weighs down your heart, so you have to be lighter than a feather to pass into blessedness.

In my seventeenth year, however, my childhood legalism was stripped from me. I was enrolled against my will in a hyper legalistic Christian "boot camp" that was guaranteed to change the participant's lives forever. This program used cult like techniques to separate the participants from family and friends. It included forced fasts, forced prayer (over many hours), forced scripture memorization, forced indoctrination, and forced evangelism. The participants were encouraged to confront the leadership if we ever believed that we were being asked to do anything unbiblical. So, confront the staff I did, pointing out that there was no scriptural precedent for forcing their religious beliefs and acts on those who did not wish to participate. In response, I was solemnly shown the scripture: "Obey them that have the rule over you, and submit yourselves: for they watch for your souls, as they that must give account, that they may do it with joy, and not with grief: for that is unprofitable for you" (Hebrews 13:17). It was at this point that something snapped inside of me, and it was as if scales had been ripped off of my eyes. Whether it was the rebellion of youth, my frontal lobes beginning to attach, or finally seeing through the manipulation, I do not know. What I do know is that I lost any faith I had possessed in the Church, spiritual authority, and even God Himself. I still believed in some abstract concept of God, but I sure didn't believe in the God that my upbringing had taught me about. Even if God did exist, I began to question what kind of God He was and why He seemed to be so indifferent to the world He had created. The most painful part of this experience was the realization that I did not really believe God cared about me. This experience was the catalyst and transition point which took me from my legalistic childhood to my antinomian youth.

Within the year, I went from identifying myself as a Christian to identifying myself as an agnostic. I felt very deceived by what I had been taught about God and the Bible and became obsessed with philosophical and theological disputations. It was at this time that I came across my first Reformed Theologians and their view of God. Their focus on His sovereignty and predestination made me even angrier; the logical conclusions of what they were postulating left God as being the author of evil and all the bad things that were happening in the world and to me. I became very aware of the philosophical "problem of evil;" I pretty much let God know, if there was a God that He could pretty much count me out as a devotee until He could provide an accounting of Himself. Since I felt I had been deceived about something as basic as God, I now began to wonder what else I had been deceived about. This began what I would later call my existential romp; I was on the road to find out. I nobly called myself a *seeker* and began to search out other explanations both philosophic and religious as to what the true nature of reality was, and what, if any, was the meaning of life. I began a systematic and thorough deconstruction of my worldview and the laws, rules, and traditions of my childhood. This was the cage from which I attempted to escape.

The fear of punishment or the hope of reward were now no longer factors in governing my behavior. The guilt and shame of my childhood could no longer be used to manipulate me into being someone I wasn't or into doing things I didn't want to do. I had become an anarchist, it was a law unto myself and did that which was right in my own eyes. I balanced my insatiable intellectual appetite with an experiential glee of sucking the marrow out of life. I realized that the forbidden fruit was the sweetest and that sacred cows provided the most delectable meat. I was committed to becoming an authentic human being and to be true to myself, but in order to do this, I first had to find out who my true self really was. I was angry at God, my family, and my subculture. I hated the church, Christianity, and Christians in general. In fact, I began to realize I did not really care for people at all and thought I could trace the source of all my problems to humanity. My solution was to leave the world of men and to dwell in the wild and waste places of the earth. I was sick and miserable. I would try almost any poison or intoxicant in an attempt to self-medicate or to find the cure. Then one day I had a horrible, but profound revelation. I was literally sitting alone on top of a mountain in the middle of nowhere; there was not even the sign or trace of another human being as far as my eye could see, yet I was still miserable and full of internal bitterness and brokenness (*Figure 17*). It was on that day that I realized the problem was not with other people, but rather with myself. God was beginning to call to me from the darkness, but I still did not have the ears to hear or the eyes to see.

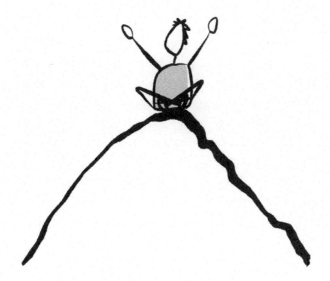

Figure 17. In the middle of nowhere.

My study of other religious traditions and various philosophic systems taught me many things and gave me many clever aphorisms to add to my collection of pithy sayings. But in the end, they were all empty and left me without answers or hope. When I used the same critiques on these systems that I had used on Christianity, they quickly collapsed under close scrutiny. Even though I was intellectually repulsed by a materialistic worldview and saw its one-dimensional emptiness, this was the default worldview with which I was left. Even during the height of my rebellion and in the times of my deepest doubt I continued to read the Bible, just in case, it turned out to be true in the end. I became obsessed with my search for God. I looked for Him under every rock and behind every tree, on desolate beaches on moonlit nights, and among the starry heavens at which I gazed for hours. Yet, the God I had once believed in earnestly during my childhood was hidden from me in my youth. I no longer had railing accusations against God, I was just lonely and beyond hope . It was out of this place of emptiness and darkness when I had been fully humbled and shown the depths of my own depravity that I heard God call my name.

In my high school years, I had the privilege to work at a camp for the developmentally disabled. It was called Camp Meteor Ranch and was run by the Wilcoxes, a loving Christian family. They contacted me and asked if I would come and be a camp counselor for the summer. I told them I would love to but that I was no longer a "believer" and did not know if they wanted someone like me to work with the campers. Without hesitation they said they would love to have me and wanted to know if I would have a problem giving the campers their night time Bible story and praying with them before they went to bed. I told them I would be happy to tell the Bible stories but would be uncomfortable praying to a god that I wasn't sure was listening. They said, "Great, we will have someone come in and pray with them and you can do the rest." So, I found myself counseling at a Christian camp not believing in Christ and a strange phenomenon began to present itself to me. On my quest to find out, I had decided that those with the greatest intellect were further along the path of true knowledge and had begun to fill my mind with the teachings of the greatest philosophers known to man. Yet there I was working with a group of mentally disabled people who had the intellect of children. When I saw these campers pray, I could tell they were actually talking to someone, and it sure seemed like someone was listening to their prayers. All my attempts at prayer were nothing more than an act of futility as I would shout at the night sky or watch my prayers bounce off the ceiling of my room. Finally, in a state of complete humility and brokenness, I asked my campers to pray for me. In all humility, I can honestly state that my IQ was probably higher than the combined total of the campers under my care, but for all my intelligence, I could not reason God out of the heavens or logically demonstrate His existence to my own satisfaction. My campers gathered around and laid their hands on me and prayed that God would reveal Himself to me. That night while reading the gospel of John, I read: "Let not your heart be troubled, you believe in God, believe also in me" (John 14:1). It was as if God had reached down and placed the seed of faith into the very core of my being, and I have never doubted His existence or felt bereft of His presence ever since that moment. I believed Jesus was God and that He loved me enough to give His life for me and had now placed His very Spirit inside of me. I still did not believe in the Bible, Church, or Christianity but I had a seed of faith which had taken root and continues to grow to this day. There would be many seasons in my new life of faith, but the inherited faith that I had taken for granted in my youth was now replaced by a genuine, personal faith. This faith became my most treasured possession.

My life began to transition from a place of lawlessness and self-rule to one of seeking the will of God for my life and being obedient to Him. This was a slow process, and I still was not done with my existential exploration. In fact, in many ways my search for truth and meaning seemed to intensify, and my life became like a pendulum swinging from one extreme to the other. My first extreme swing was to go and live with the "beautiful people" in Northern California. I joined the California Conservation Corps and became a type of second-generation hippie. I was surrounded by sex, drugs, and rock and roll but for all the freedom and love my new companions tried to share with me, I could tell that something was different and that I would never truly be one of them. I loved my time with these children of nature, and they taught me many things, but I was still a sojourner, a stranger in a strange land.

My next swing on the pendulum of life took me back to my fundamentalist roots. I figured that since I had learned so much from those on the far left of the spectrum, I should afford myself the same opportunity to learn from those on the far right. I returned to the place of my physical birth, Bob Jones University, in Greenville South Carolina. I cut my golden locks, shaved my beard, and entered into a realm of deep religious and political conservatism. I was given sound biblical and theological training, and I was sequestered from the world at large. This was a much more intense experience than the forced religious boot camp of my youth, but this time it was of my choosing, and I embraced the austerity and strict rules like a young acolyte monk of the Middle Ages. Yet, for all I learned and those whom I met, I realized that I would never truly be one of them. I always felt like an outsider looking in or a worldview tourist on holiday. The "Bob Jonesians" were good for me in many ways. They helped me overcome many of my vices and habits I had acquired during my lawless youth, and they also had instilled in me a deep sense of discipline and focus. This contributed to my transition from being outside the law (antinomian) to trying to find a new law (neonomian) and life that was pleasing to God. My doubts about the Bible, Church, and Christianity were being modified. I began to have a deep respect and trust that the Bible was God's revealed truth to man. I tried to go to church and did when it was required. But it still seemed to me that something was broken. Christianity as a religion still was not something with which I wanted to be a part or associated. It was in this period in my life that God brought me back to California but this time to the southern part of the state.

In a strange twist of fate, God brought me back to the very place where I had become an agnostic eight years earlier. It was during my freshman year at Christian Heritage College, now called San Diego Christian College, that I had lost my childhood faith. Now, I was returning as a new creation in Christ. I still remember returning to El Cajon, California which was so dark and depressing when I left on my search for truth and meaning. The first thing I noticed was how bright and cheerful the city was. It took me a while to realize that it was not the city that had changed but the very windows of my soul had been cleansed. I re-enrolled at Christian Heritage and was able to complete my undergraduate degree within a year. Now I was quite serious about my walk with Jesus and was committed to living an upright and righteous life. I was developing a great love of the scriptures but was still not too keen about other Christians. I would still go to church because it was required of all students, but I would only attend the Sunday-school class for those with developmental disabilities because these were the only church-going Christians I cared to be around. I still remembered the Sunday school workers—thanking me for coming to help with their class—I laughed and told them I was not there to help but to be one of the participants. It was at this time that I met Steve Whitten and a simple question and invitation that he gave to me changed the course of my life.

Steve Whitten was teaching church history at Christian Heritage College, and I had the privilege of being one of his first students for this course. One day after class, he asked me where I went to church. Then he wanted to know who was my spiritual shepherd and I told him I didn't have any besides Jesus. I was a freewheeling sheep that did not want to follow the herd or any human shepherds. I still had not recovered from what I saw as the abuse of spiritual authority in my youth and was not about to put myself in that position again. Then Steve asked me if I would like to come and visit his church (he told me he was a pastor of a small group of believers called Grace Fellowship). I actually laughed out loud and said, "you're a pastor?" It simply took me by surprise because Steve did not act like any pastor I had ever met previously—he was down to earth, personable, and had no trappings of clerical aloofness or authoritarianism. I agreed to visit and have been attending Grace Fellowship since then. I never would have thought that I could have felt a part of a group of people--unlike the beautiful people of Northern California or the Fundamentalists of the Deep South—I finally felt like I was among my own. It was in this context that I truly began to grow spiritually. Even though I believe God has gifted me in ways that apply more to the universal Church of Christ, it was in the context of this local fellowship that I found caretakers of my very soul.

It was also during this time that I reached a crisis point with my neonomian practices. I was trying so hard to live a righteous and Christ-centered life. Jesus had died for me, the least I could do was to live for him. I understood that salvation was by grace through faith and that not of myself, but somehow, I had gotten the idea that my sanctification (holiness and perfection) was dependent on my own self-discipline, self-effort, and obedience. The harder I tried and the higher I climbed towards spiritual perfection, the further I would fall. I read my Bible, prayed, fasted, tithed, evangelized, led Bible studies, participated in visitations, and in addition to my list of do's I had a bigger list of don'ts, like "Don't smoke, don't drink, don't chew, and don't date women who do." Yet no matter how many of my do's I did or didn't do, I would always seem to stumble somewhere along the way. When I would fail in not doing my do's and doing my don'ts, I would feel guilt and shame—guilt in that I was aware of my wrongdoing and failure, and emotional pain, shame, that could not live up to my internal standard.

That old accuser was ever on hand to mock me and tell me things like "I thought you were a Christian," "if only other people could see what you were really like," and "Jesus died for you and this is how you repay him." At this point, I would usually tell my accuser that I could take it from here, and then I would commence to psychologically beat myself up which I thought was a pious form of contrition. This would sometimes last for days or even weeks. I had no joy. I would still go to church but could not sing the hymns or participate in communion. Other Christians would ask me what was wrong, and I would tell them I was being penitent of my sins. I was actually annoyed at their apparent ambivalence because I knew that they were greater sinners than I but thought they could just say a quick "sorry, Jesus" prayer and forget about it. I thought if they were truly repentant like I was they would also be groveling like me in my remorse. What I did not realize at the time was that it was not Jesus that I had let down, but my own ego, and my penance was actually to sooth my own conscience, not to repair my relationship with Christ. After I had beat myself up enough, I would try again. I would do my do's and not do my don'ts until… Wham! I would mess up again and start the cycle all over.

GOD'S PERFECTION

Figure 18. Ladder of divine ascent.

It was a cycle of ladder climbing to holiness, falling off, beating myself up, and then climbing again (*Figure 18*). It was an exhausting practice, and by my twenty-sixth year I had had enough. I finally came to the place where I realized as long as I was alive, I would never be able to live a life of perfect holiness before God.

It was at this time that I finally read a book called "The Normal Christian Life" by Watchman Nee. I had a copy of this book for years on my bookshelf but had never read it since I figured it was a book for beginners on the Christian path. My own spiritual pride and self-efforts had blinded me to one of the most basic truths of the Christian life. The truth that Watchmen Nee pointed me to in his book was that I was already dead. The passage that Nee pointed to was Romans 6: "Knowing this, that our old man is crucified with [him], that the body of sin might be destroyed, that henceforth we should not serve sin. For he that is dead is freed from sin" (6-7). In this chapter, Paul tells us that not only did Christ die for us, but we were actually crucified with Christ. Yet, like Christ, we are resurrected in newness of life. Therefore, our "old man" is dead, but we are alive in

Jesus. I couldn't believe what I was reading, and even though I love the King James Version of the Bible, I know that sometimes the wording can be misunderstood. So, I began to cross reference to see if this was a fluke or a poor translation. Yet, rather than being a poor translation, the entire New Testament began to light up for me. Paul's teaching in Romans 6 is echoed in Romans 7:2,4, Colossians 3:1-3, Colossians 2:20, and Galatians 2:20 (see end of this section to read at length).

It was as if a great weight had been lifted from me just like the character Christian in "Pilgrim's Progress." I felt as light as a feather and filled with the light and love of God. Fred was dead and my life was hidden with Christ in God. I now had a deep and abiding joy that I had never known; because I was dead, I was free. Thank you, Jesus! Now, everything began to change. I no longer was doing good things and avoiding bad things to become something I wasn't, but I was now doing good things and avoiding bad things because of who I was in Jesus. Life became an outflow of who I was in Christ, rather than a ladder climbing to achieve some sort of perfection that was beyond me. I still fail every day, but now I thank God that he has forgiven me and remember who I am in Him. Guilt and shame, which were the tools of my own ego to measure up to some ideal image of myself, have been replaced by the conviction of the Holy Spirit. Guilt and shame could never do this because I would be driven back into the same behaviors to self sooth and medicate my condition. Instead, I began being transformed by the power of the Holy Spirit who not only brought conviction, but also provided the power to change.

Even my prayer life began to change. I now no longer asked God to help me be a better person, or to help me overcome some particular habit or sin. Now I simply asked God to help me remember who I am in Him. When I do sin, I thank him for already forgiving me and confess my sins to those I have wronged. When I find myself judging others or beating myself up, these are red flags for me, letting me know I am back on the ladder of sanctification again, and I confess this to God. When I am abiding in Christ, I have God's own mercy and compassion for others and for myself. It is out of this context that this book was written, and why I chose the title, "The Dead Have No Need of Ethics," for he that

Figure 19. Ethics in the R.A.W.

is dead is free from the law and can be *pneumanomian* (guided by the law of the Spirit). I no longer seek any righteousness or right conduct of my own. Any good that is in me is because of the one who gave Himself for me. Because my righteousness is found solely in Christ, I no longer have any need of ethics. Yet, now my life is more ethical than it ever could have been on my own for it is Christ Himself who lives in me.

The next part of this book will talk about what it means to be in Christ and what that will look like. Death is the beginning of true ethics and morality. Reckon yourselves dead to self and alive in Christ. Abide in Christ and you will bear much fruit. Walk in the Spirit and you will not fulfill the lusts of the flesh (*Figure 19*).

For additional resources and biblical references

ROMANS 6:6-14 – "Knowing this, that our old man is crucified with [him], that the body of sin might be destroyed, that henceforth we should not serve sin. For he that is dead is freed from sin. Now if we be dead with Christ, we believe that we shall also live with him: Knowing that Christ being raised from the dead dieth no more; death hath no more dominion over him. For in that he died, he died unto sin once: but in that he liveth, he liveth unto God. Likewise reckon ye also yourselves to be dead indeed unto sin, but alive unto God through Jesus Christ our Lord. Let not sin therefore reign in your mortal body, that ye should obey it in the lusts thereof. Neither yield ye your members [as] instruments of unrighteousness unto sin: but yield yourselves unto God, as those that are alive from the dead, and your members [as] instruments of righteousness unto God. For sin shall not have dominion over you: for ye are not under the law, but under grace."

ROMANS 7:2, 4 – "For the woman which hath an husband is bound by the law to [her] husband so long as he liveth; but if the husband be dead, she is loosed from the law of [her] husband. [...] Wherefore, my brethren, ye also are become dead to the law by the body of Christ; that ye should be married to another, [even] to him who is raised from the dead, that we should bring forth fruit unto God."

COLOSSIANS 3:1 – "If ye then be risen with Christ, seek those things which are above, where Christ sitteth on the right hand of God. Set your affection on things above, not on things on the earth. For ye are dead, and your life is hid with Christ in God."

COLOSSIANS 2:20 – "Wherefore if ye be dead with Christ from the rudiments of the world, why, as though living in the world, are ye subject to ordinances."

GALATIANS 2:20 – "I am crucified with Christ: nevertheless I live; yet not I, but Christ liveth in me: and the life which I now live in the flesh I live by the faith of the Son of God, who loved me, and gave himself for me."

For further additional explanation see the following video(s)

"The Dead Have No Need of Ethics." YouTube, recorded and uploaded by Fred Blackburn. 14 October 2014, https://youtu.be/H23cq41Mg8g

List of figures

Works cited

Nee, Watchman. *The Normal Christian Life.* Tyndale House P, reprinted edition, 4 Nov. 1977.

DEATH IS THE BEGINNING OF TRUE ETHICS AND MORALITY   *III*

Since death is the beginning of true ethics and morality, we are to reckon, abide, and walk. Where the Spirit of the Lord is there is liberty, and we are changed into the same image from glory to glory, even as by the Spirit of the Lord (2 Corinthians 3:17-8).

DEATH AS THE BEGINNING   *III.A*

Death is used in a variety of ways in both the Old and New Testaments. Death does not mean annihilation, but rather disconnection. The scriptures speak of both physical and spiritual death. Physical death is the separation of our spirit and soul from our body, whereas spiritual death is our separation from God. The first mention of the concept of death in the Bible is found in the book of Genesis: "But of the tree of the knowledge of good and evil, thou shalt not eat of it: for in the day that thou eatest thereof thou shalt surely die" (2:17). The day Adam and Eve ate of the forbidden fruit in an act of direct disobedience to God, placing their own will and desire above the will and desire of God, was the day they died.

The Bible refers to death as both physical and spiritual. Their physical bodies went on to live for hundreds of years subject to the curse. Yet, they died a most horrible death that day for they died spiritually and were disconnected from God. As a result of this death, brought about by elevating self over God, they passed death upon all mankind. 1 Corinthians 15:22 refers to the spiritual death of humanity which can be traced back to Adam; "For as in Adam all die, even so in Christ shall all be made alive." Similarly, Romans 5:12 states, "Wherefore, as by one man sin entered into the world, and death by sin; and so death passed upon all men, for that all have sinned." Because all were in Adam when Adam sinned, the consequences of that sin: spiritual death, was passed down to all humankind. Even though man had been created by God and was made a living soul when God breathed the breath of life into his very nostrils, man in his rebellion had spurned the gift of life and chose for himself death and separation. This became the new natural state of humanity and all future generations would be born spiritually dead from the womb. It is here that we enter into a great paradox; God's solution to the separation caused by death is to bring death to death, thus bringing a separation from separation which results in reconciliation.

Death is the great enemy of mankind and all have felt its sting. Either through the loss of a loved one or the angst and emptiness, we feel as a result of our separation from God. Yet, God used death itself to provide reconciliation between God and humankind. First, God used the death of His own Son, as an atonement (covering and payment) for our sins. Then God brought about death to our "old man" in Adam to free us from the law and from ourselves.

For further additional explanation see the following video(s)
"Death is the Beginning of True Ethics and Morally." YouTube, recorded and uploaded by Fred Blackburn. 25 April 2020, https://youtu.be/LKQN0geJdxw

For additional resources and biblical references
1 CORINTHIANS 15 – see full chapter

III.B RECKON YOURSELVES DEAD TO SELF AND ALIVE IN CHRIST

"Your sins were dealt with by His Blood, and you were dealt with by his Cross. It is an accomplished fact."
– Watchman Nee

"Knowing this, that our old man is crucified with [him], that the body of sin might be destroyed, that henceforth we should not serve sin. For he that is dead is freed from sin. [...] Likewise reckon ye also yourselves to be dead indeed unto sin, but alive unto God through Jesus Christ our Lord. [...] For the wages of sin [is] death; but the gift of God [is] eternal life through Jesus Christ our Lord." – ROMANS 6:6-7, 11, 23

"I am crucified with Christ: nevertheless I live; yet not I, but
Christ liveth in me: and the life which I now live in the flesh I live
by the faith of the Son of God, who loved me, and gave himself for
me. I do not frustrate the grace of God: for if righteousness [come]
by the law, then Christ is dead in vain." - GALATIANS 2:20-21

We are sanctified (set apart and made holy) the same way we are justified
(made righteous before God): by the person and work of Jesus. Christ lived
a perfect and sinless life and imputed (gave) His righteousness to us. If we
are in Christ, we have perfect righteousness credited to our account before
God. Because we are in Christ, when God sees us He sees us through the
precious cleansing blood of his beloved son. God sees you as He sees Jesus.

Many Christians begin well and embrace with joy the justification
they find in Christ. Yet, when the trails and affairs of this world take hold,
they find themselves struggling to live righteously before God. They plead
with God to help them overcome their besetting sins or pray that God will
make them stronger at resisting the sins which so easily overcome them.
They develop spiritual disciplines and practices to try and achieve more
holy, sanctified lives. When they try to live up to the holy standard of God
through the strength of their own efforts or a more determined will, it is
doomed to fail. What began in the Spirit and by the will of God, they try
and complete through the flesh and their own self-improvement program.

In Romans 6:6, we our told that our "old man" has been crucified
with Christ. This is past tense, and in Romans 6:11,. we are told to reckon
ourselves dead to sin in other words to count it as so. Yet, there is a tension
with Galatians 5:24 which tells us: "And they that are Christ's have crucified the flesh with the affections and lusts" (Galatians 5:24). In Romans
6, it seems as though we have been crucified by another, yet Galatians
5 could seem to imply that we are to be the ones' doing the crucifying.
Crucifixion, however, cannot be done to oneself. Through the strength of
your will, you may be able to nail down both your feet and one of your
hands, but you will still have one hand waving free. This is exactly what
we see among many Christians, through their own efforts—self-denial
and self-control—they have reached a state of being, almost crucified. In

the context of the book of Galatians, this is precisely what was occurring. The Christians in Galatia had begun by faith, but now were trying to be perfected by the law.

"O foolish Galatians, who hath bewitched you, that ye should not obey the truth, before whose eyes Jesus Christ hath been evidently set forth, crucified among you? This only would I learn of you, Received ye the Spirit by the works of the law, or by the hearing of faith? Are ye so foolish? having begun in the Spirit, are ye now made perfect by the flesh?" (Galatians 3:1-3 KJV). It is only through the Spirit that the flesh can be crucified.

Christianity is not a self-improvement program. Jesus did not come to wash us of our sins and then drop by occasionally to do touch ups if we got any new stains. Many people, Christians included, often think of Christianity as a set of beliefs or creeds. If we believe in certain doctrines, then we can count ourselves among the saved. However, Christianity is not about doctrine or creeds. While sound doctrine and creeds are very important, these are not what save you. It is quite possible to believe in the creeds but still be in Adam. Christianity is not about intellectual assent or changing behavior to live by a new set of rules even though intellect could assent and lifestyle change if a person becomes a Christian. So, what is it that happens that makes one a true believer, and not merely a cultural consenter?

III.B.1 IT IS THE INDWELLING OF THE HOLY SPIRIT THAT MAKES YOU A CHILD OF GOD

"And that ye put on the new man, which after God is created in righteousness and true holiness." - EPHESIANS 4:2

"And have put on the new [man], which is renewed in knowledge after the image of him that created him." - COLOSSIANS 3:10

This is the incredible gift of God to us; not only did Jesus die in our place and for our sins, but also He has sent His own Holy Spirit to dwell within us. We are in Him and He is in us. We were not just forgiven an unpayable debt, but God put to death our "old man" upon the cross and gave us a "new man" that was knit together with His own Spirit.

We now have a new ontological (state of being) orientation. We are a new creation. Jesus paid our debt by His blood and delivered us from ourselves by slaying our "old man" on His cross. We are still human, but more than human; our very nature has been infused with the very Spirit of God. We are now God-men and God-women—not because of our own achievements, self-correction, or self-realization but because God Himself has broken down the veil that separated us from Him and made us one with Him by making His abode within us and our abode within Him. Let me be very clear, I am not saying that we are the Creator of the universe or God almighty Himself. This is not some type of Gnostic ladder climbing in which we have understood our divine nature hiding within us or some sort of Christian Hinduism where we have pulled back the layers of ego-illusion to reveal "the god within." This is God Himself, transforming our very being and uniting our spirit with His. God took on a human form and a human nature in the person of the Son and gave to man freely what Adam and Eve had tried to take through disobedience and thievery. God became man so that men might become gods, gods in the sense that we now are the first fruits of Christ and share in His very nature. God took upon Himself humanity so that He could give man divinity.

Adam and Eve, even in their pre-fall perfection did not have the relationship with God that is available to those who are born of God. Adam and Eve talked with God in the Garden, but the Spirit of God was external from them. Their reason was not darkened but it was also not illumined by the mind of Christ. Their perception of God would come and go throughout the day, but it is not so for those who are in Christ Jesus. Even the great prophets of God from Moses to John the Baptist were given the Spirit by measure. David, a man after God's own heart, lived in fear that the Holy Spirit would be taken from him. John the Baptist said of Jesus, "For he whom God hath sent speaketh the words of God: for God giveth not the Spirit by measure [unto him]" (John 3:34).

This is the same Spirit that is given unto us, and Christ told of the work that the Holy Spirit would perform.

Death is the beginning of true ethics and morality, and while death implies an end (and it is: the end of the "old man"), it is the beginning of our "new being" in Christ. For those who are in Christ, the Spirit of Christ is in them, transforming our "new being" in Christ (Romans 12:2). This is why *The Dead Have No Need of Ethics*; we are already made perfect in Christ. Many Christians, while graciously accepting justification from the blood of Christ, foolishly try and find sanctification through their own effort and strength. We can no more sanctify ourselves than we can save ourselves; both have been and will be accomplish by Christ. Ethics, if you remember, is the theory of right conduct. Since we are no longer our own but have been bought with a price, the very blood of Christ, it is no longer us who are trying to live righteously before God. We are already as righteous as we ever possibly can be, because we have been given Christ's own righteousness. When we attempt to establish our own right-living (righteousness) through our own strength, wisdom, cleverness, or nobility of spirit, we negate the effect of the cross of Christ.

In Christ Jesus, God has provided for us wisdom, righteousness, sanctification, and redemption. All of this is the gift of God, provided by God's grace through faith. Yet, even the faith to believe this is the gift from God, we cannot even will ourselves to believe this wonderful truth through our own efforts or desire. When the Jews murmured amongst themselves because of the claims Jesus was making, he replied, "Murmur not among yourselves. No man can come to me, except the Father which hath sent me draw him: and I will raise him up at the last day" (John 6:43-44). It is not us who are seeking God, but rather God who is drawing us. And this is not because we are notably righteous or worthy, it is entirely from Him and by Him and for His glory. Outside of Christ all our righteousness is as "filthy rags"—our greatest wisdom is foolishness, our greatest strength is weakness, and our brightest moments nothing but darkness (Isaiah 64:6). Within Christ, any good that we do has been ordained by God. Any love we have for God is God loving Himself in us and through us. Any obedience we achieve is the obedience of the Spirit within us. Any abiding that is done is God abiding in Himself.

When I was a young man, I strove through my own strength of character and will to be pleasing to God. I was like an investment banker, but I was investing in the Kingdom of Heaven. I don't know if it was AWANA's, which stands for Approved Workmen Are Not Ashamed, a Christian youth organization that was like a religious version of the Boy Scouts, or my Sunday School or perhaps even my Christian Schooling that led me to a peculiar type of thinking in regards to the nature of heaven and the rewards we would receive there. All of these groups offered, ribbons, badges, prizes, accolades, and status to those who excelled in religious performance. I looked like a little brigadier general in elementary school with my uniform and all the patches and bars I had acquired for scripture reading and memorization, evangelism, and the inviting of my neighborhood friends to church or activities. But these were only a shadow of the things for which I was actually striving. Even at a young age, I was quite clever and had a capacity to reason things out to their logical conclusions. Even as a child I was aware that my life on earth was short, so I was willing to deprive myself of temporal good in exchange for eternal pleasure and payout in heaven.

In one of the stages of these religious programs, we were actually given little plastic crowns that we could pin on our uniforms. These had empty spaces that would be filled with "jewels" as we jumped through the assigned hoops to bring pleasure to both God and man—but mostly to ourselves. Similarly, as I got older, I would gather up a handful of tracks, little brochures with religious content, from the Church or school office and head down to the local Kmart and hand them out until they were gone. In high school, I would give up my lunch breaks to do door to door and street evangelism in my local town. They didn't call me "Freddy Fundamentalist" for nothing. I thought I was earning points for my "good" behavior. I read the Bible every night before I went to bed and had read it from cover to cover many times before I graduated high school. The first non-biblical books I ever read on my own were missionary adventures which took place on the Amazon. And every night before I went to bed, I would pray quite conscientiously that God would forgive me of all my sins, lest I die in my sleep and be found wanting. My behavior was a lot like "The Good Place" a contemporary tv show that depicts a "good place and bad place" dichotomy where points are awarded and lost based on human behavior. This is not Christianity; it is Zoroastrianism or Manicheaism.

In my youth, I was not alone in my striving to have the biggest mansion on the highest hill in heaven. There was a lot of competition in my Fundamentalist circles. I did have some advantages such as both my parents being "full time" Christian workers, and an aunt that was a missionary to the heathen in South East Asia but most of all I was a P.K. (the son of a preacher man) and this gave me a fantastic advantage over my peers. Around junior high, I decided to "up the ante" and began to keep the Jewish dietary laws. This was seen as extreme even among the rarified circles in which I traveled. I am not sure what my folks thought of all this or if they had any idea of what was going on inside of my head. My father did, however, make it clear that I was not to be rude when we were invited over to the parishioner's houses for Sunday dinner. Without fail it seemed that every home we were invited to would put out a baked ham, probably as a special treat because the pastor and his family were visiting. When they would offer me their dainty morsels from Babylon I would politely refuse and say, "No thank you, I don't eat unclean meat"! I was full of equal parts zeal and condescension.

One day I remember hearing another pastor preach, and he was talking about rewards in heaven which of course received my full attention. But sometime during the sermon, he quoted some obscure passage which I cannot remember to this day and from this scripture he claimed that he would receive at least one more crown than the rest of us because he was a minister of the gospel. I still remember adamantly thinking in my childhood heart, "we'll see about that," and with that challenge I redoubled my efforts. Until to my horror I became aware of the following passage in Revelation: "The four and twenty elders fall down before him that sat on the throne, and worship him that liveth for ever and ever, and cast their crowns before the throne, saying, Thou art worthy, O Lord, to receive glory and honour and power: for thou hast created all things, and for thy pleasure they are and were created" (4:10-11). I still remember thinking to myself, "what a rip-off!" Jesus has plenty of crowns of His own, what does he need mine for? I will be keeping my crowns for myself.

Looking back on this, it is easy to simply chalk it up to the immature mind of a child or perhaps as an example of the power of enculturation, in this case: a Fundamentalist subculture. Spiritually-speaking, it is easy to see the carnality of my mind and that the person I was really trying to please through my efforts was myself. However one wants to portray this situation, this mentality caused me great hardship in life. For after high school, there were no more badges or prizes. I would do my do's and not do my don'ts, but there was no treat awaiting me. Even when I was being "good," I would often have bad consequences. I couldn't seem to manipulate God into giving me what I wanted even though I would jump through the hoops, beat myself up when I was bad, or beg and plead really hard when I really wanted something. It did not seem like God treated me any differently if I was being good or being bad, and if it didn't seem to make a difference in this life, then all my eternal investment schemes seemed to perhaps have been for naught.

I believed devoutly as a child; I did not believe as a young adult, and then I believed again a few years later. Was I ever really a Christian? Did I only have the inherited faith of my family, but no true saving faith of my own? Did I lose my faith? (Yes, I know there are theological difficulties with this proposition). Experientially, it seemed like I truly believed and then experientially I really did not believe. Could God have removed my assurance as a means to humble me and to show me how worthless my own self-righteousness was? Perhaps and in many ways, I think this is the most likely scenario. When God did give me faith to believe that Jesus really did love me and had died to save me, a change began to occur. The best analogy I can come up with at this time is a type of spiritual petrification or fossilization began to take place. What I mean by this is that as I was infused by the Holy Spirit. The form of me remained, but I was being gradually replaced by the very nature of God. It has been a transforming-metamorphic process where I decrease as He increases. I am not saying that I am no longer human—I am all too human on many levels with many human frailties and failings—but I am being transformed by the renewing of my mind (Romans 12:2). Unlike a fossil, I have been quickened from the dead. Now I can say like the apostle Paul: "When I was a child, I spake as a child, I understood as a child, I thought as a child: but when I became a man, I put away childish things. For now we see through a glass, darkly; but then face to face: now I know in part; but then shall I know even as also I am known" (1 Corinthians 13:11-12).

This spiritual journey has taught me so much and who knows what I will have learned twenty years from now. The stark contrast between the Christianity of my youth and the Christ indwelling-ness of my present state is staggering. As a child, I lived for myself and was in bondage to the law. Now, I am dead to self and have perfect freedom in Christ. I strove for honors and rewards, denied myself earthly pleasures, gave of my time and resources, but it was all for nothing and is nothing but dust and ash. I received my reward for I was interested in the accolades of man and the elevation of myself over others. Now that I am dead, I have no need of recognition or of the accolades of man. Now that I am dead, I no longer feel the need to put others down so that I can elevate myself above them on an endless ladder of good works and self-proscribed spirituality. Now that I am alive in Christ, I experience ecstatic pleasure and joy in this world, and any loss I may endure is counted as gain. In my Adamic nature, I hated humanity; in Christ, I love all of mankind. When I was practicing self-discipline and self-perfection, I would constantly judge myself and others. When I am abiding in Christ, I no longer judge others, and I don't even judge myself. All the plans I had for my grandiose entrance into heaven, wearing ultra-white garments and a massive bejeweled crown that would rest precariously atop my head as I strode piously to my eternal abode, now seem like foolish madness. Now that I have my righteousness in Christ, my own depravity is so clear to me. I see that I am deserving of hell; I would proclaim this freely with all sincerity for I have seen and been given the holy standard of God. Now any good deeds I do I know do not come from me; any love I have for others is the love of Jesus flowing through me; any rewards or crowns I may one day receive I will gladly lay at His feet. Any good thing that is in my life is solely attributed to His goodness.

Because I am dead, I no longer need ethics or morality. Because I am dead, I no longer have to try and live up to some impossible standard. Because I am dead, I am no longer the slave of sin. Because I am dead, I am no longer a part of the Adamic race. Death is the end of self and the beginning of the newness of life in Christ. Because I am alive in Christ, my actions are an outflow of who I am, rather than an attempt to become someone I'm not. Because I am alive in Christ, I now have perfect righteousness. Because I am now alive in Christ, I am a partaker of the divine nature. Old things have passed away and all things have become new. Ethics, religion, and morality are for those who are still striving for self-correction and self-perfection; they all reek of the ways of Cain and are a slap in the face to the finished work of Christ. Because I am dead, I no longer have need of such things for my salvation and sanctification are found in the one who gave Himself for me, and my identity, hope, peace, and righteousness are all found in Him. Anything that is *Beautiful, Good,* or *True* in this life—any right reasoning or right living that I may achieve—is all the work and outflowing of Jesus. Those who are in Adam will never have an enough ethic that is good enough or a morality that is pleasing to God. Those who have died to their Adamic nature have no need for ethical guidelines or morals for all their righteousness and identity is found in Christ. The dead have no need of ethics.

OBJECTIONS TO "RECKONING YOURSELVES DEAD TO SELF AND ALIVE IN CHRIST"

III.B.2

At this point you may be thinking to yourself, "well that was all very fine and clever. A nice play on words, and ideas, but does this mean that for those who are in Christ there are no rules, no guidelines, and no expectations? If salvation and sanctification are the sole work of Christ, and Christ is actually the one in us keeping us from sin, and doing any good works we could possibly ever do, then is anything even required of us at all?" It has been made clear that no one is justified by the law and their own good works. Romans 5:20-1 tells us, "Moreover the law entered, that the offence might abound. But where sin abounded, grace did much more abound:

That as sin hath reigned unto death, even so might grace reign through righteousness unto eternal life by Jesus Christ our Lord." It would seem that even our failings in the end bring glory to God. The more we sin, the more grace is needed, and God is even more necessary for our salvation and sanctification.

Basically, what I have presented is a non-ethic or even an anti-ethic. This is why I chose the word *pnuemanomian* (law of the Spirit) to describe this new relation to ethics and morality. The word, *pnuemanomian,* may be of my own invention, but the concept can be found in the writings of Paul. And like Paul, I have been accused of being lawless and teaching contrary to the traditions of my people. The heretical monk Rasputin and certain sects under the umbrella term of Gnosticism taught that the body was evil, and the spirit was good. Therefore, we could sow corruption to our flesh but seek salvation for our spirit. Rasputin encouraged his followers to come and sin with him, so that the Grace of God might abound. They reasoned that if they were perfectly righteous and secure in Christ, then no deed can remove us from His love and redemption. Paul addressed this in his epistle to the Romans, "God forbid. How shall we, that are dead to sin, live any longer therein?" (6:2).

Paul, along with the other writers of the New Testament, had much to say on this topic. In this next section, I want to look at what he, and primarily the apostle John had to say about how we should live in Christ. Different theological schools of thought throughout church history have been notorious at selecting certain passages as proof texts for their positions and then neglecting or rationalizing the texts that do not align with their systematic theology. This observation could be the topic of many books, but what I want to focus on specifically is the tension that is found between the teachings on *abiding* and *striving*. The idea of *abiding* can be summarized as, "to let go and let God;" it is not up to us, but it is the work of Christ. The idea of *striving* emphasizes our personal responsibility and the importance of the choices we make. Both are taught throughout the scriptures, but it is rare to see them both embraced with equal vigor. So, how are we to avoid *antinomianism* (lawlessness, or being against the law) without becoming *neonomians* (embracers of a new law)? The solution I am suggesting is that these diametrically opposed positions can be reconciled in Christ, for in Him we are in a *pnuemanomian* (law of the Spirit) state of being (refer back to *Figure 15*).

For additional resources and biblical references
COLOSSIANS 3:1-3 - "If ye then be risen with Christ, seek those things which are above, where Christ sitteth on the right hand of God. Set your affection on things above, not on things on the earth. For ye are dead, and your life is hid with Christ in God."
2 CORINTHIANS 5:17-21 - "Therefore if any man [be] in Christ, [he is] a new creature: old things are passed away; behold, all things are become new. And all things [are] of God, who hath reconciled us to himself by Jesus Christ, and hath given to us the ministry of reconciliation; To wit, that God was in Christ, reconciling the world unto himself, not imputing their trespasses unto them; and hath committed unto us the word of reconciliation. Now then we are ambassadors for Christ, as though God did beseech [you] by us: we pray [you] in Christ's stead, be ye reconciled to God. For he hath made him [to be] sin for us, who knew no sin; that we might be made the righteousness of God in him."
ROMANS 8:1-6, 8-17 - "[There is] therefore now no condemnation to them which are in Christ Jesus, who walk not after the flesh, but after the Spirit. For the law of the Spirit of life in Christ Jesus hath made me free from the law of sin and death. For what the law could not do, in that it was weak through the flesh, God sending his own Son in the likeness of sinful flesh, and for sin, condemned sin in the flesh: That the righteousness of the law might be fulfilled in us, who walk not after the flesh, but after the Spirit. For they that are after the flesh do mind the things of the flesh; but they that are after the Spirit the things of the Spirit. For to be carnally minded [is] death; but to be spiritually minded [is] life and peace. […] So then they that are in the flesh cannot please God. But ye are not in the flesh, but in the Spirit, if so be that the Spirit of God dwell in you. Now if any man have not the Spirit of Christ, he is none of his. And if Christ [be] in you, the body [is] dead because of sin; but the Spirit [is] life because of righteousness. But if the Spirit of him that raised up Jesus from the dead dwell in you, he that raised up Christ from the dead shall also quicken your mortal bodies by his Spirit that dwelleth in you. Therefore, brethren, we are debtors, not to the flesh, to live after the flesh. For if ye live after the flesh, ye shall die: but if ye through the Spirit do mortify the deeds of the body, ye shall live. For as many as are led by the Spirit of God, they are the sons of God. For ye have not received the spirit of bondage again

to fear; but ye have received the Spirit of adoption, whereby we cry, Abba, Father. The Spirit itself beareth witness with our spirit, that we are the children of God: And if children, then heirs; heirs of God, and joint-heirs with Christ; if so be that we suffer with [him], that we may be also glorified together."

1 CORINTHIANS 3:16, 23 - "Know ye not that ye are the temple of God, and [that] the Spirit of God dwelleth in you? […]And ye are Christ's; and Christ [is] God's."

JOHN 1:12 - "But as many as received him, to them gave he power to become the sons of God, [even] to them that believe on his name."

JOHN 1:13 - "Which were born, not of blood, nor of the will of the flesh, nor of the will of man, but of God."

JOHN 3:1-2 - "Behold, what manner of love the Father hath bestowed upon us, that we should be called the sons of God: therefore the world knoweth us not, because it knew him not. Beloved, now are we the sons of God, and it doth not yet appear what we shall be: but we know that, when he shall appear, we shall be like him; for we shall see him as he is."

GALATIANS 4:6 - "And because ye are sons, God hath sent forth the Spirit of his Son into your hearts, crying, Abba, Father."

2 CORINTHIANS 5:17-21 – "Therefore if any man [be] in Christ, [he is] a new creature: old things are passed away; behold, all things are become new. And all things [are] of God, who hath reconciled us to himself by Jesus Christ, and hath given to us the ministry of reconciliation; To wit, that God was in Christ, reconciling the world unto himself, not imputing their trespasses unto them; and hath committed unto us the word of reconciliation. Now then we are ambassadors for Christ, as though God did beseech [you] by us: we pray [you] in Christ's stead, be ye reconciled to God. For he hath made him [to be] sin for us, who knew no sin; that we might be made the righteousness of God in him."

EPHESIANS 2:15 – "Having abolished in his flesh the enmity, [even] the law of commandments [contained] in ordinances; for to make in himself of twain one new man, [so] making peace;"

EPHESIANS 2 – see full chapter

JOHN 16: 7-15 – "Nevertheless I tell you the truth; It is expedient for you that I go away: for if I go not away, the Comforter will not come unto you; but if I depart, I will send him unto you. And when he is come, he will reprove the world of sin, and of righteousness, and of judgment: Of sin, because they believe not on me; Of righteousness, because I go to my Father, and ye see me no more; Of judgment, because the prince of this world is judged. I have yet many things to say unto you, but ye cannot bear them now. Howbeit when he, the Spirit of truth, is come, he will guide you into all truth: for he shall not speak of himself; but whatsoever he shall hear, [that] shall he speak: and he will shew you things to come. He shall glorify me: for he shall receive of mine, and shall shew [it] unto you. All things that the Father hath are mine: therefore said I, that he shall take of mine, and shall shew [it] unto you."

2 CORINTHIANS 5:17-21 - "For Christ sent me not to baptize, but to preach the gospel: not with wisdom of words, lest the cross of Christ should be made of none effect. For the preaching of the cross is to them that perish foolishness; but unto us which are saved it is the power of God. For it is written, I will destroy the wisdom of the wise, and will bring to nothing the understanding of the prudent. Where [is] the wise? where [is] the scribe? where [is] the disputer of this world? hath not God made foolish the wisdom of this world? For after that in the wisdom of God the world by wisdom knew not God, it pleased God by the foolishness of preaching to save them that believe. For the Jews require a sign, and the Greeks seek after wisdom: But we preach Christ crucified, unto the Jews a stumblingblock, and unto the Greeks foolishness; But unto them which are called, both Jews and Greeks, Christ the power of God, and the wisdom of God. Because the foolishness of God is wiser than men; and the weakness of God is stronger than men. For ye see your calling, brethren, how that not many wise men after the flesh, not many mighty, not many noble, [are called]: But God hath chosen the foolish things of the world to confound the wise; and God hath chosen the weak things of the world to confound the things which are mighty; And base things of the world, and things which are despised, hath God chosen, [yea], and things which are not, to bring to nought things that are: That no flesh should glory in his presence. But of him are ye in Christ Jesus, who of God is made unto us wisdom, and righteousness, and sanctification, and redemption: That, according as it is written, He that glorieth, let him glory in the Lord."

Works cited

Nee, Watchman. The Normal Christian Life. Tyndale House P, reprinted edition, 4 Nov. 1977.

ABIDING AND STRIVING   *III.C*

One of the most beloved passages in the Bible on *abiding* is from the fifteenth chapter of the gospel of John. Jesus declares that He is the vine and we are the branches. Those who are in Christ will bear much fruit, but those who try and produce fruit through their own effort and strength apart from the vine will be barren, withered, and dead and will be thrown into the fire. This passage is beautiful in that it shows our complete dependence upon Christ, yet it is also terrifying to see the consequences of trying to bear fruit (good works) through our own strength. On the one hand, it seems to be a teaching that any fruit we produce is actually dependent on the vitality of Christ passing through our lives. Yet, on the other hand, this metaphor comes with a qualifier. "If you love me, keep my commandments".

III.B.2 JOHN 15

"I am the true vine, and my Father is the husbandman. Every branch in me that beareth not fruit he taketh away: and every [branch] that beareth fruit, he purgeth it, that it may bring forth more fruit. Now ye are clean through the word which I have spoken unto you. Abide in me, and I in you. As the branch cannot bear fruit of itself, except it abide in the vine; no more can ye, except ye abide in me. I am the vine, ye [are] the branches: He that abideth in me, and I in him, the same bringeth forth much fruit: for without me ye can do nothing. If a man abide not in me, he is cast forth as a branch, and is withered; and men gather them, and cast [them] into the fire, and they are burned. If ye abide in me, and my words abide in you, ye shall ask what ye will, and it shall be done unto you. Herein is my Father glorified, that ye bear much fruit; so shall ye be my disciples. As the Father hath loved me, so have I loved you: continue ye in my love. If ye keep my commandments, ye shall abide in my love; even as I have kept my Father's commandments, and abide in his love. These things have I spoken unto you, that my joy might remain in you, and [that] your joy might be full. This is my commandment, That ye love one another, as I have loved you. Greater love hath no man than this, that a man lay down his life for his friends. Ye are my friends, if ye do whatsoever I command you. Henceforth I call you not servants; for the servant knoweth not what his lord doeth: but

I have called you friends; for all things that I have heard of my
Father I have made known unto you. Ye have not chosen me, but
I have chosen you, and ordained you, that ye should go and bring
forth fruit, and [that] your fruit should remain: that whatsoever
ye shall ask of the Father in my name, he may give it you. These
things I command you, that ye love one another." (John 15:1-17)

What begins as a beautiful passage can quickly turn to feelings of inade-
quacy, fear, and despair: "If ye keep my commandments, ye shall abide in
my love; even as I have kept my Father's commandments, and abide in his
love" (John 15:10). If I could have kept His commandments, then Jesus
never would have needed to die for me. So, why is He now making it a
condition for me to be able to abide in Him? This passage, rather than
bringing me peace and joy, for many years brought me fear and insecurity.
It became one of my proof texts on why salvation is not eternally secure
but is dependent on obedience. Would Jesus cut me off if I did not follow
the rules? What if I was having a dry spell and there didn't seem to be any
fruit in my life? Would Jesus, cast my withered branch into the flames? If
Jesus spoke these things that our joy might be full, then why was it bringing
me such anxiety?

The problem was that I was looking at this passage from the perspective of one who believed he had been saved by Christ, but that it was now
up to me to show how much I loved him by bearing much fruit. I had
inadvertently reverted back to the way of Cain. Instead of obeying God, I
tried to please God through my own efforts and on my own terms. When I
finally realized that not only had Jesus died for me, but that I too had been
crucified with Him, my whole understanding of this passage changed. I
was no longer afraid of not bearing fruit, because the fruit was not being
produced by me. I was no longer wondering day to day if I was keeping
His commandment to "love one another" because the very love of God
flowed through me. I no longer even worried about abiding in Him as
if through the strength of my will I could cling a little tighter to Christ.
I now had the very Spirit of Christ dwelling in and flowing through me,
clinging to himself. Now bearing fruit is simply a natural outflow of who

Figure 20. The vine and the branches.

I am in Christ (*Figure 20*). It is not something I am trying to do to show Christ how much I love Him, rather it is because His love is in me that I can love God, others, and even myself.

For further additional explanation see the following video(s)
"Abiding and Striving." YouTube, recorded and uploaded by Fred Blackburn. 14 April 2020, https://youtu.be/TXPUmz3DAEo

FRUIT OF THE SPIRIT

> "But the fruit of the Spirit is love, joy, peace, longsuffering, gentleness, goodness, faith, Meekness, temperance: against such there is no law. And they that are Christ's have crucified the flesh with the affections and lusts." - Galatians 5:22-24

When we look at the fruit of the Spirit that is produced by abiding in the vine of Christ, we see the very nature of Jesus being manifested. Yet, this passage also seems to come with a qualifier; those that are in Christ have crucified the flesh. Once again, if we have an improper understanding of our identity in Christ, we will attempt countless techniques of self-denial, self-mortification, and self-control. When we realize that it is actually the work of the Spirit that crucifies the "old man," we can then experience the denial of self and an embracing of our new being who has the fruit of the Spirit as part of one's new creation in Christ.

In the teachings of Paul, there appear to be numerous logical fallacies and contradictions. Paul is adamant that our salvation and sanctification are both accomplished in Christ. Without taking a breath, Paul will then exhort us to mortify the flesh, buffet our bodies, run the race, seek the prize, and fight the good fight (1 Corinthians 9:24). If we are signed, sealed, and delivered in Jesus, and our eternal abode is secure in Him. Then why is Paul so concerned about our mortal and moral conduct? Why does Paul spend so much time talking about the raging battle between the flesh and the Spirit if Christ has already reconciled us to himself? Because we are in Christ, we are to put to death the works of the flesh (*sarx*). The order is important: we do not put to death the flesh to be in Christ, but rather it is because we are in Christ that this is possible (Colossians 3:1-11).

Just as we saw in the teachings of the apostle John, the apostle Paul seems to combine that which has already been accomplished with that which is occurring in the present and that which will be made manifest in the future. Paul jumps from the practical outworking of our new life in Christ in everyday living to our glorified state of who we are in Jesus without pause or missing a beat. Paul sees everything through the lens of eternity, but at the same time, he speaks of eternal things in the context

Figure 21. Four-eyed fish.

of space and time. This paradigm reminds me of the bizarre four eyed fish (*Figure 21*). Its irises are actually split, so that it has what appears to be two eyes which rest above the surface of the water to see that which is above and two eyes below the water to see what lies beneath. This is the reality of our god-man ontological position. We still have human bodies with a human nature, but our human nature is no longer that of our old being in Adam, but is a new nature, created in Christ Jesus. We have mortal bodies, which are indwelt by both a human and a divine nature, so it is natural that we would have both physical and spiritual concerns and perspectives.

In order to understand the context of this paradigm, read 1 Corinthians 9:24-27, Philippians 3:14, 2 Timothy 4:7-8, and Ephesians 6:11-17. From these verses, it is easy to see how someone could formulate a *neonomian* (new law) position with regards to our sanctification and perhaps even our salvation. Paul shows the struggle, discipline, and striving which are involved in living a Christ-centered life here on earth. He talks about how we should have the mindset of an athlete or a warrior. We are to be in training, bringing our bodies into submission, temperate, self-controlled, and striving for victory. When you take these passages in context of Paul's overall teachings or even in the context of the passages themselves, we see a complete dependence and empowerment on the Spirit of God to accomplish any of these things. In Ephesians 6:11-17 discusses what it means to put on the armor of God; look how the meaning changes if we read verses

10 and 18 from the same passage: "Finally, my brethren, be strong in the Lord, and in the power of his might. [...] Praying always with all prayer and supplication in the Spirit, and watching thereunto with all perseverance and supplication for all saints." By reading this famous passage in context, it becomes clear that it is not in our own strength and power that we put to death the flesh. God is not giving us a better set of tools or armor for protection in our fight against the evil one (which is then dependent on our own self-discipline will and strength), but rather putting to death the flesh is only accomplished by being in the Lord and through God's own power, accomplished in the Spirit: "Put on the whole armour of God, that ye may be able to stand against the wiles of the devil (*Figure 22*). For we wrestle not against flesh and blood, but against principalities, against powers, against the rulers of the darkness of this world, against spiritual wickedness in high places" (Ephesians 6:11-12).

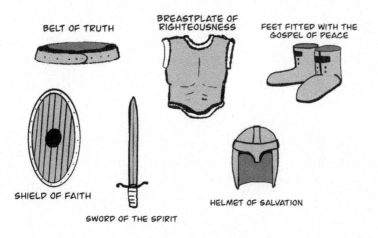

Figure 22. Armor of God.

> "Know ye not that the unrighteous shall not inherit the kingdom
> of God? Be not deceived: neither fornicators, nor idolaters, nor
> adulterers, nor effeminate, nor abusers of themselves with man-
> kind, Nor thieves, nor covetous, nor drunkards, nor revilers, nor
> extortioners, shall inherit the kingdom of God." – 1 Corinthians
> 6:9-10

This may be one of the all-time favorite passages in the Bible that
people will quote as a proof text to condemn all sorts of behaviors that they
find personally repulsive. The list includes drunks, the sexually immoral,
homosexuals, thieves, and other practices. If that isn't enough, the list starts
off with the broad category of the unrighteous which allows you to use
this passage to condemn everyone. Paul then goes on to talk specifically
on why sexual immorality and prostitution are so wrong because we are
the temple of the Holy Spirit. The latter part of this passage can then be
used to condemn people for what they eat, drink, or take into their bodies. Paul is quite clear that those who commit such things will not enter
the kingdom of heaven. It amazes me how people will use this passage
to condemn others, but then somehow give themselves a pass as if their
besetting sins did not make the list, forgetting that the whole list starts out
with "the unrighteous shall not inherit the kingdom of God," including
everyone born of Adam (1 Corinthians 6:10).

Fortunately, Paul adds an amazing statement: "And such were some
of you: but ye are washed, but ye are sanctified, but ye are justified in the
name of the Lord Jesus, and by the Spirit of our God" (1 Corinthians 6:11).
Those who are in Christ have been washed, sanctified, and justified by
the Spirit of our God. This has already been accomplished; it is in the past
tense not present or future. This passage ends with statements of wonder
at our relationship with the Spirit, rather than statements of fear of what
will happen if we do not measure up to God's holiness. 1 Corinthians
6:19-20 states, "What? know ye not that your body is the temple of the
Holy Ghost [which is] in you, which ye have of God, and ye are not your
own? For ye are bought with a price: therefore glorify God in your body,
and in your spirit, which are God's." Once again, it is because of who we

are in Christ that our behaviors should be an outflow of our new creation. We glorify God in our bodies because we are indwelt by the Holy Spirit. This passage is not a check off list of things not to do so that we can be holy before God; it is because we are Holy in God that we no longer have to walk in the flesh.

Paul says something even more shocking in 1 Corinthians 9 which is often rationalized away or neglected. He states, "All things are lawful unto me, but all things are not expedient: all things are lawful for me, but I will not be brought under the power of any" (1 Corinthians 9:12). Is Paul suggesting that he is a *metanomian* (beyond the law)? He does qualify his statement by saying that even though all things may be lawful for him, not all things are good for him. And he does not want to be brought under the power of any—in context I would say it is under the power of any besides the power of Christ. And this brings us full circle back to Romans 6 which I hope we will meditate on in its entirety. It is through death to our "old man" by the Spirit of God that we have been made free. There is now therefore no condemnation to those who are in Christ Jesus. We find our identity, strength, and hope in God and abide in perfect peace and righteousness through Christ. At the same time, we are striving and in a raging battle, between the flesh and the Spirit, yet the war has already been won, and our victory is secure in Jesus Christ our Lord.

QUESTIONS REGARDING ABIDING AND STRIVING   *III.C.3*

At this point you may now be thinking, "did Blackburn really just try to argue that we are beyond the law? Is he suggesting that our behavior isn't what saves us and that someone could be a liar, thief, drunkard, homosexual, fornicator—and still be in Christ? The reconciliation between the paradox of abiding and striving was intellectually interesting, but how does that apply to daily life, and righteous living? I love Jesus, but seem to be daily overcome by besetting sins, this all looks good on paper, but how does reckoning myself dead to self and alive in Christ translate into ethical living? Oh, right, you don't believe in ethics." Let me rephrase that, "how are we supposed to live, if there are no longer any rules, and all things are lawful for us?"

These questions will all be dealt with in the next section, which is named after Galatians 5:16: "Walk in the Spirit, and you will not fulfill the lusts of the flesh."

For additional resources and biblical references
COLOSSIANS 3:1-11 – "If ye then be risen with Christ, seek those things which are above, where Christ sitteth on the right hand of God. Set your affection on things above, not on things on the earth. For ye are dead, and your life is hid with Christ in God. When Christ, [who is] our life, shall appear, then shall ye also appear with him in glory. Mortify therefore your members which are upon the earth; fornication, uncleanness, inordinate affection, evil concupiscence, and covetousness, which is idolatry: For which things' sake the wrath of God cometh on the children of disobedience: In the which ye also walked some time, when ye lived in them. But now ye also put off all these; anger, wrath, malice, blasphemy, filthy communication out of your mouth. Lie not one to another, seeing that ye have put off the old man with his deeds; And have put on the new [man], which is renewed in knowledge after the image of him that created him: Where there is neither Greek nor Jew, circumcision nor uncircumcision, Barbarian, Scythian, bond [nor] free: but Christ [is] all, and in all."
1 CORINTHIANS 9:24-27 – "Know ye not that they which run in a race run all, but one receiveth the prize? So run, that ye may obtain. And every man that striveth for the mastery is temperate in all things. Now they [do it] to obtain a corruptible crown; but we an incorruptible. I therefore so run, not as uncertainly; so fight I, not as one that beateth the air: But I keep under my body, and bring [it] into subjection: lest that by any means, when I have preached to others, I myself should be a castaway."
PHILIPPIANS 3:14 – "I press toward the mark for the prize of the high calling of God in Christ Jesus."
2 TIMOTHY 4:7-8 – "I have fought a good fight, I have finished [my] course, I have kept the faith: 8 Henceforth there is laid up for me a crown of righteousness, which the Lord, the righteous judge, shall give me at that day: and not to me only, but unto all them also that love his appearing."
EPHESIANS 6:11-17 – ""Put on the whole armour of God, that ye may be able to stand against the wiles of the devil. For we wrestle not against flesh and blood, but against principalities, against powers, against the rulers of the darkness of this world, against spiritual wickedness in high [places]. Wherefore take unto you the whole armour of God, that ye may be able to withstand in the evil day, and having done all, to stand. Stand therefore, having your loins

girt about with truth, and having on the breastplate of righteousness; And your feet shod with the preparation of the gospel of peace; Above all, taking the shield of faith, wherewith ye shall be able to quench all the fiery darts of the wicked. And take the helmet of salvation, and the sword of the Spirit, which is the word of God."

1 CORINTHIANS 6:9-20 – "Know ye not that the unrighteous shall not inherit the kingdom of God? Be not deceived: neither fornicators, nor idolaters, nor adulterers, nor effeminate, nor abusers of themselves with mankind, Nor thieves, nor covetous, nor drunkards, nor revilers, nor extortioners, shall inherit the kingdom of God. And such were some of you: but ye are washed, but ye are sanctified, but ye are justified in the name of the Lord Jesus, and by the Spirit of our God. All things are lawful unto me, but all things are not expedient: all things are lawful for me, but I will not be brought under the power of any. Meats for the belly, and the belly for meats: but God shall destroy both it and them. Now the body [is] not for fornication, but for the Lord; and the Lord for the body. And God hath both raised up the Lord, and will also raise up us by his own power. Know ye not that your bodies are the members of Christ? shall I then take the members of Christ, and make [them] the members of an harlot? God forbid. What? know ye not that he which is joined to an harlot is one body? for two, saith he, shall be one flesh. But he that is joined unto the Lord is one spirit. Flee fornication. Every sin that a man doeth is without the body; but he that committeth fornication sinneth against his own body. What? know ye not that your body is the temple of the Holy Ghost [which is] in you, which ye have of God, and ye are not your own? For ye are bought with a price: therefore glorify God in your body, and in your spirit, which are God's."

List of figures

III.D WALK IN THE SPIRIT AND YOU WILL NOT FULFILL THE LUSTS OF THE FLESH

> "I say then, Walk in the Spirit, and ye shall not fulfil the lust of the flesh. For the flesh lusteth against the Spirit, and the Spirit against the flesh: and these are contrary the one to the other: so that ye cannot do the things that ye would. But if ye be led of the Spirit, ye are not under the law." – Galatians 5:16-18

So far, we have talked about what it means to reckon ourselves dead to self and alive in Christ. We have looked at the tension between *abiding* and *striving*, but both can only be accomplished by the power of the Holy Spirit not by trying to accomplish these things through the strength of our own will. It is because we are a new creation in Christ and have been indwelt by God's own Holy Spirit that we now have the power and ability to live a Christ-like life. At the very beginning of this journey, I critiqued "Christian Ethics." Although I pointed out why Christian Ethics was a superior theory of ethics, its glaring flaw was that it was so superior and perfect that the only one who could live up to it was Christ himself. Yet, this is the great news, Christ is actually in you if you be His, and it is actually He who is living out the Christian life in you. This is accomplished by the power of the Holy Spirit. If we live in the Spirit, then we should also walk in the Spirit.

Human beings are amazing creatures, and even though we have been made in the image of God, we are bound by certain limitations. One of these limitations is that we cannot do two things at the same time. Multitasking is a myth. Although some people can switch between two or more tasks more quickly and efficiently than others, all people are limited to only being able to do one thing at a time. This is a good thing especially in context of the above verse. What this means is that you cannot simultaneously be walking in the flesh and in the Spirit. If you are walking in the Spirit, you will not even be able to fulfill the lusts of the flesh.

At this point, it will be helpful if we define exactly what the *flesh* is. Confusion on this point has created great problems philosophically and theologically. It is out of this confusion that Gnostic heresies (the belief that the flesh was evil, and the spirit was good) were born. And it is out of this confusion that many have set up a vast array of rules and taboos to keep us from fleshly desires. The Greek love of philosophy led them to develop a very precise language with which to discuss the subtleties of abstract concepts and ideas. The first Greek word I want to discuss is the word *soma*, which is translated as *body* in the English language and is used to refer to our physical form. The second Greek word I want to discuss is the word *sarx*, which is usually translated as *flesh*. *Flesh* can refer to either our physical flesh or a nonphysical impulse or desire such as the desire for food, sex, sleep, shelter, or whatever pertains to the self. Both of these words can be found in Romans 8:13: "For if ye live after the flesh (*sarx*), ye shall die: but if ye through the Spirit do mortify the deeds of the body (*soma*), ye shall live."

The problem is that in some translations of the Bible the word *sarx* is translated as "sin nature." For example, "For I know that good itself does not dwell in me, that is, in my sinful nature [*sarx*]. For I have the desire to do what is good, but I cannot carry it out. [...] Thanks be to God, who delivers me through Jesus Christ our Lord! So then, I myself in my mind am a slave to God's law, but in my sinful nature [*sarx*] a slave to the law of sin" (Romans 7:18, 25 NIV). The NIV, New International Version, has recently revised this translation, back to the English word *flesh*, as is found in the King James and many other versions of the Bible. Why is this important? It is important because *sin* is not a thing. Even though the word sin can have both a noun and a verb form, *sin* itself is a negation, or a negative relationship to the commands of God. Quite simply, something is righteous or good if it measures up to God's standard which is perfection. Something is unrighteous or sinful if it falls short of God's standard or misses the mark of God's perfection. Everything God created was good, including man and woman. Yet, because of the "lust of the flesh, the lust of the eyes and the pride of life," Adam and Eve choose to give into the desires of their flesh, rather than obeying the commandments and will of God (1 John 2:16). This is the root of all sin and disobedience: placing self over God.

If we make the word *flesh* into *sarx* synonymous with sinful or sin nature, what do we do with other passages in the New Testament that tell us Christ has come in the flesh? John 1:14 reads, "And the Word was made flesh (*sarx*), and dwelt among us, (and we beheld his glory, the glory as of the only begotten of the Father,) full of grace and truth." In this is verse, "the Word" (*logos*) is made flesh (*sarx*), yet the Word who is Jesus had no sin or sin nature. It is problematic to equate *sarx* with that which is evil. Similarly 1 John 4:2-3 and 2 John 1:7 are prob,kematic is *sarx* is evil. These passages are so important since many of the earliest heresies (false teachings) involved the nature of Christ. For those who believed the physical body was evil, it was inconceivable to them that Jesus could have an actual physical form lest he be tainted. This led to a host of false teachings about the nature of Christ; some claimed He was a phantom or ghost or that the Spirit of Christ possessed the man Jesus but was not tainted by the evil of human flesh. This is why John is so clear in his epistle that those who deny that Christ has come in the *flesh* are false teachers and antichrists. The scriptures are quite clear. Even though Jesus came in the flesh, He had no sin. Jesus had both a human and a divine nature, but He was not a demigod (half man, half god) like Hercules. Jesus was fully God and fully man. Yet, in Him no sin was found.

2 Corinthians 5:21 makes it clear that "For he hath made him [to be] sin for us, who knew no sin; that we might be made the righteousness of God in him." Even though Jesus was in a body of flesh, he lived a sinless life and exchanges our sin for his righteousness. This is one of the most amazing verses in the Bible and is at the heart of the gospel. Christ accomplished in the flesh what we could never do through the strength of our own will. We see this tension in the book of Romans 7. Paul wants to do what is right and pleasing to God, but he finds another principle working in his flesh (*sarx*). Flesh wants what flesh wants, and if it is not checked by the higher part of man, our *nous* and *logos*, then it will run rampant and pursue natural desires in an unlawful manner. The *sarx* wants what is pleasing to it, comfort, shelter, food, drink, medication, sex, and, ultimately, its own way. If these desires have no restraint, the desire for pleasure will lead to hedonism (pleasure is the highest good); the desire for shelter will lead us to covet the shelter of our neighbor; the desire for food will lead to gluttony; the desire for drink will lead to drunkenness; the desire for medication will lead to

addiction; the desire for sex will lead to all manners of sexual immorality; and the desire for satisfying the ego will bring about envy, wrath, anger, jealousy and malice towards all those who thwart our egocentric desires. Unfortunately, our mind is not able to keep our fleshly desires in check. We may do well for a season, but the flesh is relentless and overtime wears away at our will until the lower aspects of our soul overcomes the higher aspects of our mind.

Paul acknowledges that in his flesh there is no good thing, so with his *sarx* he serves the law of sin which brings about death, but with his *nous* he serves the law of God. What a horrible position to live in, having the desire to do that which is right in one part of our soul, yet seeing our baser part constantly thwart our efforts. This dilemma can be found in Romans 7:21-5, where Paul sees two laws at war within him; "I find then a law, that, when I would do good, evil is present with me. For I delight in the law of God after the inward man: But I see another law in my members, warring against the law of my mind, and bringing me into captivity to the law of sin which is in my members. O wretched man that I am! who shall deliver me from the body of this death? I thank God through Jesus Christ our Lord. So then with the mind I myself serve the law of God; but with the flesh the law of sin."

Fortunately, this is not where the story ends. Paul continues in Romans 8 and shows us the hope and deliverance that can be found in Christ; "For what the law could not do, in that it was weak through the flesh, God sending his own Son in the likeness of sinful flesh, and for sin, condemned sin in the flesh" (Romans 8:3). The law, rather than providing us a way to be righteous before God, actually incited the flesh all the more and showed us how sinful we actually are. Even those without the Law of Moses, could not live up to the law in their own conscience (Romans 1). The law was never meant to redeem us; it was given to show us our desperate need for a redeemer. Unfortunately, many who come to Christ with great joy for their justification turn to the strength of their flesh to try and live out a Christ like life. Or they try and keep the law through the power of their own will, thinking that they must keep the law to be pleasing to God. What foolish madness, and this is what Paul tried to convey to the Galatians. If you have been saved by grace through faith, why then would you try to seek perfection through the law? Romans 8:3 tells us clearly that God sent His own Son in the likeness of sinful flesh to condemn sin in the flesh. What the law could not do because of the weakness of our flesh, Christ was able to fulfill for even though He lived as a man in the flesh He walked continuously, by the power and Spirit of God.

This is the same power and Spirit that is available to everyone who is in Christ Jesus. The power our flesh had over us is broken. That which our own mind or strength of will could not accomplish has already been accomplished in Christ. Therefore, stop trying to live out a Christian life by the strength of your own effort and will. Reckon yourself dead to the "old man," to the power of the flesh, abide in Christ, and walk in the Spirit. Jesus made it clear in John 8:34-36, "Verily, verily, I say unto you, Whosoever committeth sin is the servant of sin. And the servant abideth not in the house for ever: [but] the Son abideth ever. If the Son therefore shall make you free, ye shall be free indeed." Jesus made it clear that those who sin are enslaved by it, yet if Jesus has made you free, you are free to walk in the Spirit and not satisfy the lusts of the flesh.

HOW DO WE KNOW WE ARE WALKING IN THE SPIRIT AND THAT WE ARE NOT JUST JUSTIFYING OUR FLESHLY DESIRES?

The idea of reckoning, abiding, and walking in the Spirit may sound very appealing to you. What incredible freedom compared to living by a set of rules let alone the law of God! Yet, we know the heart is desperately wicked, who can know it? We may be afraid that we might think we are walking in the Spirit, but in reality are only using the Spirit as a justification for living out our own carnal desires. I can't tell you how many times people have told me it was God's will for them to do a certain activity which to me was so obviously not of God, and I freely admit that I myself am not beyond self-deception. So, how can we really tell if our lives are being lived by the power and Spirit of God? Have we simply found a new sophisticated and incredibly pious way to justify our own desires?

People have often claimed to know God's will throughout history; but even with the best of intentions, it can have horrific results. The apostle

Paul, while he was called Saul, thought he was doing the will of God by persecuting the early church. The battle cry of the crusades was "Deus Volt," which means God wills it. Manifest destiny was the justification in America to either kill or confine the native populations so that God's chosen people, "the Christian Americans," could rule from sea to shining sea. In the antebellum South, God fearing men and women justified owning slaves, believing that God created some people as masters and others as servants and that to violate this order would be a direct rebellion against God. This later was applied to the idea that interracial marriages were against God's plan since God divided the races at the tower of Babel—what God actually divided at Babel was language, but I have never yet, heard anyone say, that learning another language was an act of rebellion against God. I have heard men and women justify premarital sex or divorcing their spouses because it was God's will for them to be happy. Or people involved in homosexual relationships claiming, "how could it be wrong, if God made me this way?" After all this work and effort is ethics and morality really just relative and subjective after all? If everyone has a different understanding of what God's will is, how can we tell what is coming from God? Even though the "old man" is crucified with Christ, if we are not walking in the Spirit we will fall back to our old ways and patterns formed through our upbringing, enculturation, and biases.

For additional resources and biblical references
1 JOHN 4:2-3 - "Hereby know ye the Spirit of God: Every spirit that confesseth that Jesus Christ is come in the flesh [sarx] is of God: And every spirit that confesseth not that Jesus Christ is come in the flesh [sarx] is not of God: and this is that [spirit] of antichrist, whereof ye have heard that it should come; and even now already is it in the world."
2 JOHN 1:7 - For many deceivers are entered into the world, who confess not that Jesus Christ is come in the flesh [sarx]. This is a deceiver and an antichrist."
1 JOHN 3:5 - "And ye know that he was manifested to take away our sins; and in him is no sin."
HEBREWS 4:15 – "For we have not an high priest which cannot be touched with the feeling of our infirmities; but was in all points tempted like as [we are, yet] without sin."
1 PETER 2:22-24 – "Who did no sin, neither was guile found in his mouth:

Who, when he was reviled, reviled not again; when he suffered, he threatened not; but committed [himself] to him that judgeth righteously: Who his own self bare our sins in his own body on the tree, that we, being dead to sins, should live unto righteousness: by whose stripes ye were healed."

2 CORINTHIANS 5:19-21 - "To wit, that God was in Christ, reconciling the world unto himself, not imputing their trespasses unto them; and hath committed unto us the word of reconciliation. Now then we are ambassadors for Christ, as though God did beseech [you] by us: we pray [you] in Christ's stead, be ye reconciled to God. For he hath made him [to be] sin for us, who knew no sin; that we might be made the righteousness of God in him."

ROMANS 8:1-11 - "[There is] therefore now no condemnation to them which are in Christ Jesus, who walk not after the flesh, but after the Spirit. For the law of the Spirit of life in Christ Jesus hath made me free from the law of sin and death. For what the law could not do, in that it was weak through the flesh, God sending his own Son in the likeness of sinful flesh, and for sin, condemned sin in the flesh: That the righteousness of the law might be fulfilled in us, who walk not after the flesh, but after the Spirit. For they that are after the flesh do mind the things of the flesh; but they that are after the Spirit the things of the Spirit. For to be carnally minded [is] death; but to be spiritually minded [is] life and peace. Because the carnal mind [is] enmity against God: for it is not subject to the law of God, neither indeed can be. So then they that are in the flesh cannot please God. But ye are not in the flesh, but in the Spirit, if so be that the Spirit of God dwell in you. Now if any man have not the Spirit of Christ, he is none of his. And if Christ [be] in you, the body [is] dead because of sin; but the Spirit [is] life because of righteousness. But if the Spirit of him that raised up Jesus from the dead dwell in you, he that raised up Christ from the dead shall also quicken your mortal bodies by his Spirit that dwelleth in you."

ROMANS 3:20 – "Therefore by the deeds of the law there shall no flesh be justified in his sight: for by the law [is] the knowledge of sin."

ROMANS 6:6, 16-7, 20, 23 – "Knowing this, that our old man is crucified with [him], that the body of sin might be destroyed, that henceforth we should not serve sin. [...] Know ye not, that to whom ye yield yourselves servants to obey, his servants ye are to whom ye obey; whether of sin unto death, or of obedience unto righteousness? But God be thanked, that ye were the servants of sin, but ye have obeyed from the heart that form of doctrine which was delivered you. [...] For when ye were the servants of sin, ye were free from righteousness. [...] For the wages of sin [is] death; but the gift of God [is] eternal life through Jesus Christ our Lord."

KNOW THYSELF

To know if something is from God or from us, we must first know our-selves. Socrates exhorted his followers that they must first know themselves if they are to have any hope of knowing anything else. We have to be honest and know what is coming from our own hearts and desires. I am not even talking about the desires of the "old man," but simple human desires. We still desire self-preservation, comfort, pleasure, exaltation, and our own way. Yet, once we understand what the self, the ego desires, it becomes easier to contrast this with the desire of the Holy Spirit. Who is the final authority in your life? Is it you, or the Holy Spirit? In John 12:24-6, Jesus tells us that we must lose our own desires, ambitions, and egocentric goals in order to enter into life eternal; "Verily, verily, I say unto you, Except a corn of wheat fall into the ground and die, it abideth alone: but if it die, it bringeth forth much fruit. He that loveth his life shall lose it; and he that hateth his life in this world shall keep it unto life eternal. If any man serve me, let him follow me; and where I am, there shall also my servant be: if any man serve me, him will [my] Father honour." The challenge is identifying who sits on the throne of your will. We love to talk about our new lives in Christ, but often we forget that it comes at a great cost. I am not just talking about the cost Christ paid, but the cost is your own former life. In 1 Corinthians 6:19-20, we are told that even our bodies are now the dwelling place of the Spirit of God, so we are to honor God in both our physical behavior and soul life (mind, will, emotion); "What? know ye not that your body is the temple of the Holy Ghost [which is] in you, which ye have of God, and ye are not your own? For ye are bought with a price: therefore glorify God in your body, and in your spirit, which are God's." So, the key is to know yourself well enough to distinguish what is coming from you and what is coming from the Spirit dwelling within you.

THE WINDOW

One psycological construct that can be helpful in understanding the com-plexity of knowing oneself is the Johari window *(Figure 23)*. The Johari window is a psychological tool which was developed by Joseph Luft and

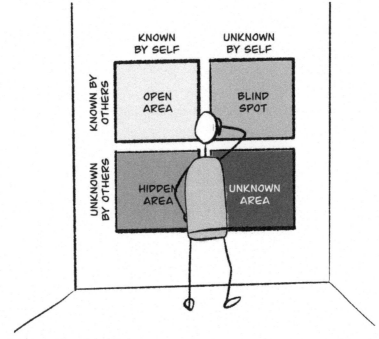

Figure 23. The Johari Window.

Harry Ingham in 1955; it identifies the complexity of knowing oneself beyond the surface.

I have always found the narratives people create to make sense of their lives fascinating. These narratives are quite revealing and can often pull back the curtain on one's "hidden window-pane." Countless examples could be given from political parties to religious denominations, but what I am most interested in are the stories we tell ourselves and others about who we are and why we think and act the way we do. If you think your personal narrative is synonymous with objective reality, I have an exercise for you. Find a close relation or friend and begin to critique their personal narrative and fill them in on some of their blind spots. I can almost guarantee you that they will return the favor and all of a sudden you will get a glimpse of what everyone else perceives about you that you did not perceive yourself. It can also happen when your narrative is not working and the stories you tell yourselves are shown as the shadow puppets they really are.

I can already hear the critics clamoring, what they heard was, "there is no objective Truth" what I am suggesting is not that there is *no* objective Truth, rather that type of knowledge is beyond our subjective range. You can make all sorts of Truth claims, but I do not know of any that can transcend your experiences. You may take offense and place your trust in all sorts of things from God to science, faith to reason, or religion to the scientific method. Regardless of your source of Truth, it is *you,* the subjective individual, who seeks to align your personal beliefs with what you belief to be True, thus formulating your personal narrative.

Truth is conventionally defined as that which corresponds to facts and/or reality.

This definition begs a couple of questions, "what are facts?" and more importantly, "what is reality." We also have to account for our own limitations, biases, and blind spots if we are to have any hope at all of being aligned with the Truth; for example, the truth of who we are. Yet, even then we must acknowledge our limitations and I believe it is wise to make qualifications when pronouncing Truth claims.

I have many friends and acquaintances who are naturalistic materialists. They see the world through a scientific lens and for them reality is quite physical. I have other friends who are eastern mystics and deny the existence of the material world and perceive reality as mind and consciousness. I fall somewhere in between; I believe in the existence of the material world, but I am also an idealist and romantic, not to mention my belief in non-material, spiritual beings and the role of Spirit in animating all living things.

> We are reality generating beings
> Living in a Reality that has already been generated
> How well does your reality align with Reality?
> And how do you know?

LOVE AND OBEDIENCE III.D.2

Love and obedience to God are indications that we are walking in the Spirit. Obedience to God cannot be accomplished through the strength of our own will. If it could be, then there would have been no need for Christ to die. Jesus tells us in John 15, "If you love me, keep my commandments" (15:14). What are Jesus' commandments? It is simple: "To love one another" (John 15:17). If you want a law or rule to follow, this is it, the law of the Spirit, for is the law of love. When Jesus was confronted by the Sadducees and the Pharisees, a lawyer among them asked, "Master, which [is] the great commandment in the law? Jesus said unto him, Thou shalt love the Lord thy God with all thy heart, and with all thy soul, and with all thy mind. This is the first and great commandment. And the second [is] like unto it, Thou shalt love thy neighbour as thyself. On these two commandments hang all the law and the prophets" (Matthew 22:36-40). Once again to be very clear, we cannot obey either of these commandments through the strength of our will, the "old man" only truly loves our old selves. So even our loving of God is only done out of self-interest. Once we have died to the "old man" and have been made alive in Christ. The very Spirit of God in us is able to perfectly love God and to perfectly love others. We know if we are true believers and disciples, if we love one another. Even though I really like the provocative title of this book, "The Dead Have No Need of Ethics," it could have just as easily been called, "An Ethic of Love," or "Holy Spirit Ethics." The apostle John makes it brutally clear in his epistle that love and obedience are the great indicators of whether or not we are in Christ.

In 1 John 3:4-9, John here hits us with a "one, two, punch" of love and obedience. The love part sounds so good, warm, and cozy, but then he tells us that "whoever is born of God does not commit sin" (John 3:6). How can this be? In the first chapter of John's epistle, he tells us that all have sinned which we can easily affirm. Is he now telling us that whoever abides in Jesus does not sin? Some translations render these verses as: "do not continue in sin," (1 John 3:9 NIV) or "make a practice of sinning" (1 John 3:9 ESV). But let us ask ourselves, do we just accidently sin on occasion, or is sin crouching daily at our door? Do we still have besetting sins or habits that have continued to plague us even though the "old man" has been put to death? Do we put ourselves above others—even above Jesus—on a daily basis? That sounds like continuing in sin to me. This passage should lead us to some serious "soul searching." If we still sin, are we really saved or even a Christian? Some preachers and theologians will attempt to explain this by saying that as long as you have a physical body you are going to sin, and until we have a glorified body in heaven, sin will always be a part of our earthly existence. What a curious thing to say. It reeks of gnostic heresy, making our physical bodies the problem and culpable for our sin. While our bodies are under the curse, our physical bodies (*soma*) do not cause us to sin. Jesus had a *soma*, but he also had no sin. Does your fist just randomly strike someone or do your genitals force you to have illicit sex? Does your mouth cause you to curse or your hand cause you to steal? What foolish nonsense!

One of my nephews, who came to live with me when he was eleven, was listening to a famous radio evangelist with me on the way to school one morning. This preacher's text for the day was 1 John 3. After he read the above passage, he paused for a commercial break. When he came back from the break, he chuckled mildly to himself and in his old timey country voice said, "Beloved, I bet that passage had you worried, but don't worry, you will continue to go on sinning as long as you have a body" (J. Vernon McGee). I was so startled by what I had just heard that I almost crashed the car. Instead, I immediately reached out with my right hand and began to "choke" my young nephew by throttling his neck. I asked him, "Who's choking you? Me or my hand?" He replied, "You are uncle." At which point I released him and said, "And don't ever forget this." Our bodies can do nothing without our consent. Even though I have a great deal of appreciation and respect for this radio preacher, I thought that his understanding on this topic was quite dangerous, and I didn't want my nephew to let this teaching take root in his life. Our bodies are not sinful or promoting evil, it is the intentions and desires of the heart which animate the actions of the body. This is a prime example that even though someone might be a profound and solid preacher, it can be easy to place blame on our mortal frame for a problem that ultimately resides in the soul.

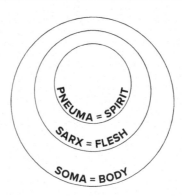

Figure 24. Soma, Sarx, Pneuma.

Sins are not the result of our body (*soma*) but come from our flesh (*sarx*) (*Figure 24*). I know I am being redundant, but I want so badly for you to understand what we are discussing here. The very flesh that made it impossible for us to keep the law of God, the likeness of which was taken on by Jesus, he put to death sin in the flesh. In a very real sense, now when we sin, it is no longer us who are doing it, rather it is sin that dwells within us. This is evident in Romans 7:20; "Now if I do that I would not, it is no more I that do it, but sin that dwelleth in me."

Have you experienced this phenomenon? You know you love God, and you have been redeemed. But you find yourself participating in the vilest acts of lust, anger, covetousness, and others. Yet, when the feelings and urges pass, it is almost as if you awoke and are back in your right mind, wondering what that was all about. It is rather like the psychological condition called a *fugue state* in which an individual will actually take on mannerisms and a countenance of someone else and do not even realize they are doing it until it is over. I call it "spiritual zombie land," where our "old man" who has been crucified is animated and walking around, trying to take control of our life even though he has already been put to death on the cross of Christ. Just like a corpse, the "old man" is a stinking rotting mess. When we are back in the mind of Christ, we cannot even believe that that putrefied flesh held any appeal to us, and we are repulsed and confess our sin. Fortunately, God is faithful and just to forgive us our sins and to cleanse us from all unrighteousness (1 John 1:9). The issue here once again is identity. Who are you? If you are in Christ, you are a new creation; if you abide in Christ, it is impossible for you to sin; if you walk in the Spirit, you will not fulfill the lusts of the flesh. If, however, you walk in the flesh, you are capable of the most horrific acts imaginable. A life in the flesh brings death, but a life in the Spirit brings life. This concept is clearly articulated in 1 John 3:9; "Whosoever is born of God doth not commit sin; for his seed remaineth in him: and he cannot sin, because he is born of God." Who's seed remains in you? It is the very seed of God. I will talk more of this in the later section on *theosis* (the deification of the believer). It is not us being loving and obedient that gets us right with God. It is by having the Spirit of Christ, God's seed, in us that we are capable of being loving and obedient towards God. Those that are in Christ model His love and obedience because when believers walk in the Spirit, the *sarx* no longer has control.

THE FRUIT OF THE SPIRIT   *III.D.3*

Another way we can know if we are walking in the Spirit is by the fruit that is being produced in our lives (*Figure 25*). Jesus tells us, "Either make

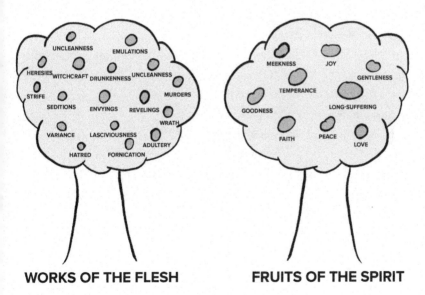

WORKS OF THE FLESH   **FRUITS OF THE SPIRIT**

Figure 25. Fruit of the Spirit; works of the flesh.

the tree good, and his fruit good; or else make the tree corrupt, and his fruit corrupt: for the tree is known by [his] fruit. [...] A good man out of the good treasure of the heart bringeth forth good things: and an evil man out of the evil treasure bringeth forth evil things" (Mat 12:33, 35 KJV). When we look at the fruit that is being produced in our lives, it is clear whether this fruit is coming from the flesh or from the Spirit.

III.D.4 THE TRANSFORMATION OF THE MIND

The very part of our mind that was separated from God by the fall is now being renewed by the power of the Holy Spirit. We actually begin to reason from a new perspective, and we have access to the very mind of Christ. That which once seemed like foolishness to us, we now see as the power and mercy of God. We no longer are limited to a human perspective, but through Christ we have access to a divine point of view. Our judgments and values are no longer based on our own self-interests or bias. We now have access to God's own heart and desire. Ephesians 4:22-4 states, "That ye put off concerning the former conversation the old man, which is corrupt according to the deceitful lusts; And be renewed in the spirit of your mind; And that ye put on the new man, which after God is created in righteousness and true holiness."

Similarly, 1 Corinthians 2 points out that the foolishness of God is greater than the wisdom of men; "Because the foolishness of God is wiser than men; and the weakness of God is stronger than men" (2:25). The carnal mind cannot understand the things of God. It is foolishness to those who have not been regenerated by the Holy Spirit. We know that we are in Christ partly because what we once could not understand through the strength of our own reason or through the recollection of our personal experiences has been made know to us by God himself. When we were spiritually dead, we could not know the things of God because they can only be spiritually discerned. Once Christ quickened our spirits and united us with His own, we no longer were left to lean on our own understanding, but with our new life—God gave us the very mind of Christ.

THE TESTIMONY OF GOD'S SPIRIT TO OUR SPIRIT   *III.D.5*

The same way we can know that we are walking in the Spirit is the same way we can know that we are saved and are in Christ Jesus. The Holy Spirit bears witness with our spirit that we are the sons and daughters of God. The Spirit bears witness with our spirit that we are the children of God; Romans 8:12-17 conveys this saying, "Therefore, brethren, we are debtors, not to the flesh, to live after the flesh. For if ye live after the flesh, ye shall die: but if ye through the Spirit do mortify the deeds of the body, ye shall live. For as many as are led by the Spirit of God, they are the sons of God. For ye have not received the spirit of bondage again to fear; but ye have received the Spirit of adoption, whereby we cry, Abba, Father. The Spirit itself beareth witness with our spirit, that we are the children of God: And if children, then heirs; heirs of God, and joint-heirs with Christ; if so be that we suffer with [him], that we may be also glorified together." Also, Romans 8:23 and 26 add that the Spirit not only confirms our pedigree, but also intercedes on our behalf: "And not only [they], but ourselves also, which have the firstfruits of the Spirit, even we ourselves groan within ourselves, waiting for the adoption, [to wit], the redemption of our body. [...] Likewise the Spirit also helpeth our infirmities: for we know not what we should pray for as we ought: but the Spirit itself maketh intercession for us with groanings which cannot be uttered." The reason we have assurace is because we have the very Spirit of God within us. God's testimony bears witness in us to us; "Hereby know we that we dwell in him, and he in us, because he hath given us of his Spirit" (1 John 4:13).

When people ask me how I know what I believe in is true, I do not talk about reason, evidence, or even quote the Bible at them. I look them straight in the eye and tell them that I know that God is real and that Jesus, His son, came to reconcile me to Himself through His own precious blood, and I know this not because of some fabulously devised tales, iron age mythologies, or even wishful thinking. I know this because I have the Holy Spirit within me, and His Spirit bears witness with my spirit that I am His and He is mine. I believe it is possible to grieve the Holy Spirit, but I do not believe He will ever leave us or forsake us. People who are indwelled by the Holy Spirit but are not walking in the Spirit and instead walk the flesh, may not have the kind of assurance I am talking about. I am not suggesting that they are not saved or have lost their salvation, but they have lost that fellowship which could so easily assure them of their new identity in Christ. We are God's workmanship. Our new lives may involve us, but they are not dependent on us. 2 Timothy 1:12 clarifies this saying, "for I know whom I have believed, and am persuaded that he is able to keep that which I have committed unto him against that day."

For further additional explanation see the following video(s)
"Walk in the Spirit." YouTube, recorded and uploaded by Fred Blackburn. 18 April 2020, https://youtu.be/q3j2TOBP9VM
"Neoplatonism and Gnosticism." YouTube, recorded and uploaded by Fred Blackburn. 19 November 2019, https://youtu.be/nabAko23a_s
"Exploration of the Self." YouTube, recorded and uploaded by Fred Blackburn. 15 January 2019, https://youtu.be/rgCXmTVlo7Y

For additional resources and biblical references
Luft, J, H. Ingham. "The Johari window, a graphic model of interpersonal awareness." *Proceedings of the Western Training Laboratory in Group Development*, Los Angeles: U of California, 1955.
1 JOHN 4:1-11 - "Beloved, let us love one another: for love is of God; and every one that loveth is born of God, and knoweth God. He that loveth not knoweth not God; for God is love. In this was manifested the love of God toward us, because that God sent his only begotten Son into the world, that we might live through him. Herein is love, not that we loved God, but that he loved us, and sent his Son [to be] the propitiation for our sins. Beloved, if God so loved us, we ought also to love one another."
1 JOHN 3:4-9 - "Whosoever committeth sin transgresseth also the law: for sin is the transgression of the law. And ye know that he was manifested to take away our sins; and in him is no sin. Whosoever abideth in him sinneth not: whosoever sinneth hath not seen him, neither known him. Little children, let no man deceive you: he that doeth righteousness is righteous, even as he is righteous. He that committeth sin is of the devil; for the devil sinneth from the beginning. For this purpose the Son of God was manifested, that he might destroy the works of the devil. Whosoever is born of God doth not commit sin; for his seed remaineth in him: and he cannot sin, because he is born of God."
MATTHEW 15:16-20 - "And Jesus said, Are ye also yet without understanding? Do not ye yet understand, that whatsoever entereth in at the mouth

goeth into the belly, and is cast out into the draught? But those things which proceed out of the mouth come forth from the heart; and they defile the man. For out of the heart proceed evil thoughts, murders, adulteries, fornications, thefts, false witness, blasphemies: These are [the things] which defile a man: but to eat with unwashen hands defileth not a man."

JAMES 4:1-5 - "From whence [come] wars and fightings among you? [come they] not hence, [even] of your lusts that war in your members? Ye lust, and have not: ye kill, and desire to have, and cannot obtain: ye fight and war, yet ye have not, because ye ask not. Ye ask, and receive not, because ye ask amiss, that ye may consume [it] upon your lusts. Ye adulterers and adulteresses, know ye not that the friendship of the world is enmity with God? whosoever therefore will be a friend of the world is the enemy of God. Do ye think that the scripture saith in vain, The spirit that dwelleth in us lusteth to envy?"

GALATIANS 5:17 - "For the flesh lusteth against the Spirit, and the Spirit against the flesh: and these are contrary the one to the other: so that ye cannot do the things that ye would."

ROMANS 8:5-11 - "For they that are after the flesh do mind the things of the flesh; but they that are after the Spirit the things of the Spirit. For to be carnally minded [is] death; but to be spiritually minded [is] life and peace. Because the carnal mind [is] enmity against God: for it is not subject to the law of God, neither indeed can be. So then they that are in the flesh cannot please God. But ye are not in the flesh, but in the Spirit, if so be that the Spirit of God dwell in you. Now if any man have not the Spirit of Christ, he is none of his. And if Christ [be] in you, the body [is] dead because of sin; but the Spirit [is] life because of righteousness. But if the Spirit of him that raised up Jesus from the dead dwell in you, he that raised up Christ from the dead shall also quicken your mortal bodies by his Spirit that dwelleth in you."

GALATIANS 5:19-25 - "Now the works of the flesh are manifest, which are [these]; Adultery, fornication, uncleanness, lasciviousness, Idolatry, witchcraft, hatred, variance, emulations, wrath, strife, seditions, heresies, Envyings, murders, drunkenness, revellings, and such like: of the which I tell you before, as I have also told [you] in time past, that they which do such things shall not inherit the kingdom of God. But the fruit of the Spirit is love, joy, peace, longsuffering, gentleness, goodness, faith, Meekness, temperance: against such there is no law. And they that are Christ's have crucified the flesh with the affections and lusts. If we live in the Spirit, let us also walk in the Spirit."

PSALM 1:3 - "And he shall be like a tree planted by the rivers of water, that bringeth forth his fruit in his season; his leaf also shall not wither; and whatsoever he doeth shall prosper."

JOHN 15:5 - "I am the vine, ye [are] the branches: He that abideth in me, and I in him, the same bringeth forth much fruit: for without me ye can do nothing."

ROMANS 6:22 – "But now being made free from sin, and become servants to God, ye have your fruit unto holiness, and the end everlasting life."

EPHESIANS 4:17-24 - "This I say therefore, and testify in the Lord, that ye henceforth walk not as other Gentiles walk, in the vanity of their mind, Having the understanding darkened, being alienated from the life of God through the ignorance that is in them, because of the blindness of their heart: Who being past feeling have given themselves over unto lasciviousness, to work all uncleanness with greediness. But ye have not so learned Christ; If so be that ye have heard him, and have been taught by him, as the truth is in Jesus: That ye put off concerning the former conversation the old man, which is corrupt according to the deceitful lusts; And be renewed in the spirit of your mind; And that ye put on the new man, which after God is created in righteousness and true holiness."

1 CORINTHIANS 2 - see full chapter

List of figures

Fig. 23. The Johari Window.

Fig. 24. Soma, Sarx, Pneuma.

Fig. 25. Fruit of the Spirit; works of the flesh.

III.E GLORIFICATION AND *THEOSIS*

"For our light affliction, which is but for a moment, worketh for us a far more exceeding [and] eternal weight of glory." – 2 Corinthians 4:17

So far, we have talked about how we are washed, sanctified, and justified in the name of the Lord Jesus, and by the Spirit of our God (1 Corinthians 6:11). Yet, the end goal of Christ's work in our lives is the glorification of the believer, and in our glorification, God is glorified. Glory is mentioned throughout the Old and New Testaments. Glory can refer to what is of great weight or consequence or to that which is lifted up and exalted. It covers the full spectrum of height and depth, gravity and loftiness, dread and magnificence. Lucifer was the most exalted and glorious of all of God's celestial creation, yet he craved more and tried to exalt his glory over the very glory of God. Man was made as the crowning glory of terrestrial creation, and woman was created as the glory of man. This is stated in Psalm 8:5, "he is the image and glory of God: but the woman is the glory of the man" (1 Corinthians 11:7). There is the glory of kings and the glory of beasts, the glory of the sun and the glory of the moon, the glory of a raging storm or the glory of a peaceful land, yet none of these can compare to the glory of Christ.

Man's glory was marred when he chose to exalt his self-will over the will of God. As it was in Eden, so it is every time we choose self over God. However, God had compassion upon us and gave to us freely what we tried to take by theft. Adam and Eve in their attempt to become like God, became debased in their imaginations and their hearts were darkened.

In His wonder, God has chosen to manifest His glory through the brokenness of man. This treasure is in earthen vessels which is our mortal frame. It is actually through our cracks, blemishes, and weaknesses that the glory and goodness of God shines most brightly. We try so hard to patch up our flaws and shortcomings so that God and others will not see our deficiencies. But it is in these very flaws that the light of God shines forth most clearly. The apostle Paul tells us how God would not remove "the thorn in his flesh," but rather left the thorn so as to keep Paul completely dependent on God rather than his own strength (2 Corinthians 12:7). Paul realizes that it is in his weaknesses he must be completely dependent on God, yet that is exactly where Paul wants to be; "And he said unto me, My grace is sufficient for thee: for my strength is made perfect in weakness. Most gladly therefore will I rather glory in my infirmities, that the power of Christ may rest upon me. Therefore I take pleasure in infirmities, in reproaches, in necessities, in persecutions, in distresses for Christ's sake: for when I am weak, then am I strong" (2 Corinthians 12:9-10). This is the power and paradox of the cross.

Though man was created in glory a little lower than the angels, his fall debased him to the level of the beasts (Psalm 8:5). Yet, God in His great mercy, exalted fallen man above the angels by His own Son fulfilling the righteous judgment of God and transforming the brokenness of humanity into the glorious image of His Son. 1 Corinthians 15:49 says, "And as we

Figure 26. Jesus is the light of the world.

have borne the image of the earthy, we shall also bear the image of the heavenly." Through man's fall and Christ's redemption, that which is earthly becomes heavenly—the far off become near, the fallen are exalted, the dead are made alive, sinners are made righteous, strangers are made sons, mortality is exchanged for immortality, the filthy are made clean—and we who once walked in darkness are the bearers of God's own glorious light. This is why John 8:12 says, "Then spake Jesus again unto them, saying, I am the light of the world: he that followeth me shall not walk in darkness, but shall have the light of life (Figure 26). And in Matthew 5:16 He turns it to us: "Let your light so shine before men, that they may see your good works, and glorify your Father which is in heaven."

It is at this point I want to turn to the most mysterious and glorious part of this journey we have taken together. So far, we have talked about how we are justified by grace through faith, not of ourselves since it is the "gift of God lest any man should boast" (Ephesians 2:8-9), We have seen we are sanctified the same way we are justified by the power and work of Christ. (1 Corinthians 6:11). Finally, I have shown how we are glorified—

not because of what we have done, but because of who we are in Christ. Yet, there is a final movement, something so wonderful and otherworldly that I tremble at the very thought of trying to put it into words. This final mystery is that we are no longer mere mortals. We have become more than humans; we have become partakers of the divine nature and in so doing we have become gods.

THEOSIS (THE DEIFICATION OF THE BELIEVER)

> "For this is why the Word became man, and the Son of God became the Son of man, so that man, by entering into communion with the Word and thus receiving divine sonship, might become a son of God." - Saint Irenaeus

> "God became man so that men might become gods." – Saint Athanasius

> "The Son of God took on human nature so that the sons of man might be partakers of the divine nature." – Darkwaterhermit

Theosis is the teaching that our human spirit is actually united with the spirit of God. We become partakers of God's nature by God's grace. This goes far beyond being imitators of Christ to being partakers of Christ's divine nature through the indwelling of the Holy Spirit. We literally are no longer merely humans although we still have a human nature; now we have also been united with the divine nature, thus making us god-men and god-women. Adam and Eve in all their pre-Fall perfection and glory, even though they were made in the image of God, did not partake of the divine nature. They were perfect humans but still only humans. Despite all the tragedy, death, and separation that accompanied the Fall, it actually set into place God's plan of redemption. Not only did God reconcile us to himself through the sacrifice of his son, but he gave to us something that Adam and Eve never had. God imparted to us His own nature; the very seed of God is in those who have been conceived by the indwelling of the Holy Spirit (1 John 3:9).

Jesus Christ is the model of this new type of being. Jesus, the Son, in union with the Father and the Holy Spirit make up the Holy Trinity. These are the three persons of the Godhead. One God in three persons. Philippians 2:6-7 identifies Jesus's relation in the Trinity saying, "Who, being in the form of God, thought it not robbery to be equal with God: But made himself of no reputation, and took upon him the form of a servant, and was made in the likeness of men." It is crucial to understand that Jesus is co-equal and co-eternal with the other members of the Godhead. Additionally, "God sending his own Son in the likeness of sinful flesh, and for sin, condemned sin in the flesh;" by having a physical human body, Christ put sin to death through His own death (Romans 8:3). Jesus as God took on human nature and form and by his sacrifice provided the means by which humans can take on the divine nature.

For additional resources and biblical references
ROMANS 8:30 – "Moreover whom he did predestinate, them he also called: and whom he called, them he also justified: and whom he justified, them he also glorified."
2 THESSALONIANS 2:13-14 – "But we are bound to give thanks alway to God for you, brethren beloved of the Lord, because God hath from the beginning chosen you to salvation through sanctification of the Spirit and belief of the truth: Whereunto he called you by our gospel, to the obtaining of the glory of our Lord Jesus Christ."
2 CORINTHIANS 4:4, 6-7, 16-18 – "In whom the god of this world hath blinded the minds of them which believe not, lest the light of the glorious gospel of Christ, who is the image of God, should shine unto them. [...] For God, who commanded the light to shine out of darkness, hath shined in our hearts, to [give] the light of the knowledge of the glory of God in the face of Jesus Christ. But we have this treasure in earthen vessels, that the excellency of the power may be of God, and not of us. [...] For which cause we faint not; but though our outward man perish, yet the inward [man] is renewed day by day. For our light affliction, which is but for a moment, worketh for us a far more exceeding [and] eternal weight of glory; While we look not at the things which are seen, but at the things which are not seen: for the things which are seen [are] temporal; but the things which are not seen [are] eternal."
1 CORINTHIANS 15:22, 45-49 – "For as in Adam all die, even so in Christ shall all be made alive. [...] And so it is written, The first man Adam was made

a living soul; the last Adam [was made] a quickening spirit. Howbeit that [was] not first which is spiritual, but that which is natural; and afterward that which is spiritual. The first man [is] of the earth, earthy: the second man [is] the Lord from heaven. As [is] the earthy, such [are] they also that are earthy: and as [is] the heavenly, such [are] they also that are heavenly. And as we have borne the image of the earthy, we shall also bear the image of the heavenly." JOHN 1:1-5, 9-13 – "In the beginning was the Word, and the Word was with God, and the Word was God. The same was in the beginning with God. All things were made by him; and without him was not any thing made that was made. In him was life; and the life was the light of men. And the light shineth in darkness; and the darkness comprehended it not. [...] [That] was the true Light, which lighteth every man that cometh into the world. He was in the world, and the world was made by him, and the world knew him not. He came unto his own, and his own received him not. But as many as received him, to them gave he power to become the sons of God, [even] to them that believe on his name: Which were born, not of blood, nor of the will of the flesh, nor of the will of man, but of God."

MARY AND THE HOLY GHOST   *III.E.1*

"But while he thought on these things, behold, the angel of the Lord appeared unto him in a dream, saying, Joseph, thou son of David, fear not to take unto thee Mary thy wife: for that which is conceived in her is of the Holy Ghost." – Matthew 1:20

In Roman Catholic theology, Mary is referred to as the "Mother of God" because she gave birth to the Son of God. In Eastern Orthodoxy, Mary is referred to as the *theotokos*, which means God-bearer. I prefer the Eastern Orthodox terminology; even though Mary was the earthly mother of Jesus, she was not the mother of God in the sense that God came from her, but rather the Spirit of God came upon her, and she had the highly favored position of bearing God within herself. Yet, all those have Christ in them are also *theotokos*, for we bear the very nature of God within ourselves in the person of the Holy Spirit. When Mary gave birth to Jesus, she no longer had the divine nature within her, until she later received the gift of the Holy Spirit in the same way that we receive the indwelling of the Holy Spirit.

God, through the person of the Son, took on human nature. This is known as the *hypostatic union* in theology which in this context is one person with two natures. Jesus is fully God and fully man, having both a divine and human nature. Jesus is not half-God and half-man, but fully God and fully man. Yet, even though Jesus is the only begotten Son of the Father, He is the firstborn of a whole new creation: a new type of lineage, a new type of being. Jesus is the firstborn of God; but because of His Spirit, we too are born of God: "For whom he did foreknow, he also did predestinate [to be] conformed to the image of his Son, that he might be the firstborn among many brethren" (Roman 8:29). Our "old man" was in Adam, but our "new man" is in Christ. Our Adamic nature has been put to death on the cross, and our new nature is found in Christ. Since flesh and blood will not enter the kingdom of heaven, when Jesus conveys this idea to Nicodemus, He made it quite clear to we must be *born again*.

III.E.2 BORN AGAIN

> "Jesus answered and said unto him, Verily, verily, I say unto thee,
> Except a man be born again, he cannot see the kingdom of
> God." – John 3:3

It is our new birth in the Spirit that makes us of Christ. We are made new; "Therefore if any man [be] in Christ, [he is] a new creature: old things are passed away; behold, all things are become new" (2 Corinthians 5:17). This is also articulated in 2 Peter 1:3-4, "According as his divine power hath given unto us all things that [pertain] unto life and godliness, through the knowledge of him that hath called us to glory and virtue: Whereby are given unto us exceeding great and precious promises: that by these ye might be partakers of the divine nature, having escaped the corruption that is in the world through lust." It is through the divine power of Jesus Christ our Lord that he has made us partakers of the divine nature. Now that we have the Spirit of God within us, we are already the Children of God: "Behold, what manner of love the Father hath bestowed upon us, that we should be called the sons of God: therefore the world knoweth us not, because it knew him not. Beloved, now are we the sons of God, and it doth not yet appear what we shall be: but we know that, when he shall appear, we shall be like him; for we shall see him as he is" (1 John 3:1-2). Being called children of God, being transformed, changes everything. When we discussed 1 John 3 earlier, I made a critical point and I shall say it again for emphasis: the reason we cannot commit sin is because it is the very seed of God that puts his living Spirit inside of us and that is our new identity in Christ (1 John 3:9-11). Just as in Romans 7 where Paul disassociated himself with the sin principle which is at work in his members, he identifies that his identity is with the Spirit of God that has been knit together with his own Spirit.

Just as Christ has two natures, divine and human, and will have these two natures throughout eternity; in Christ we also now have two natures, human and divine, which we too will have throughout eternity. Christ, out of His divinity, took on humanity. It is in Christ that our humanity is united with divinity; "But he that is joined unto the Lord is one spirit" (1 Corinthians 6:17). The context of the above verse is that Paul is admonishing believers not to engage in sexual immorality, in this case not to join our bodies to that of a prostitute, "for the two shall become one flesh" thus doing a play on ideas (1 Corinthians 6:16). Paul is using graphic sexual imagery to demonstrate what is happening to us spiritually when we are joined to the Lord. We still have a human spirit, but it becomes one with God's indwelling Spirit when we are joined with it. Like Christ we share in having two natures, but unlike Christ we are indwelt by two persons. One person is our new man, created in Christ which is fully human, and the other person is the Holy Spirit, which is fully God. This is an important distinction between the Christian doctrine of *theosis* and the false teachings of divine self-realization found in Gnosticism and Hinduism, or the Buddhist teaching of the annihilation of the self.

In the Gnostic, Hindu, and various types of Eastern Mysticism or New Age spirituality, the idea is that we are all divine. These religions teach that all people have the spark of the divine within that simply needs to be realized and manifested. This belief is as if we are indwelt by a god with amnesia whom we are able to bring back into conscious awareness by getting in touch with our *true* divine self. This is the ultimate form of self-deception and echoes the sin of Lucifer and that of Adam and Eve. God's highest created celestial and terrestrial beings both rebelled against their maker and tried to claim divinity for themselves. In contrast, the Buddhist tradition teaches that there is no self. Rather than your true self being God within, there is no self. The Buddhist practice of self-annihilation attempts to remove the false ego self and to reveal nothing within. Yet, for this type of Buddhist nothingness, called Nirvana, is actually everything-ness which makes the enlightened Buddhist one with everything or in other words: God. All of the above examples are humans trying to obtain the divine, just like Adam and Eve trying to obtain divine knowledge in the garden of Eden. In contrast, *Theosis* is god brining divinity to humanity.

Even though *theosis* is the Christian teaching of becoming united with the divine, it stops short of claiming that we are God. In Christ, we do not become the fourth member of the trinity. We do not take on the attributes which belong to God alone to be part of His eternal nature. We do not become eternal although we are given everlasting life; we do not become all powerful although we have the power of God within us. We do not become all knowing although we have access to the mind of God; we do not become everywhere present even though God is ever present with us, and we do not become the creator and sustainer of all things even though he has created within us a new life and sustains us. Rather it is by the gift of God that He has united us with Himself in His Son. It is in Jesus we have light and life. It is in Jesus that we have union with the Father. It is because we are given the mind of Christ that we can know the mind of God: "For who hath known the mind of the Lord, that he may instruct him? But we have the mind of Christ" (1 Corinthians 2:16). This is not achieved by realizing our true nature or by annihilating our false self. It is by being given a new nature by God and being indwelt by His own nature in the person of the Holy Spirit.

THE UNITY PRAYER OF JESUS   *III.E.3*

"Neither pray I for these alone, but for them also which shall believe on me through their word; That they all may be one; as thou, Father, [art] in me, and I in thee, that they also may be one in us: that the world may believe that thou hast sent me. And the glory which thou gavest me I have given them; that they may be one, even as we are one: I in them, and thou in me, that they may be made perfect in one; and that the world may know that thou hast sent me, and hast loved them, as thou hast loved me. Father, I will that they also, whom thou hast given me, be with me where I am; that they may behold my glory, which thou hast given me: for thou lovedst me before the foundation of the world. O righteous Father, the world hath not known thee: but I have known thee, and these have known that thou hast sent me. And I have declared unto them thy name, and will declare [it]: that the love wherewith thou hast loved me may be in them, and I in them." - John 17:20-26

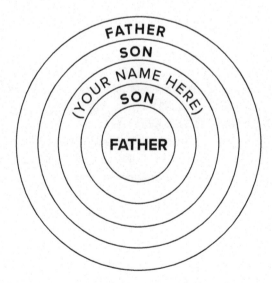

Figure 27. Depiction of John 17.

In Christ we do not cease being human, instead we become the humans that God always intended us to be. For the first time in our lives we can actually be authentic and true to ourselves. Our "old man" was born dead in sin and through our flesh or strength of our will we never could free ourselves of the bondage in which we were held. Christ put sin to death in the flesh and made us a new creation. Now having put on the new being, we are no longer the slaves of sin, but we are now the slaves of Christ. Yet, in being the slaves of Christ, we are now free for the first time. It is by the power of God's own Holy Spirit that dwells within us that we can remain free and alive in Him. Adam Fred is crucified with Christ. Nevertheless, Fred lives; yet it is not Fred, but Christ who lives in me, and the life which Fred now lives in the flesh Fred lives by the faith of the Son of God, who loves Fred, and gave himself for Fred (Galatians 2:20). The human Fred partaking of the divine nature of Jesus lives in perfect liberty and freedom in Christ. This allows me, Fred, to be the person God always intended me to be and to live the life that God always intended me to live.

For further additional explanation see the following video(s)
"Glorification and Theosis." YouTube, recorded and uploaded by Fred Blackburn. 25 April 2020, https://youtu.be/RMDsNLLR1nE

For additional resources and biblical references
LUKE 1:30-35 - "And the angel said unto her, Fear not, Mary: for thou hast found favour with God. And, behold, thou shalt conceive in thy womb, and bring forth a son, and shalt call his name JESUS. He shall be great, and shall be called the Son of the Highest: and the Lord God shall give unto him the throne of his father David: And he shall reign over the house of Jacob for ever; and of his kingdom there shall be no end. Then said Mary unto the angel, How shall this be, seeing I know not a man? And the angel answered and said unto her, The Holy Ghost shall come upon thee, and the power of the Highest shall overshadow thee: therefore also that holy thing which shall be born of thee shall be called the Son of God."
HEBREWS 2:9, 16-18 – "But we see Jesus, who was made a little lower than the angels for the suffering of death, crowned with glory and honour; that he by the grace of God should taste death for every man. [...] For verily he took not on [him the nature of] angels; but he took on [him] the seed of Abraham. Wherefore in all things it behoved him to be made like unto [his] brethren,

that he might be a merciful and faithful high priest in things [pertaining] to God, to make reconciliation for the sins of the people. For in that he himself hath suffered being tempted, he is able to succour them that are tempted."

HEBREWS 4:14-15 – "Seeing then that we have a great high priest, that is passed into the heavens, Jesus the Son of God, let us hold fast [our] profession. For we have not an high priest which cannot be touched with the feeling of our infirmities; but was in all points tempted like as [we are, yet] without sin."

JOHN 1:14 – "Jesus is the only begotten Son of God. "And the Word was made flesh, and dwelt among us, (and we beheld his glory, the glory as of the only begotten of the Father,) full of grace and truth."

JOHN 3:16 – "For God so loved the world, that he gave his only begotten Son, that whosoever believeth in him should not perish, but have everlasting life."

JOHN 3:3-8 – "Jesus answered and said unto him, Verily, verily, I say unto thee, Except a man be born again, he cannot see the kingdom of God. Nicodemus saith unto him, How can a man be born when he is old? can he enter the second time into his mother's womb, and be born? Jesus answered, Verily, verily, I say unto thee, Except a man be born of water and [of] the Spirit, he cannot enter into the kingdom of God. That which is born of the flesh is flesh; and that which is born of the Spirit is spirit. Marvel not that I said unto thee, Ye must be born again. The wind bloweth where it listeth, and thou hearest the sound thereof, but canst not tell whence it cometh, and whither it goeth: so is every one that is born of the Spirit."

JOHN 1:12-13 – "But as many as received him, to them gave he power to become the sons of God, [even] to them that believe on his name: Which were born, not of blood, nor of the will of the flesh, nor of the will of man, but of God."

1 JOHN 3:9-11, 24 – "Whosoever is born of God doth not commit sin; for his seed remaineth in him: and he cannot sin, because he is born of God. In this the children of God are manifest, and the children of the devil: whosoever doeth not righteousness is not of God, neither he that loveth not his brother. For this is the message that ye heard from the beginning, that we should love one another. [...] And he that keepeth his commandments dwelleth in him, and he in him. And hereby we know that he abideth in us, by the Spirit which he hath given us."

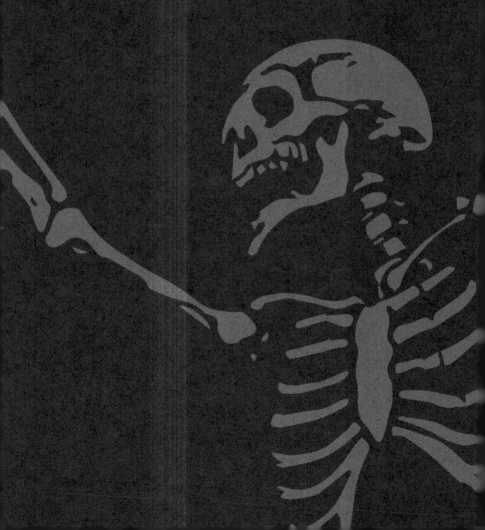

PART 3

Critique, Process, and Application

§

PREFACE

In this third and final part of the book, I thought it would only be fair to subject my own theory to a formal critique. This will include an objective summary and critique of *The Dead Have No Need of Ethics*, just like I critiqued the other theories in Part 1. I also thought it may be of interest to share my personal ethic and the process I go through in making ethical decisions and navigating moral dilemmas. My personal ethic will include my highest *good*, why I believe I'm here on earth, what empowers me to live out my ethic, and what I believe will happen to me when I die. I will also discuss how I deal with moral success and failure on a personal level as well as how my prayer life has changed. I do believe it is important to discuss the tension between human free will and God's sovereignty as it relates to ethics and morality.

Finally, I want to end the book with an ethical topic sampler. I will show you how I arrive at various convictions through my discussion of environmental issues, capital punishment, war, civil disobedience (specifically how it relates to government authority and personal reasonability), and euthanasia. I will show you how I personally navigate these issues in the hopes that it will help you as you engage these and other ethical topics. If you had not guessed it by now, this non-ethic, or Holy Spirit led ethic, could lead to a variety of ethical and moral decisions and personal convictions. I hope this third and final part is a blessing to you and will help you as you yield to the Spirit and embrace Christ's righteousness as your own.

II CRITIQUE OF *THE DEAD HAVE NO NEED OF ETHICS*

II.A ETHICS AND RELIGION

I think it has become self-evident by this point that I have a love/hate relationship with both ethics and religion. I have dedicated my life to the study of these disciplines which try to answer such fundamental questions as "what is the meaning and purpose of life?" "Where did I come from?" "Why am I here?" "What is the right way to live and what enables me to do so?" "Is there a God, and if so, how do I have right relationship with the Deity?" "What happens to me when I die?" Ethics and religion deal with such questions and more. Ethics and religion are lofty in their thoughts and ideals and bring a certain order, hope, and beauty to our world. However, they are also often self-serving and manipulative, using either shame and guilt as means of control or sometimes outright temporal power and authority forcing others to conform to their point of view.

I have been more than happy to critique other worldviews, religions, and ethical theories, so I thought it would only be good form to return the favor on my own personal beliefs. I hope you enjoy this critical thinking exorcise and that it will aid you in your own critiques of not only the ethical and religious beliefs of others, but also of your own.

II.B FORMAL CRITIQUE OF *THE DEAD HAVE NO NEED OF ETHICS*

In my formal critique of my own theory, I will begin with an objective summary—at least as objective as a subjective individual can produce. This will be followed by a list of objective strengths followed by a list of objective weaknesses. I will conclude my critique with a subjective opinion about this book and an alternative to human based ethics that is presented in Part 2.

II.B.1 SUMMARY

The Dead Have No Need of Ethics is a thought-provoking book on the topic of ethics. It is quite clearly coming from a Christian worldview and takes the Bible as authoritative and applicable. By quoting and relying on the

Bible for content and conclusions, this book presupposes the existence of God and that God has revealed His will through the Scriptures and other types of revelation. The preface explains what ethics and morality are, followed by an overview of the power of presuppositions on our thoughts and beliefs. Part 1 deals primarily with a presentation and critique of the major Western theories of Ethics. Part 1 concludes that all human efforts of right living fail because none of them can produce the perfect standard required by God. Part 2 presents the author's personal journey and how he concluded that his personal ethic did not align with his understanding of how he is reconciled to God by grace through faith. The author goes on to tell us how death to self and new life in Christ is by the indwelling of the Holy Spirit which becomes the true source of ethics and morality, a term he calls "pneumanomian." The author discusses the tension between abiding and striving and how his only hope of living a life that is pleasing to God comes by having the Spirit of God within him and then yielding to that Spirit. The end goal of this type of living is that God is glorified, and the believer is deified.

STRENGTHS   *II.B.2*

a. This book effectively shows the disparity between an ethic that is based on self-discipline, achievement, and control with an ethic that is based on the finished work of Christ.

b. This book provides hope for those who realize they can never measure up to "God's standard."

c. This book, although written in a very logical and reasonable manner, does not depend on logic or reason for right living.

d. This book places all that is *Good, True,* and *Beautiful* in the domain of God

e. The "ethic" laid out in this book can free people from guilt and shame and the impossible task of living up to God's perfect standard.

II.B.3 WEAKNESSES

a. This book will carry very little weight or authority for those who do not share the author's presuppositions.

b. This book did not prove there is a God, let alone which is the *true* God. There is also the concern of Scriptural authority, suggesting that the God in question not only is correctly portrayed in the Bible but also authored the Bible.

c. It appears one could justify any behavior or activity if one claimed it was the Will of God or one acting in the freedom provided by God. Even if the author's presuppositions are true, one could justify "sinful" behavior on the grounds that "where sin abounds, grace abounds more."

d. It does not have a system of checks and balances to assure that partakers of this ethic do not abuse their "freedom" since this is not a common ethic among churches and Christians and does not lend itself to external, social input.

e. The whole idea of *theosis,* or deification of the believer, sounds quite fantastical and not within mainline, western Christian teaching.

II.B.4 PERSONAL CONCLUSION

What I liked most about my book was the way I attempted to reconcile my belief in a grace-based salvation with a works-based sanctification (being made holy). I liked how I spent time discussing the difficult topic of ethics and made sure readers would understand the presence and power of presuppositions. I liked how each theory in Part 1 was objectively critiqued and how the conclusion found all ethical theories insufficient. Part 2 is more personal and even pastoral. And it was cathartic to share my life and struggles with readers. Even though I was not able to reconcile my previous ethic with my salvation and sanctification, I came to realize that both are dependent on the person and work of Jesus Christ. My book reveals that the freedom, hope, and joy that comes from knowing I am reconciled to God has replaced my spiritual workout which always left me falling short. Now, instead of trying to become someone I am not, I am able to be the person God has always intended me to be. I have been forgiven, justified, and sanctified (all in the past tense), and now I am free to live in right relationship with God because of the sacrifice of the Son and the indwelling of the Holy Spirit. My book sought to help readers, and myself, understand that both right relationship to God and right living are accomplished by the Spirit; therefore, there is no longer a need for ethical theories to offer a standard of morality.

HOW I APPROACH ETHICAL DILEMMAS   *III*

In this next section, I want to discuss how I personally approach ethics and morality. I will explain some overarching biblical and personal principles that can be applied to ethics at large and to specific moral dilemmas. I will show how I am guided by the Scriptures and the Holy Spirit in navigating the right way God wants me to live. It is only through His power and Spirit that I am able to live in right relationship with Him and His will.

GENERAL GUIDELINES   *III.A*

First, as stated in Part 2 of this book, it is important to know thyself. This becomes key if we hope to distinguish what is coming from ourselves and what is coming from God. Secondly, we must know God, specifically, how the Holy Spirit operates. The first way we can know God is through general revelation. This would include creation, and the highest thoughts of man found in our *nous*. Ideas such as the *Good*, the *True*, and the *Beautiful* come from God, and concepts like eternity and perfection can only be known *a priori* (prior to experience) since no human has seen or experienced these concepts yet we all have them because we are made in the image and likeness of God. Even our ability and desire to critique and evaluate things implies an internal if not eternal template by which we judge ourselves, others, and things.

The second way we can know about God is through special revelation. This would include prophecy, signs, omens, visions, dreams, and the direct illumination, or revelation of the Holy Spirit. I believe the Bible is made up of previous revelations given by the Holy Spirit that was then written down under the Holy Spirit's direction. I distinguish *illumination* from *revelation* by defining *revelation* as truth revealed that was not gained through personal experience or insight. *Illumination* is the ability to understand revelation. In addition to the Bible, I believe God speaks to us directly, even today, through the Holy Spirit.

It is at this point, however, that I would like to add a word of caution. We can have many ideas, thoughts, or promptings, pop into our heads—not all of them may be the Spirit. It is imperative that we test the spirits and use the revelation previously given by the Holy Spirit, and the Holy Spirit within us, to compare what we believe we are being shown or told with what the Holy Spirit has previously revealed. I do not believe the Holy Spirit contradicts Himself, but as I will discuss later in, the "my process" section, the Holy Spirit does sometimes change our understanding of what we thought we had known before, perhaps even changing our previous interpretation of Scripture.

III.A.1 I MUST RECKON MYSELF DEAD TO SELF, BUT ALIVE IN CHRIST (ROMANS 6).

It is only by recalling that I am no longer alive in Adam that I can access the life I have in Christ. This is the beginning of true ethics and morality and is accomplished by the work of the Spirit. This makes ethics and morality an identity issue rather than a formula or rules for good behavior. When I remember who I now am in Christ and am walking in the Spirit, I can keep my ego and personal desires out of the ethical decision-making process.

I MUST ABIDE IN CHRIST, ONLY IN CHRIST DO I HAVE LIFE AND THE ABILITY TO BEAR THE FRUIT OF THE SPIRIT (JOHN 15).

If I try and produce any good apart from Christ, I am merely displaying my own efforts and personal goodness which are not out of obedience. This I alluded to as participating in the ways of Cain. Whenever we choose how we will worship, and obey God, we are trying to accomplish God's commands through our own efforts. God has made it brutally clear that the greatest goodness of man outside of Christ is like a branch that has been separated from the tree. A cut off branch will wither and die and is good for nothing but to be cast into the fire. The good news, however, is that if we do abide in Christ, bearing the fruit of the Spirit will be a natural outflow of who we now are in Jesus.

I MUST WALK IN THE SPIRIT TO NOT FULFILL THE LUSTS OF THE FLESH (GALATIANS 5).

Galatians 5:16 tells me that if I walk in the Spirit, I will not fulfill the lusts of the flesh, and in verse 18, Paul tells me that if I am led by the Spirit, I am not under the law. This is one of the blessings of not being able to multitask as humans, I can only do one thing at a time. If I'm in the flesh I can not be in the Spirit; conversely, if I am in the Spirit, I can not be in the flesh. The way I can tell if I am in the flesh or the Spirit is by the fruit or works that are being produced in my life. If I am in the Spirit, I will produce the fruit of the Spirit, but if I am in the flesh, I will produce the works of the flesh.

I AM FREE, BUT I AM NOT TO USE MY FREEDOM AS A LICENSE TO SIN (GALATIANS 5).

Galatians 5:13-14 tells me that I have been called to freedom. I am not to use my freedom as an excuse to sin, but rather I am to use it to love and serve others. For all the law is fulfilled in the maxim "to love my neighbor as myself." I love my freedom, but if I am not wise and led by the Spirit, my freedom can easily turn into bondage or self-serving behaviors. The reason God has given me freedom is so I can better love and care for others. This is a principle that is difficult to navigate and cannot be done through the strength of my own will or cleverness of my own reason. This freedom can only be navigated by the one who gave it and it is only in Him that I can use my freedom in a way that glorifies God and serves my fellow man.

III.A.5 I AM NOT TO JUDGE OTHERS FOR THEIR FREEDOM, AND I AM NOT TO ALLOW MY FREEDOM TO CAUSE OTHERS TO SIN (ROMANS 14).

This is perhaps one of the hardest principles to learn and to apply. In Romans 14, Paul talks about how I am no longer under the law and unto the pure all things are pure. He gives examples of how some people do not eat meat or feel the need to worship on a particular day or will only drink certain things. The point Paul is making is that whatever I do, I do it unto the Lord. The Lord is the master of all, and I have no business judging another's servant. I am to serve God, and it is God who has the right to judge or to justify my actions. One day I will give an account to God. Additionally, Paul gives a different type of admonition: to no longer judge one another, but rather to not do things that cause others to sin. If I have freedom and liberty to do a particular activity or eat a particular thing, I should thank God for my freedom and not destroy others with the freedoms God has given me.

In the end, I am to be thankful to God for the freedom he has given me, yet I also need to be considerate of those who do not share my freedom (Romans 14). Consider that the passage ends with the thought that whatever is not of faith is sin (Romans 14:23). If I have faith that what I am doing is allowed by and pleasing to God I may proceed, but if I encourage others by word or deed to participate in things, they think are wrong, both they and I have sinned. They have sinned because they have not acted according to faith, and I have sinned because I have not considered how my freedom may affect them and their relationship to God.

PERSONAL ETHIC

The first assignment I give my students in Ethics is to write their own personal ethic. I use this as a benchmark, so they can compare what they wrote at the beginning of the course with where they are at the end. Since many of my students have never previously written out their own ethic, I give them a series of prompts which I will now personally answer according to my own beliefs.

WHAT IS MY HIGHEST GOOD?

My highest good is God. In fact, I believe "God = *Good.*" If you asked me to define God or *Good,* I would say that which is whole and perfect, lacking nothing, eternal, the beginning and the end, complete in and of itself. I believe these definitions would also apply to that which is *true* and *beautiful.* God = *the Good, the True,* and *the Beautiful.*

WHAT IS MY PURPOSE IN LIFE?

I believe I was made by God and given life to glorify Him. I believe God is glorified by me, being filled with and walking in His Spirit. I believe I am a conduit of the Divine and God's love, grace, mercy, and fruit of His Spirit are meant to flow through me.

WHAT EMPOWERS ME TO LIVE OUT MY PURPOSE IN LIFE?

I believe it is only through the power and regeneration of the Holy Spirit that I can live out God's purpose for my life. God will be glorified whether I live in obedience or rebellion, but I desire to be aligned with the will of God rather than to be crushed by it. It is the Holy Spirit which allows me to live out this life in the way God desires.

WHAT HAPPENS TO ME WHEN I DIE?

This is a bit of a tricky question especially considering how I have dealt with the concept of death in this book. I was born dead in Adam and am found wanting because of both the federal sin committed in Adam and the personal sins I have committed myself. I have already died to my "old man" in Adam, and now live a resurrected life in Christ. At the end of my mortal frame's existence, I believe God will give me a glorified body to house my immortal soul and spirit and I will live forever with the One who gave me life.

III.C PERSONAL PROCESS

This section holds a little irony for me, for like my great teacher Soren Kierkegaard, I too reject systems, categories, and formulas. I believe the Spirit is like the wind and blows where it wills, I can hear the sound of it, but do not know where it is coming from and where it is going, and so is everyone who is born of the Spirit (John 3:8). When I encounter an ethical dilemma or moral crisis in my life, there is a type of process I go through to try and discern the will of God.

III.C.1 SEEK PREVIOUS REVELATION FROM THE SPIRIT.

If the issue I am dealing with has already been addressed by the Spirit, such as previous revelation recorded in Scripture, then I want to consult what the Spirit has already said. This requires a knowledge on my part of the Scriptures and a yielding to the Holy Spirit's illumination to help me understand correctly. If my dilemma is not something the Spirit has previously addressed or at least recorded in Scripture, then I seek to extrapolate His will from what He has previously revealed. I also believe the Holy Spirit is fully capable of directly revealing His will to me. This often comes from promptings directly from His Spirit to my spirit. I liken this to an intuitive type of knowledge that is a direct knowing not acquired through sense perception or experience, it is knowledge coming directly from God. This is not arrived at through my human reason or study, neither does it come from my feelings and emotions. It is from God's own Spirit, to my *nous* which is being renewed. After this insight is given, I can think about it rationally or have feelings about it emotionally, but such revelation, insight, or prompting was not generated from my reason or emotions, rather from the very Spirit of God. I know I am capable of imaginative thoughts and seem to have a knack for self-deception, so in order to address novel insight or promptings with spiritual discernment, I will consult with others in which I can see the Spirit living and moving.

SEEK WISDOM AND PERSPECTIVE FROM THOSE CURRENTLY WALKING IN THE SPIRIT.

III.C.2

I find it helpful to have fellowship in my life with other people who are also walking in the Spirit. I believe they are a valuable source of wisdom in discerning what the will of the Spirit is and how the Spirit would have me act. This of course must come with not only an understanding of myself, but also to know the people I am consulting. It is difficult at times to separate my or my companions' perspectives from that being provided by the Holy Spirit. For example, years ago I was being sued in a court of law by someone who I believed was also a Christian. Following my process, I first consulted the scriptures and remembered this issue being addressed by the apostle Paul in 1 Corinthians 6. He makes it quite clear that believers are not to take other believers to court, rather it would be better to suffer loss than to disparage the name of Christ. With this scriptural knowledge in mind, I asked the advice of friends and family that I believed were Spirit led. Without exception they advised me to get a lawyer and counter sue the litigant. When I mentioned Paul's teaching about lawsuits against believers, they responded, "well, the other person obviously is not a believer because they are suing you!" Even though I had great respect for these people and could see the Holy Spirit in their lives, I had no peace or rest in my spirit with their recommendations. I believed they had let their love for me and the offense they had taken on my behalf to cloud their judgement and they were speaking from their flesh (revenge, retribution, preservation of self) rather than communicating to me what the Spirit wanted me to do. I wrestled with this issue for weeks until I was reading a passage out of the Tao Te Ching, the passage spoke about how no harm could come to our true self externally, that kind of harm could only be caused from within. Even though this was not the Christian Bible, the Holy Spirit used this to illumine my understanding and to be at peace not counter suing. To do otherwise would violate my conscience and what I believed was the right thing to do based on my understanding of the scriptures and how God wanted me to respond to my litigator. I told the person that was suing me that I loved them and would not resist their efforts. Thank God they dropped their lawsuit, but regardless I was at peace either way. I was willing to have my wages garnished for the rest of my life rather than violating my sense of self in Christ and what I thought the Spirit wanted me to do. If I would have counter sued, I would have ruined my testimony to this person, and I would have violated my own inner promptings of the Spirit, and what I believed was a clear teaching in Scripture.

III.C.3 DIRECTLY SEEK GUIDANCE FROM THE SPIRIT.

The Holy Spirit is the Third Person of the Godhead. The Holy Spirit is not an it, or a force, but rather a person. The Spirit is the very one that gives us life and creates a new spirit within us. The Holy Spirit then knits His very Spirit with our renewed human spirit (I Corinthians 6:17). The Spirit literally guides believers into all truth (John 16:13). The Holy Spirit is active and at work in the lives of believers. It would be incredibly beneficial to study the work of the Holy Spirit; many people have written books on the subject and if you would like to take this topic deeper, I recommend you look into adding several books on the Holy Spirit to your own library.

III.C.3.a THE SPIRIT IS CONSISTENT.

The Holy Spirit like the other Persons of the Godhead is eternal and unchanging, yet the Spirit is also full of life and power and is constantly at work. Therefore, it is important to understand the Holy Spirit's work and revelation in the past so we can see how He is working in the present. I have noticed that my prayer life has begun to change, the more I acknowledge the Person and work of the Holy Spirit in my life. I still direct my prayers to the Father, through the Son, but it is the Holy Spirit that directs me how to pray and intercedes to the Father on my behalf (Romans 8:26). This is why I believe it is important to not only know the scriptures which I believe is the Spirit's previous revelation, but also to actually know the Spirit for myself. If I have some new "revelation" or illumination that I believe is coming from the Holy Spirit, I need to test it against who the Spirit is and what He has previously revealed. If my new understanding is contrary to either the past revelation or current character of the Spirit, I need to reevaluate what I think the Spirit is trying to tell me and ask for clarification and guidance as to what is His will for my life.

THE SPIRIT MAY CHANGE MY UNDERSTANDING OF THE TRUTH RATHER THAN CHANGE THE TRUTH.

III.C.3.b

Due to who the Holy Spirit is, His *Truth* does not change. If the Holy Spirit has previously revealed the will of God, this will is True and stands. In Matthew 5:17-18, Jesus tells me he has not come to destroy the law but to fulfill it, and not one jot or tittle shall pass away from the law until all is fulfilled. In context, I believe Jesus is talking about the law of Moses, but because of Jesus and God giving us His own Spirit, I now have the law of God written on my own heart (Ezekiel 36:26, Hebrews 8:10).

Does this mean I must live in accordance with over 613 laws given in the Old Testament? Do I still need to offer sacrifices for my sins? Do I need to apply God's capital punishment requirements on others and even myself if I am found to have broken the law?

God forbid, no! The law is *Holy* and *Good*, but it never saved anyone. The law gave me God's standard and showed me my inability to keep it. The only one who could keep it was Jesus who is God in the flesh. Thank God, Jesus kept the law perfectly and gave his righteousness to me in exchange for my sinfulness (2 Corinthians 5:21). In Galatians 5:18, I am told that if I am led by the Spirit I am not under the law. Hallelujah! Now I do not have to go by some external standard that is imposed upon me with the threat of eternal death if I fail, instead I have the very Lawgiver living inside me, joined together with my own spirit. And He can illumine the law to me, but better still, He empowers me to be able to live in accordance with the will of God.

In different passages of the New Testament, questions arise about the law, concerning the parts that should be applied to the believer. These included issues such as circumcision, dietary laws, and corporate worship. In some passages, like Paul's admonition to Timothy, Timothy is charged to keep the custom of circumcision so as not to cause offense to those he ministered to (Acts 16). Yet, in other writings he condemns the gentile believers for wanting to be circumcised and claims if they hope to be justified by the law they have fallen from grace (Galatians 5). At the council of Jerusalem, the apostle Peter makes a strong case for the freedom of the gentile believers which I would like to quote in its entirety:

"And God, which knoweth the hearts, bare them witness, giving them the Holy Ghost, even as he did unto us; And put no difference between us and them, purifying their hearts by faith. Now therefore why tempt ye God, to put a yoke upon the neck of the disciples, which neither our fathers nor we were able to bear? But we believe that through the grace of the LORD Jesus Christ we shall be saved, even as they." (Acts 15:8-11)

At the conclusion of the matter, James under the guidance of the Holy Spirit, only applied four of the Mosaic laws to gentile believers. These included not eating blood, things polluted by idols, or animals that have been strangled; apart from these dietary laws, believers were not to fornicate. An interesting list to be sure, but even this list was later challenged and revised, at least regarding food offered to idols by the apostle Paul (Acts 15:20, Romans 14). The council of Jerusalem was not claiming the law had changed, rather they were acknowledging that it was the grace through faith in Christ that saved them rather than the keeping of the law. I think it is interesting to note that Peter's testimony came from his encounter with the Holy Spirit which corrected his understanding of what and who was clean and unclean. I think it is also interesting that different believers had different requirements they were held to. This relates back to the general guidelines with which I started this section, where some folks could eat food offered to idols with thanksgiving, and for others to eat the same food would be a sin for them because they had not acted in faith and violated their conscience.

I would like to end this section with an example of how the Holy Spirit changed Peter's understanding of the law without changing the law itself. This example comes from Acts 10. In this passage of Scripture, Peter is on a missionary trip to Joppa and is up on a rooftop awaiting the preparation of food when he falls into a trance. During this trance, he had a vision of a sheet being let down from heaven filled with all manner of unclean animals. Then he heard a voice say, "arise, slay and eat." Peter responded by saying no, that he has never eaten an unclean thing. This happens three times and the voice responded to Peter by saying, "what God has cleansed do not call common." At this time there ,was a knock on the door and three gentiles (unclean in Jewish eyes) had arrived to talk to Peter. It was the Jewish custom to not entertain gentile guests because they were unclean, this vision Peter understood to mean that God's grace was extended to all people not just the Jews and he was not to call unclean what God had made clean. This does not mean that the unclean animals listed in the law of Moses were now kosher, rather God was using this to correct Peter's misunderstanding about the place of gentiles within the body of Christ. The previous truth of the Scriptures had not been altered, but rather Peter's understanding of it.

HOW DO I RESPOND WHEN I SUCCEED OR FAIL IN MY MORALITY?

III.D

In this section, I would like to discuss how my understanding has changed with regards to my moral failings and successes. Such challenges have greatly affected how I treat myself and others in relation to righteousness and sin, and it has even affected my prayer life

SUCCESS MEANS ALL GLORY GOES TO GOD

III.D.1

This part of my journey has been easier to deal with than my failures. Once I realized that the only *Good* in me comes from God Himself, it has been very easy to attribute any goodness I see in my life to the One who is doing it. I will be more than happy to lay any crowns I receive at the feet of Jesus, because it is only from the work of Jesus that I would receive any crowns at all. This is part of how I know I belong to God and that His Spirit dwells within me. When I see love and the other fruit of the Spirit being produced in my life, I know it is coming from God and not my innate goodness or good deeds. I, Fred in Adam, loved only myself or others in that they had some benefit for me. Now I see a love for others in me that I know comes from God Himself and when this love flows out towards others, I know that it is because of the love of God in me.

III.D.2 FAILURE MEANS I NEED TO ACKNOWLEDGE GOD'S PERSPECTIVE OVER MY OWN

Unfortunately, even though I now know who I am in Christ, I forget daily and live as though I am still in Adam. Even though my "old man" is dead and has been crucified with Christ, it has an uncanny ability to act as though it is still alive and tries to take control of my body (Romans 6:6, Romans 7). This is what I like to refer to as a spiritual zombie, my "old man" is dead, yet it acts like it is still alive and is ravenous to fulfill the cravings of the flesh. When I forget who I am in Christ, I am capable of any atrocity or depravity. I referred to this way of living like being in a fugue state—where I am in a fog of flesh and forget who I now am in Christ, but when the fog lifts and I am back in my right mind of Christ, I am repulsed by what I have allowed my old dead man to do.

In the past, I would have begun my process of self-flagellation until I had satisfied my own guilt and shame and was willing to try and climb the ladder of self-perfection again. Praise be to God, this is one thing that has changed since I have realized I am already perfect in Christ. Now when I fail, I no longer beat myself up, rather I boldly and honestly confess my sins and thank God that He has already forgiven me.

III.D.2.a CONFESSION

I no longer ask God to forgive me for my sins because I have already been forgiven. I do, however, confess my sins and acknowledge that I have not been living in the Spirit.

THANKFULNESS

I thank God for already forgiving me. And for not only His discipline in my life, but also for the daily grace and mercy He showers upon me. The fear of the Lord is the beginning of wisdom, but it is the love of God that brings me to a place of repentance, the changing of my ways (Proverbs 9:10, Romans 2:4). I am eternally thankful for the love of God.

I PRAY TO BE REMINDED OF WHO I NOW AM—IT'S AN IDENTITY ISSUE

When I was still climbing the ladder of moral perfectionism, I would pray things like, "God please help me overcome this or that besetting sin, God please give me the strength to do my do's and not do my don'ts." My prayers gave away my spiritual condition, I was still trying to accomplish through the strength of my own will but with God's help what Christ had already accomplished. I was asking God to empower me, instead of reckoning myself dead to my Adamic nature. I was asking God to allow that nature to succeed. God's solution was to put me to death with His Son and raise me in newness of life with Him. The solution is not to have a new and improved Adamic nature, but rather to reckon that "old man" dead, to realize my new life is in Christ. And now that I am a partaker of the divine nature, when I pray, I acknowledge my sins, thank God for forgiving me, and most of all I ask Him to remind me of who I already am in His Son. I am signed, sealed, and delivered and as pleasing and righteous before God as I ever will be. Now instead of asking for God's help against my wandering desires, I ask God to change those very desires to ones that align with Him.

STRIVE TO ABIDE, LABOR TO REST

This does not mean our striving leads to abiding and we are not laboring so we can rest! Instead, it means we must strive to understand that it is He who *keeps us abiding* and it *was* His labor, not ours, that *allows us* to enter into His rest (Hebrews 4:11). This means our labor is to stop laboring and all our striving is to *abide*. Thank you, Jesus!

III.D.4 WARNING SIGNS TO LET ME KNOW IF I AM THINKING FROM A
CARNAL MIND AND NOT THE MIND OF CHRIST

I want to reflect on my ladder climbing analogy for it is here I can often
gage who's mind I currently have. If I judge or evaluate others based on
where I see them in relation to me on the ladder of self-perfection, I have
slipped into a carnal mindset. If I condemn others or for that matter, even
myself, I have taken upon myself the role and rights of my Lord. If I beat
myself up when I fail, I am trying to achieve my own righteousness and
have forgotten that I am already as righteous as I can ever be in Christ.
These are good "red flags" to let me know, I am no longer in the mind of
Christ, and I need to remember my true identity in Him.

IV HUMAN FREE WILL AND THE SOVEREIGNTY OF GOD

I thought it was important to at least mention the issue of the sovereignty
of God and the free will of humans as it relates to ethics and morality. If
human thoughts and actions are completely determined by God, then
ethics and morality really have no meaning or point since everyone is
simply doing what God predestined them to do. If, however, ethics and
morality are dependent upon us, then to whatever degree humans exercise
freedom, the sovereignty of God is diminished. I would love to formally
discuss the paradox of free will and sovereignty at length but that would
take another book. For those who would like a more detailed discussion
of sovereignty and free will, watch the video at the end of this section.

I personally believe the Bible teaches both the sovereignty of God
and the free will of man. Many theologians and philosophers will choose
one at the expense of the other since they are logically mutually exclusive.
My thumbnail solution to this dilemma is what I like to call "bracketed
freedom." What I mean by this is that God's sovereignty is over all and
cannot be changed by another; however, within God's sovereignty, He
has allowed real choices with real consequences. These choices can have
an eternal effect on the ones who make them and even others. But God's
purpose and plan can never be altered, and He can reconcile all choices
into the fulfillment of His will.

In *The Dead Have No Need of Ethics*, Part 2, I placed salvation and sanctification securely in the arms of God. It is entirely the work of God that allows me to be reconciled to Him and to live the life He would have me live. Yet, even so, there is still a role and a choice for me to make. First, I must accept the gift of the Holy Spirit along with the grace, faith, and perfect righteousness given to me through the Son. Then I have a choice: to yield to the Spirit or to yield to the flesh. This choice will have temporal and eternal consequences, but all these choices and consequences take place within the overarching sovereignty of God.

GOD IS THE AUTHOR AND FINISHER OF MY FAITH   *IV.A*

Hebrews 12:2 tells us that Jesus is the author and finisher of our faith. When the Jews murmured about Jesus claiming that he was the bread sent down from heaven, Jesus responded, "murmur not among yourselves. No man can come to me, except the Father which hath sent me draw him; and I will raise him up at the last day" (John 6:43-44). Jesus makes it very clear to that no one will come to Him apart from the Father's calling. Saving faith is a gift from God and cannot be self-generated. Faith comes from God, but I still get to chose whether to live by faith in God or to trust in my own ways and understanding.

GOD GIVES FAITH BY MEASURE   *IV.B*

Romans 12:3 tells us that God has dealt every man the measure of faith. It doesn't clarify if this is a quantity or quality of faith, but it reinforces the idea, that faith is given by God. Having faith, however, is not enough for James makes it quite clear that faith without works (action) is dead (James 2:17). This helped me, personally, to stop comparing myself to others. When I first met a friend of mine, Steve Whitten, I wanted to be like him and minister to people like he did. Steve was (and is) a true pastor: the way he would enter into people's pain and suffering; his home was always open to people in need. He is gregarious and personable, and while you could say some of this is his personality, certainty some of it is the work of the Spirit. Later on, Steve remarked that he wished he had a patience to minister to some of the people that I invest in. That is when I realized that the application of our faith and ministry looks different not because one person is better than the other, but because the Holy Spirit had enabled us in different ways. Steve is a minister to "the white sheep" the ones that are willing to come into the fold, people who are in the church and seeking that kind of pastoral care. I see my calling to relate more to the "black sheep" the people that do not come into the fold, have been hurt by the church, or do not fit into the traditional confines of faith and religion. I have created a ministry out of this posture called "Black Shepherd Ministries" (*Figure 28*). We are able to reach more people, different people, as we both walking the Spirit.

Figure 28. Black Shepherd Ministries

IV.C I CAN YIELD TO THE FLESH OR TO THE SPIRIT

Even though the gift of faith is solely dependent of God, what I do with it is largely up to me. Galatians 5 tells me that I get to choose to whom I shall yield, the flesh or the Spirit. Paul goes on in Romans 6:13 to direct that I am not to yield my members as instruments of unrighteousness but to yield myself to God. Since I am now alive from the dead, I am to use my body as an instrument of righteousness.

BRACKETED FREEDOM   *IV.D*

What I mean by "bracketed freedom" is that I have real choices with real consequences, but they are bracketed within the sovereign will of God. I did not get to choose my sex, ethnicity, country of origin, physical stature, or intellectual abilities. But I do get to choose how I use them and how I live with the abilities and deficiencies God has given me.

EXAMPLES OF FAULTY THINKING REGARDING SOVEREIGNTY   *IV.E*
AND FREEDOM AND HOW IT AFFECTS ETHICS AND MORALITY

When a person embraces either free will or sovereignty they do so at the expense of the other. To the degree that humans are free, God's sovereignty is logically limited. And to the degree in which God is sovereign, human freedom is limited. However, like I mentioned previously, I believe the Scriptures teach both. Those who wreck in the ditch of human freedom, have an anemic God who is no longer in control, but rather has limited power and authority. Those who wreck in the ditch of sovereignty without human freedom, make God the author of evil and responsible for all that is wrong with the world. I have heard people say things like, "if it's not God's will, it will not happen." Although this is true in one sense, it removes personal responsibility from one's own actions. I have also heard people say, "I don't need to worry about viruses, my days are numbered, and God already knows when I'm going to die. Nothing I do will add or take away from my appointed lifespan." Once again, this is true in one sense, God does know our appointed days and time of our death, but God also knew if you were going to chose not to protect yourself or others. Our choices still have real consequences to ourselves and others and we will give an account of our choices one day before God.

For further additional explanation see the following video(s)
"Free will and predestination." YouTube, recorded and uploaded by Fred Blackburn. 2 February 2016, https://youtu.be/Q-S_lsEQJ44

V APPLICATION OF THE DEAD HAVE NO NEED OF ETHICS TO A SAMPLER OF ETHICAL TOPICS

In this last section of the book, I thought it would be helpful if you could see how I apply a Spirit led ethic to a variety of ethical dilemmas. I want to be quite clear at the outset that the conclusions and convictions I reach after going through my "process" may not be the same conclusions or convictions at which you arrive. This is to be expected for a variety of reasons. Firstly, we are all unique individuals coming from different backgrounds, life experiences, and perspectives. Secondly, we are all in different places in our spiritual and moral transformation. Thirdly, we are all given a different measure of faith, and what you may have the freedom to do, I may have convictions against. In such cases, I am not to judge you and you are not to cause me to sin by encouraging me to do something I think is wrong. The inverse is also true, you are not to judge me for my freedoms, but I am not to encourage you to do something you think is wrong. Fourthly, we all have biases and presuppositions. I believe that in the Spirit these types of prejudices can be overcome, but we should be aware of how our presuppositions and confirmation bias affects our ethical decision-making process. I hope this list of topics and how I approach them is a blessing to you, even if you disagree with my personal conclusions.

V.A ENVIRONMENTAL ISSUES

Environmental Issues is a broad topic category that could include everything from conservationism (conserve the resources we have left) to protectionism (we should leave the wild places of the world wild). This topic deals with our natural environment and our relationship to it. From a Christian perspective there have traditionally been two broad ways of thinking on this topic. Historically the church has embraced a dominion type of theology, but this has been challenged since the latter part of the twentieth century by a stewardship type of theology.

In dominion theology, God created the world and gave man dominion over it. This can be found in Genesis 1:26-28 where we are told that man was given dominion over the earth, this is a very strong term and implies authority and control. Some adherents of this view believe the earth was made for man and we can do with it as we will. Even though I believe human authority over God's creation is taught in Scripture, I also believe Scripture teaches that we will give an account to how we treat the works of God's hands.

Stewardship theology shifts the emphasis from man and his control over the environment to man and his caregiving of the creation. The idea of stewardship can also be found in the Genesis account. In Genesis 2:15, we are told that God put man into the garden of Eden where he was to preserve and protect it. In both types of theology, man has authority over creation. However, who creation belongs to and who we, as caretakers of creation, are accountable to for our treatment of it is very different with regards to stewardship theology and dominion theology.

When I look at the creation, God's letter-less book, there is much I can learn about the Creator. I can see the order and patterns of creation, and the multiplicity and diversity of forms. God seems to enjoy variations of a theme, and yet He also has created the world as interdependent parts of a whole. The more we learn about the world in which we live, the more we begin to understand the love, precision, and care provided by the Creator. The earth, and especially the untrammeled parts of it, speak to me of the majesty and power of God. It only takes one look up on a starlit night to show me my place, and to adjust my perspective. I may loom large in my classroom or in my home; but in the mountains, I am but animated dust, and my passing would not alter the turning of the earth in the slightest. Yet, herein lies a great paradox, for even though my life is but a vapor, the Lord of Creation cares for me (James 4:14).

In the Scriptures, we are told the earth is the LORD's along with all it's inhabitants (Psalms 24:1). Revelation 4:11 tells us God is worthy of all glory and honor for He has created all things, and for His glory and pleasure, they were created. Romans 1 tells us that man is without excuse because creation itself shows forth God's eternal power and points to God. In the Mosaic law, animals, plants, and even the land received a sabbath rest. Animals got to rest one day a week just like humans (Deuteronomy 5:14). And trees and fields got to rest one year out of seven in which they were not to be pruned or tilled, and any fruit that grew was to be for the undomesticated animals, the poor, or strangers in the land (Leviticus 25:4). The Bible tells us how we are to treat, not only one another, but also God's creation.

I find it a helpful analogy to think of God's creative works as we would think of the works of an artist. The artist's creations are not the artist, but they come from and tell us much about him. Just as you can recognize the creator of a piece of art or music, the same goes for the Creator of the entire world. When we disrespect or disabuse the works of God's hands, whether that is the earth, it's inhabitants, or other humans who are made in God's image, we are disrespecting the Creator. When we show, care, cultivation, and protection, towards the works of God's hands, we honor the Creator and the role He has given us on this earth.

I have encountered a broad array of perspectives on this topic, from militant earth firsters whose motto is, "no compromise in the defense of Mother earth," to spoilers and wasters who believe it's all going to burn anyways, so we might as well get what we can while we can. When I was a young man, I worked in the California Conservation Corps. We were focused on energy conservation and recycling. Our goal was to conserve the resources we have and to focus on renewable energy. A few of my peers were a bit more radical and I would call them preservationists. They saw humans as a cancerous plague that was consuming the earth and needed to be stopped. They wanted a complete moratorium on development and would oppose anything that led to a loss of wilderness or added to the climate burden humans had placed on the environment. Their highest good was the environment; they reasoned that without a healthy life sustaining planet, all other socio-political issues were a moot point.

I was certainly influenced by and continue to share many of the ideals and practices I learned while in the California Conservation Corps. I do my best to recycle and to limit my impact on the environment in a negative way. Unlike my more militant companions, I do not see humans as a virus, and I would not kill a person to save a tree or whale, but I do agree certain areas should remain untouched and free so we can see what nature looks like without human interference. We, humanity, change creation for good and bad; we leave a mark on it. So, I just love to see it as is, untouched. Because I feel like it gives me a glimpse of the beautiful temple designed by God in the wilderness. For example, there is a beauty surrounding a night sky far from city light pollution or numerous satellites. It is something you have to see to vividly understand on an experiential, spiritual level. This leads me to my personal take on environmental issues which includes conservationism and some aspects of preservationism yet, in many ways, my stance goes beyond both.

When I was a young man, I loved to learn about the indigenous peoples of the Americas, and even though they were coming from more of an animistic or polytheistic world view, many of their teachings resonated with me and I hold them to this day. Humans were seen by many tribes as an integral and interdependent part of creation. Like the Biblical idea of stewardship, they saw our role as caretakers of the land—for the land was something no human could own, but would remain after their generation had passed away. Our use of the land, along with the beings that share it with us, needed to be done with respect and an understanding that our decisions would affect those who came after us. Hence, whenever a major undertaking was being discussed, the consequences would also need to be considered with regards to how it would impact up to seven generations into the future.

I love the idea of wilderness areas where we let nature be. Since we can have a powerful impact on the earth for good or. evil, we need to be cognizant of our interactions with the land like identifying the repercussions of forest management versus clear cutting. Humanity, as caretakers, can help a forest recover and be healthy in a fraction of the time it would take to get there if left to natural processes. Yet, we can also bring great harm and destruction to the earth if we treat it as a consumer rather than a caretaker. I do not confuse the creation with the Creator, but rather it is because of my love of the Creator that I want to honor and care for His creation. Of all the different groups people throughout the world, I would think Christians ought to be the most avid environmentalists because we believe the world was made by and belongs to our Heavenly Father. Unlike my conservationists or preservationists' friends, I am seeking something much more radical which I like to call *restorationism*. This idea can be found in Romans 8:18-25 where Paul talks about how creation suffers because of the sin of man, but as man is reconciled to God, so too will creation. My ideal for how to interact with the environment comes down to partaking in God's restoration of the creation. We may use it but ought not to abuse it; we respect it because of the One who made it; and become conduits of His reconciliation. Because when I am in right relationship with God, it naturally follows that I am in right relationship with other creation. I understand my place and my purpose, thus abiding as a caretaker. This means that I am treating the world as a mindful steward rather than a waster or destroyer. As God reconciles me to Himself, that reconciliation is extended to all creation; just as creation suffered because of man's disobedience, so to creation will be blessed by man's obedience. How the redemption of man and the creation fits in with a new heaven and new earth I do not know, but I do believe that the works of God's hands need to be treated with respect and in doing so we respect our Creator.

VB CAPITAL PUNISHMENT, WAR, AND CIVIL DISOBEDIENCE

The next three ethical topics I am going to discuss inconjunction, since religious communities tend to adhere to opposing positions, pitting two passages of Scripture against each other or choosing one set of verses that confirm their view and ignore those that speak against them. Since I believe the Scripture was authored by the Holy Spirit, and I have already mentioned I do not believe the Holy Spirit contradicts Himself, we must find a way to navigate the passages that seem to be advocating opposite guidelines for right living. There are certainly non-Biblical arguments both for and against the above topics, but I will be focused more on the Biblical teachings because there are too many arguments to discuss all perspectives at this time.

Regarding capital punishment, war, and civil disobedience, two of the passages in apparent conflict are Matthew 5 and Romans 13. Matthew 5 has several verses that seem to indicate retribution and killing are categorically prohibited for those who claim to follow Christ's teachings. Matthew 5:21

reaffirms the teaching in the 10 commandments, "Thou shalt not kill." Yet in verse 22, Jesus goes on to say that those who are angry with another are in danger of the same judgement as those who kill. Rather than lessening the Mosaic law, Jesus adds intention to action. Murderous thoughts in the heart are seen by God the same way as physical murder. The weight of thoughts and intentions is reiterated on the topic of lust where lustful thoughts are portrayed as equivalent to lustful actions (Matthew 5:28). In Matthew 5:38, Jesus appears to be alluding to Leviticus 24:20, "You have heard that it hath been said, An eye for an eye, and a tooth for a tooth." In Leviticus 24:21, the commandment extends to a life for a life. Yet, Jesus goes on to say in Matthew 5:39: do not resist evil, and then He gives examples of how we are to respond to physical, economic, and social assaults on our person. In each case, we are to respond with gentleness and meekness, rather than with retribution or violence.

The last biblical example I wish to mention from Matthew 5 is found in verses 43 and 44. Once again, Jesus quotes from the law of Moses, and Jesus reiterates how radical his standard of right living is: "Ye, have heard that it hath been said, thou shalt love thy neighbor, and hate thine enemy. But I say unto you, Love your enemies, bless them that curse you, do good to them that hate you, and pray for them which despitefully use you, and persecute you: That you may be the children of your Father which is in heaven: for he maketh his sun to rise on the evil and on the good, and sendeth rain on the just and on the unjust" (Matthew 5:43-45). I hope you are already thinking ahead as to how Matthew 5 relates to capital punishment, war, and civil disobedience, but before I work out the opposing arguments, I want to share Romans 13.

In Romans 13:1-7, Paul is discussing authority and where it comes from. The passage begins with all authority coming from God, so those who resist authority are in effect resisting God. In verse 4, we are told that the authority does not bear "the sword" in vain; it does not say whip or rod, but sword. This is significant because the sword is an instrument of death, not of corporal punishment. Corporal punishment is a physical retribution that stops short of maiming or death, and in biblical times it was often done by the use of a whip or a rod. It goes on to say that those in authority are the ministers of God and bring revenge and wrath upon those that do evil (Romans 13:4).

So, here is the dilemma. On the one hand, Scripture seems to clearly teach that we are not to kill and that revenge belongs to God alone. Even in Romans 12:19, Paul tells us not to avenge ourselves or give way to wrath for vengeance belongs to God. Yet, In Romans 13 it seems equally clear, that those in authority are acting under God's authority and vengeance can be carried out by them. So, as believers, are we to participate or permit violence and retribution? How does taking Scripture as authoritative influence our convictions?

Some folks have tried to reconcile this apparent contradiction by claiming Jesus is talking about individuals in the book of Matthew, but Paul is talking about civil authority in Romans 13. This conclusion is valid, and could be an easy solution. But what if the person in civil authority is also a follower of Jesus? How does a follower of Christ reconcile their individual ethic and mores with those which pertain to their role as a civil authority, judge, juror, or executioner? Some would claim the state has the right and obligation to enforce civil laws, but the individual is not to seek personal revenge. In other words, this view holds that we are not to seek vigilante justice but are to let the powers that be fulfill their roles as representatives of God.

At this point, some of you might object that this idea of deferring to governmental justice would be valid if we had a godly government. But since we do not have such a government, how can we expect them to carry out right judgements? In response to this I think it is important to note, that Paul wrote Romans 13 during the reign of emperor Nero, one of the most horrific rulers in the history of the world. Paul advocated to submit to authority even while under an authority that was slaughtering and murdering at will.

Other Christian thinkers such as Leo Tolstoy in his book, "The Kingdom of God is Within You," believes Christians should not be involved in civil authority, either as soldiers, police, judges, or jurors for in such a position we may be asked to do things like judge or kill. Tolstoy believed war and violence were not compatible with the God of love that he read about in the New Testament. Also, Tolstoy was not able to reconcile the actions of the God of the Old Testament (in which God permitted and commanded various acts of violence) with that of the New Testament (where God is primarily portrayed as the God of love and mercy). Unfortunately, in my opinion, Tolstoy had an incomplete view of God. Yes, God is a God of love, but He is also a God of wrath; He is the Lord of Mercy, but He is also just and justice requires retribution.

CAPITAL PUNISHMENT   *V.B.1*

First, I would like to give my personal conclusion and conviction regarding Capital Punishment. I do not believe God wants me to kill anyone for their crimes or sins. This does not mean I turn a blind eye or do not believe there are consequences for certain capital crimes under United States Law, regarding anything from treason, mutilation/torture, first degree murder, to kidnapping where the victim dies. Rather than death, I advocate for incarceration and a call to repentance and reconciliation. Those that break the law will not escape judgement even if they are not put to death in this life.

Second, I do not believe the practice of punishment is appropriate for the believer. And I think you will be hard put to find any Biblical examples of God punishing His children, those born of the Holy Spirit in Christ. God is clear that He disciplines those He loves; God's wrath and punishment was taken on by Christ and in exchange, we become the beneficiaries of not only God's mercy, but also Christ's own righteousness. To make the distinction clear, punishment brings about retribution or revenge, it is payback for what someone has done. God retains this privilege unto Himself which is clear in Romans 12; but He also grants authority to those who are His "ministers" to carry out His wrath (Romans 13). God does, however, discipline His children. Discipline is motivated out of care and concern and the intention is to change behavior for the well being of the recipient rather than retribution for what they have done. I believe this applies to the application of corporal as well as capital punishment, neither are appropriate for someone who has been forgiven by God. My response should be to forgive others because God has forgiven me. This does not mean to deny or ignore one's wrongdoings, we still have a duty to protect others by restricting criminal's behavior, whether this comes through rehabilitation or incarceration.

In the parable of the unforgiving servant, Matthew 18:21-35, Jesus tells the story of a servant who owed an unpayable dept. When this servant begged for mercy, his master forgave him. Yet, this same servant went out and found another servant who owed him a pittance and would not have mercy on him. When the master found out that the servant whom he forgave would not forgive another, he brought his wrath and justice down on that unforgiving servant. We are to forgive just as we are forgiven. This concept is also mentioned in "the Lord's Prayer" where we are instructed to ask for forgiveness for our trespasses as we forgive those who trespass against us (Matthew 6:9-13). If we are unwilling or unable to forgive others, I believe it shows we do not really understand God's forgiveness in our own lives. Those who have received God's mercy should be willing and excited to extend mercy to others.

In conclusion, God forgive me for my sins, the consequences of which demand an eternal death and separation from God; He did not ignore or forget about our sins but provided a way for them to be paid by the sacrifice of His Son. Because I have been forgiven an eternal debt, I now rejoice to forgive others for I have God's very Spirit of mercy and reconciliation within me. So, in dilemmas containing the option of capital punishment, I ought to choose forgiveness over vindictiveness "for judgment is without mercy to the one who has shown no mercy. Mercy triumphs over judgment" (James 2:13 NKJV).

V.B.2 WAR

The Bible is full of passages that either describe or in some instances prescribe war and violence. This includes the Old Testament accounts of conquest and even genocide, the New Testament accounts of Christians being part of the Roman military, and the affirmation the government's right to capital punishment in Romans 13. The early church was largely pacifistic, and its members either fled persecution or received a martyr's crown because of it. I do not know of any New Testament examples where Christians were instructed to physically, let alone violently, resist the government. Yet, those who came to Christ as members of the military were not asked to resign their commissions, but rather to be honorable—to not do violence or extort money—in their military office (Luke 3:14). In the fourth century A.D., the Roman empire not only legalized Christianity, but by 380 A.D. made it the state religion. Now the Church, instead of being outlawed and underground, held the keys to temporal wealth and power. It was in this context that the church first dealt with "Just War Theory" which was developed by Saint Augustine.

When the Church and Christians assumed a role in the Roman Empire rather than being persecuted by it, questions arose about the role of Christians in government and the responsibilities had to govern in a godly manner. Saint Augustine addressed the issue of Christians at war by making a few qualifying distinctions. Augustine believed that for a war to be just, it must meet two criteria—I personally believe there is a third, and even stronger criteria, but I'll get to that later—Augustine first distinguishes between *just* and *unjust* wars. A *just* war would be a war of defense against an aggressor, or intervening on behalf of another person, group, or country, that was being unjustly assaulted. The second qualifier is that the war had to be fought justly, and even though this was written sixteen centuries before the Geneva convention, Augustine's ideals are quite similar to their prescribed conclusions.

In theory, I agree with Saint Augustine, but based on world history, I think one would be hard put to find an example of a post-first century war where both qualifiers were followed. The other problem is perspective. Just War Theory is complicated if all both sides see their position as just or at times both positions go as far as to claim, "God is on our side." The ultimate qualifier, as to what constitutes a "just war," I believe is if God command's or wills it. *Deus Volt*! (God Wills It!) was the battle cry of the crusaders. And even far more recently, the American president George W. Bush declared it was God's will that he invade Iraq and Afghanistan and create a Palestinian state. I am fairly confident that the crusades were not God's will (but rather the product of humanity's free will, arrogance, and ignorance); although some of the crusaders may have had godly intent, many did not and the atrocities committed in the name of God are still a stain upon Christendom to this day. Whether or not God told President Bush to go to war I do not know (as I am not he), but for me to go to war I would need God to communicate His will to me directly.

Just as with the issue of capital punishment, there is a huge spectrum of Christian belief on the topic of war. Some Christians believe war is a tool God uses to bring about His will, check evil, and expand the Kingdom of Heaven. Others, like Leo Tolstoy, claimed they would not even defend their own wives and children if that defense included violence. Often this issue is portrayed as an "either/or" proposition between pacifism and activism, passivity versus patriotism. Personally, I see it more of a spectrum and prefer the term non-violence to pacifism since pacifism seems to imply passivity and indifference. I believe one can be quite active in resisting evil, but resorting to violence is not the means one ought to choose to achieve peace. I am impressed by Tolstoy's commitment to non-violence, but I also I believe certain people have been put under my protection and care. God forbid that I would have to use violence to protect them, but I do not think I could remain completely passive if I saw oppression and violence towards anyone. Violence ought to be a last resort; I want to act out of faith and duty rather than anger or fear. I know Christians who are pacifists and Christians who are in the military and law enforcement. Unfortunately, it is easy to vilify those who have different convictions and roles; God may have one person be a courageous police officer whilst another a bold protestor of police brutality. It is not my place to question the validity or genuineness of different Christian's convictions. We are all accountable to God. He is the judge, not me. Often these opposites see each other as violating God's will, but I would say, if God has given you the faith to renounce violence as a solution: praise Jesus! But if God has called you into law enforcement or national security: by God's grace, may you be salt and light where God has placed you and may you use your authority to protect and serve rather than to extort and oppress!

CIVIL DISOBEDIENCE

Even though I started off discussing how Matthew 5 appears to contradict Romans 13, for the following section, I would like to include several additional Scriptural examples from the Old and New Testament. The book of Daniel has several explicit accounts of civil disobedience which bear the potential of Capital Punishment. In Daniel 3, we are told the story of Nebuchadnezzar's golden idol which he erected on the plains of Shinar. The great king ordered all to worship the idol on pain of death for disobedience. Shadrack, Meshack, and Abednego famously disobeyed the king's order for they would only worship the God of Abraham, Isaac, and Jacob. In Daniel 6, King Darius demands to be worshiped as God and all prayers were to be directed only towards him. Daniel, like his Hebrew companions before him, refused to worship or pray to anyone besides *YHWH*. In the book of Acts, the apostles Peter and John are arrested by the Jewish religious authorities and are commanded not to preach about Jesus (Acts 4). Peter boldly asked the Jewish leaders who he should obey, God or man? It is clear that there is a conflict when it comes to to obedience and authority.

Romans 13 strongly indicates that all authority comes from God and disobeying authority is tantamount to disobeying God. Yet, there are numerous Biblical accounts of people refusing to obey the authority in their lives and God seems to bless their disobedience. I personally believe that the Holy Spirit authored the book of Daniel and the book of Romans, and I do not believe the Spirit contradicts Himself. This begs the question: what makes some disobedience equivalent to rebellion against God, whereas other disobedience is to the Glory of God? In all the examples mentioned above and in other Biblical examples where disobedience is praised and even rewarded, the unifying theme is that God's law is higher than man's law. And if the commands of men are contrary to the commands of God, we are to obey God even if it means temporal loss or suffering.

In addition to the primacy of God's law, the examples mentioned above have another trait in common: the attitude of the law breakers. The Hebrews in the book of Daniel as well as Peter and John in the book of Acts, all displayed deference and submission to those in authority over them. Even though they were not able to obey because it violated their loyalty to God, it is clear that their behavior was not merely of rebellion or personal taste. This I believe is a key component in godly civil disobedience. Attitude and actions must both be yielded to the Spirit.

There is a difference between submission and obedience. And a good friend of mine, the Reverend Father, Steve Whitten, helped me see how both are taught in Scripture but submission is unconditional whereas obedience is conditional. In my antinomian youth, I greatly struggled with authority (and to a degree still do so to this day). Romans 13 really pricked against my flesh for it is easy to be a judge of the law and those in authority rather than to be submissive and obedient in my actions. As the Spirit worked to renew my heart, I wanted to be more and more obedient to Him, but still my reason allowed me to rationalize that an unjust and ungodly government did not have authority over me, a child of God. Yet, Scripture cannot be broken, and Romans 13 caused me extensive cognitive dissonance because I was being told to submit myself to an authority that in many situations was far from godly. It was at this point that Steve Whitten pointed out to me that Romans 13 categorically commands us to submit, but obedience is conditional. What a liberating distinction of terms and a very helpful realization for reconciling civil disobedience with obeying the authorities God has placed over us!

The command in Romans 13 is submission which is an attitude of the heart and is to be given to the just and unjust ruler. It is absolute and not qualified. Obedience on the other hand is conditional, and our obedience is to be qualified by what the authority asks us to do. One response is an attitude while the other is an action: the attitude of submission is absolute, we are to respect authority, while obedience is dependent on what is being asked. For example, if the government commands you to wear a mask (whether or not it is during a pandemic), your attitude needs to be one of submission to authority. Your response needs to have a humble attitude (not to lash out or disrespect their commands) whether or not we favor it.

In order to be disobedient, an authority's request would need to violate a command from God. And even in disobedience, you need to be submissive; rather than shouting that the government is not the boss of you or that they cannot limit your freedom, you ought to respectfully listen to their commands and honor God with your attitude and actions. According to Romans 14, if any authority in our lives asks us to do something contrary to the will of God or violates our own conscience or walk of faith, we are to submissively disobey. Submission is an attitude of the heart and is honoring to God; obedience is contingent on what is being commanded and we are always to obey God rather than man.

Submission is an attitude of the heart and is pleasing to God. This attitude exemplifies the fruit of the Spirit in its forms of gentleness, long-suffering, kindness, meekness, and love. If your civil disobedience exhibits the works of the flesh (anger, wrath, malice, rebellion, sedition, etc.), then it is coming from the flesh and not the Spirit. James 1:20 tells us the anger of man does not accomplish the righteousness of God. If those in authority over us command us to do something contrary to the Law of God, then we are to submissively disobey. If the government commands us to do things, regardless how inane or personally annoying or inconvenient they may seem to us, we are to obey as unto the Lord, and we are to do it with a submissive attitude. This is very hard area of my life to give to God but as I submit to those in authority over me, I do it as an act of worship and obedience to the One I love, and I encourage you to do the same.

EUTHANASIA

The final dilemma with which I will show how I approach and parse out my convictions (at least in this book) is Euthanasia. The word itself means "good" or "happy death." It has been described by its adherents as "the right to die" or "mercy killing." Normally when one person kills another it is called homicide, and if a person kills themselves it is called suicide. Euthanasia is seeking a different designation because the intention is to end pain and suffering; it is usually done out of compassion for oneself or others, rather than out of malice, anger, fear, or greed. Euthanasia has been practiced since antiquity and is becoming more socially acceptable in the United States of America. As of the writing of this book, ten U.S. States have physician-assisted death, or "medical aid in dying," legal in their jurisdictions.

The proponents of this theory believe it is immoral to keep someone alive against their will or to prolong chronic pain and suffering. Allowing people to die or assisting them in their death is seen as an act of lovingkindness and compassion, not just for the one who's life is ending, but also in providing closure for their family and loved ones. Their reasoning is that if we advocate for mercy killing of animals, how much more so, should we advocate for the same mercy for humans.

Those that oppose euthanasia may refer to the ten commandments and the injunction, "thou shalt not kill" (Exodus 20:13). This applies to killing others and oneself. Even though the intentions may come from a place of mercy and compassion, the result is the taking of a life. Suffering is not an enjoyable experience, but it can also be a great teacher. God can even use our pain and misery to perfect us and bring Glory to Himself. Our lives are not our own, and our days are numbered by God. If we take our own or another's life, even with the best of intentions we are interjecting our will and perspective onto that which should be the sole prerogative of God. We do not know the future, and we do not have the foresight or wisdom to know if this was the right decision, and if we hasten death, we may rob the individual of God's intervention.

For me, this dilemma comes down to, who does life belong to? If our lives belong to us, then we should have the right to decide when we want to end it. But if our lives belong to God, He is the one with the final say on how long we will remain in our mortal frame. He does not guarantee us a life free of pain and suffering, so how can I use pain as an excuse for ending one? Do we have the free will to take our own or another's life? Yes, but just because God allows us to make such weighty choices does not necessarily mean we should do so.

We have already covered the Biblical injunctions against taking a human life, but are there any examples of euthanasia in the Scriptures and are they portrayed in a favorable or unfavorable light? The only clear example that I recall of euthanasia or "mercy killing" in the Scriptures is in 1 Samuel 31:4. In this passage, King Saul has been mortally wounded on the battlefield and asks his armourbearer to take his life. His armourbearer refused, and Saul chose to fall on his own sword, thus ending his life before the Philistines could end it for him. Saul is not condemned explicitly for taking his own life; the prophet Samuel had already told Saul that he would die that day with his sons. There is no explicit commentary on Saul's action; there is no condemnation here, so we are left with a neutral example. It is interesting to note however that the person who later claimed to have killed Saul, lost his own life because of it. The only other example which could be considered euthanasia (which I think is a bit of a stretch) is found in the New Testament.

In John 10:18, Jesus claims that no man can take his life, but Christ has the power to lay down his life and to take it up again. How could mankind possibly kill God? Mankind couldn't. Jesus laid down His life; He let it go. In a very broad sense, one could say that Jesus' death was an act of mercy, not only for himself, but for the sins of the world. According to the above passage, it appears as though Jesus took His own life for the good of the world. In Philippians 1:21, the apostle Paul tells us, "to live is Christ, but to die is gain." In 1 John 3:16, John tells us that just as Jesus laid down his life for us, we ought to lay down our lives for the brethren. These New Testament passages are very theologically interesting, but I do not think they are addressing the topic of euthanasia but rather emphasizing that whether we live or die it is to be unto Christ . The Old Testament passage of Saul's euthanasia/suicide is recorded in Scripture as something that happened rather than a prescription of how we are supposed to act.

The passage that most resonates with me on this topic and answers my initial question of "who does our life belong to?" is found in 1 Corinthians 6:19-20: "What? know ye not that your body is the temple of the Holy Ghost which is in you, which ye have of God, and ye are not your own? For ye are bought with a price: therefore glorify God in your body, and in your spirit, which are God's." This passage is primarily focused on how we are to care for the body God has given us especially, considering it is indwelt by the Holy Spirit. Since our lives are not our own, but belong to Christ, it is Christ who gets to decide when we are free to leave our mortal bodies.

When I was a boy, I grew up in the country and was taught how to treat and care for both domestic and wild animals. When my family hunted or butchered our animals for food, it was always done with respect and with as little pain and suffering as possible. When a family pet got too old and was in constant pain, we did not have a vet that we went to, we felt it was our responsibly to end their suffering at home. I will never forget a little white mouse I had as a pet. One day I was playing with him outside and I was afraid he was going to get away and accidently broke his back trying to catch him. I felt so bad, but I was raised not to be cruel or let animals suffer. So, with many tears and sadness I sent my little white mouse to meet his maker. This was part of my enculturation and occurred long before I considered the ethical or Scriptural ramifications of euthanasia.

Years later, after I was aware of the ethical dilemma of euthanasia and had been teaching ethics for over a decade, I had another incident that had the potential of ending with euthanasia. This time instead of a mouse, it was my oldest nephew's cockatiel. I had gotten my nephew Jordan a pair of cockatiels for pets. The female was called Fiona and the male was Orick. They were free roaming companions, and one day when I came home from work, I accidently stepped on Orick, square in the back, dislocating both his wings. Once again, based on my upbringing, I felt compelled to end his suffering. But then I thought of my classes on ethics and euthanasia and how death was so final; also, I traumatized my eleven-year-old nephew, who was convinced that I had stepped on Oricck on purpose. Instead of permanently putting Orick out of his pain, I wrapped him up and made him as comfortable as possible. I assured my nephew that I did not step on Orick on purpose. And I set my alarm early for the next morning, planning to dispatch what I expected to be a deceased bird before my nephew awoke. Much to my surprise, the following day not only was Orick not dead, but he was active and limping around his cage. I left him some food and water and prayed for the little feller throughout the day. Within a week, his wings were back in place and after a month he was able to fly again. This situation made an deep impression on me and helped me realize that I could not always know when another's time is up, and since I was not able to give life, I should be very hesitant to be quick to take it.

I understand we live in a pluralistic society and not everyone shares my presuppositions or beliefs. I certainly do not want to force someone to stay alive against their will, and I think it would be cruel to do so even though I personally would not feel able to help them in terminating their life. Although I believe all life belongs to God, I think the Christian should be very hesitant about using euthanasia. For me, it would be an act of fear and disbelief in the Sovereignty of God. I am all for alleviating the pain, both physical and emotional, of those who suffer, but I do not believe mercy killing should be the means to that end.

It is important when dealing with the topic of euthanasia to mention that there are different kinds. Broadly speaking there is active and passive euthanasia. Active euthanasia would be actively terminating one's own or another's life. This can be done through things like guns, pills, or suffocation. Passive euthanasia could range from not eating to not providing life support or the artificial means of maintaining life. I am personally opposed to active euthanasia as it would likely violate my conscience. Yet, I do not want to prolong someone's pain or suffering by keeping them alive by artificial means, especially against their will. This is part of why it is important to have the hard conversation of potential euthanasia with friends and loved ones while you are able to and can formally put your wishes in a living will or trust.

This topic is not just theoretical for me. I have had to watch several loved ones die in extreme pain and suffering, and I have been asked to be part of the decision making process on when to unplug a loved one from life support. The emotional rawness of such a decision on friends and family is profound, and it is rare to have everyone in agreement on what should be done. Our current technology has created new ethical dilemmas the likes of which people in the past did not have to address. Formerly, people would get sick and die just like today, but now we have the capability to keep someone's body functioning even after we think that the inhabitant of that body has departed.

My first encounter with euthanasia was with my grandma, Nana, who was eighty-three years old. She had contracted some type of illness and her health was deteriorating rapidly. They did not have any plan or hope for her recovery and she was given hospice assistance. Part of what hospice does is to try to comfort the dying along with their family and help them prepare for death. They also can help manage pain, but sometimes there is a limit to how much pain they can alleviate. I will never forget walking into my grandma's hospital room and seeing her writhing in agony. I argued with the hospice and hospital staff over medications and told them I did not want to see her in pain. Whether it was the illness that killed her or the morphine, I do not know, but at that point in my life all I could think of was, this is my grandma, please stop her suffering.

Unfortunately, I had an even more involved case of passive euthanasia when Logan, another of my nephews, came to the end of his struggle with cystic fibrosis. He battled bravely for every breath in his twenty-one years of life, but he had finally gotten to a point where he could no longer breathe on his own. The family had great hopes of a lung transplant, and my nephew had been moved to the top of the list. Sadly, when my nephew got an infection and he was no longer eligible for the transplant. This crushed our hope. The machine that was meant to keep him alive while awaiting a transplant was now the only thing keeping his soul attached to his body. When all options had been exhausted, including a transplant that could no longer take place, the family along with the hospital staff had to make the hard decision. We could keep Logan alive but unconscious for an indeterminate amount of time or we could let him go. Even though I do not believe in actively taking someone's life to end their pain, I also do not believe in prolonging someone's death especially if they are suffering. With great prayer and emotional wrestling, the family finally agreed to unplug him from his life support and let him go. His will to live was so strong that he continued to struggle for each breath even after he had been extubated for several hours. This was the hardest situation I have ever had to be a part of, but even though we love Logan dearly, we believed that it was out of our love for him that we needed to let him go.

V.D AFTERWORD TO THIS SECTION

I did not realize how much more difficult it would be to write about ethical topics than it is to teach about them in class. I hope this small sampler of topics gives you at least an idea about how I approach ethical dilemmas and try to form personal convictions about them. Even though I know what I believe and why, I realize the limitations of my knowledge and understanding. I am constantly revaluating and learning about different approaches and understandings of the above topics and more. I think it is helpful to try and work through ethical topics while they are still theoretical and have not yet become personal. Once our emotions are involved, it is often difficult to engage our *logos*, let alone our *nous*. At other times, we are forced to make very rapid decisions. In these cases, I make the best decisions that I can with the light that is within me and have the assurance that even my poor choices can work together for good and bring glory to God: "And we know that all things work together for good to them that love God, to them who are the called according to his purpose" (Romans 8:28). This is a balance between not tempting God, not taking His grace for granted while at the same time being completely dependent on His grace. Hopefully, I have adequately explained the complexity of not only making ethical decisions, but also comprehending our own humanness with God's redemption in our lives (*Figure 28*).

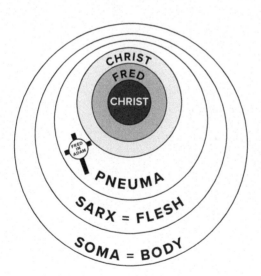

Figure 28. The layers of humanness. - In Adam crucified; in Christ alive.

Perhaps someday I will compose a book dedicated solely to ethical topics and moral dilemmas, but until then I would like to leave you with some closing thoughts that I have woven into poetry:

Reason and emotion are co-conspirators
both in the thrall of *Desire*. They are not to be trusted.
My reason can perform
intellectual feats of wonder,
but it is directed by my desire,
therefore, my reason and logos
can be impeccable,
but only insofar as it is a self-referential loop created by desire,
The *TRUTH* is beyond its grasp.
My emotions reflect
whether my desires are being met
and whether I feel like I got what I wanted
when and how I wanted it.
If I didn't get my desire
or felt like it was being thwarted
I can assure you my feelings are rather
less pleasant than when I get
what I want.
These are just a few of the reasons
I no longer trust my head
or my heart.

I want my *logos* (reason),
my *kardia* (emotions),
and most of all
my quickened *nous* (mind)
to be illumined and led,
convicted and empowered
by the Holy Spirit.
It is in the Spirit,
I wish to live and move and have my being.
When my greatest desire is to love and glorify God
rather than to gratify myself
then even my desire will have been sanctified
and its role in my thinking and feeling will
have been redeemed.
Thank you, Jesus, and thank you, Father,
for sending us your Spirit
Who He Himself is one of
The Three In One.
And thank you, Spirit, for life, light, love,
and your relentless work
of transforming us into the image of the Son.

VI *Postface*

In the preface of the book, I mentioned what a difficult task lay before me. I did not know the half of it. I can with complete assurance tell you that I am no more ethical or moral than I was at the beginning of this project. Praise be to God! My ethics and morality are not dependent on me but are provided to me by the One who gave me His righteousness in exchange for my sin. Although my personal righteousness has not increased, my understanding for the need of a redeemer sure has. I can see now more than ever my utter and complete dependence on Jesus for my righteousness. I can also see what happens when I walk in the flesh rather than in the Spirit. My gratitude towards the Father and His love towards us has grown exponentially, and it is His love that keeps drawing me to Himself.

I want to thank all my friends, family, and students who have put up with me and my dialectical mind over the years. I know many of you have been involved in "knock-down drag 'em out" arguments with me or have felt the tension that surrounds so many of these issues. I especially want to thank my earlier students for enduring my classes which I describe as a "crucible" and a "trial by fire." I have gotten much mellower in my later years, but still work the students like a taskmaster, trying to get them to confront what they believe and why. Please know that I was so intense with you because I love you and care about the wellbeing of your souls.

My prayer is that each one of you who are reading this book or going through my classes can find that perfect freedom and righteousness that can only be known in Christ. All praise and glory to the Father, eternal gratitude to the Son, and daily thanksgiving for the life and love of the Holy Spirit. May God grant you: life in His Son, and a peace that passes understanding knowing that you have been reconciled to the Three in One.

Glossary of Terms

A Posteriori After experience, scientific, tangible.

A Priori Before experience, gained through reason, intuition.

Agnostic Not sure if there is a God. Does not believe there is enough evidence either way.

Allegory One group of things used to represent another (parables).

Anarchist One with no external authority.

Animism Everything has a soul or spirit, including inanimate objects. Collective spirit or soul-Innua (ants, seals, fish, etc.)

Anthropomorphic Applying human traits to non-human things, like plants, animals or even to God; e.g., the face of God, His right hand.

Antinomianism Your own experiences are the highest authority.

Asceticism A way of life in which one believes that by controlling or diminishing the body, one could free and release the Spirit, carnal is bad and spiritual is good.

Beautiful That which is whole, complete, and lacking nothing, eternal and perfect, not subject to change. (Throughout this book, the Beautiful = God's perfection, beautiful = humanity's insufficient conception of the perfect ideal).

Christian One who has been reconciled to God by Jesus Christ and is indwelt by the Holy Spirit, follower of Christ.

Consequentialism Ethical theory emphasizing outcomes over intentions.

Cultural Relativism Is descriptive. It simply points out that in diverse times and places people do things in different ways and have different values and beliefs.

Death It does not mean end of existence, but rather separation. This could be separation of one's spirit to their body, or more profoundly, a separation from God.

Deism Detached God. God created the world but has left it largely to its own devices. There are many different degrees of deistic thinking.

Deontological Ethics Intention and duty based ethical theories.

Dialectic A point-counter-point approach to problem solving. It can also refer to questions and answers between two people.

Divine Command Theory Ethical theory claiming God is the highest good. God's commands are good; His prohibitions are evil.

Egoism Ethical theory claiming self-interest is the highest good.

Empirical Facts, hard observable evidences. Knowledge is gained through sense perception.

Environmentalism A care and concern for the environment, the physical surrounding location, in which one lives.

Epicureans Pleasure is the highest good, get rid of fears of gods, death, afterlife.

Epignosco Experiential knowledge

Epistemology Theory of knowledge. How do we gain knowledge? Are there absolutes? Can we know things? How?

Ethical Relativism Is prescriptive. Values and morals are based on the culture in which you are living. "When in Rome..."

Ethics Theory of right conduct.

Ethics of Care Ethical theory developed by Carol Gilligan in which she argues for the inclusion of feminine virtues into the study of ethics and morality, good = what is caring and loving

Ethical Relativism Ethical theory claiming that one's culture determines the highest good.

Ethical Topics Ethics is applied to specific topics or dilemmas.

Evangelical One who holds to the fundamentals of the faith and actively seeks to convert and influence others.

Existentialism Experientially based knowledge. Only what you have or are experiencing is what you "truly" know. Emphasis is placed on the individual, free will, personal responsibility, living an authentic life and searching for meaning and purpose through the despair and meaninglessness of the universe. Angst refers to existential dread, which is a composite of fear and anxiety, over no one knows what.

Faith On the high end, it is absolute assurance that comes from God. On the low end, it could be "wishful thinking."

Foreknowledge God's omniscience means He knows everything including that which will happen.

Fideism Faith over reason. Faith is a Gift from God and is more certain and can give you greater knowledge than reason.

Free will The ability to make real choices with real consequences.

Fundamentalist One who holds firmly to foundational beliefs.

Good That which is whole, complete, and lacking nothing, eternal and perfect, not subject to change. (Throughout this book, the Good = God's perfection, good = humanity's insufficient conception of the perfect ideal).

Glorification This term refers to that which has great weight or consequence, lifted up for exalted.

Gnosticism A first century philosophical\religious movement, which was very eclectic in forming a synthesis of all know beliefs and wisdom held by men including the "mysteries", which would be revealed to the initiated as they climbed the ladder of spiritual enlightenment and perfection. This is similar to what we find in the New Age movement today. The main distinction of all the various flavors of Gnosticism is its emphasis on Dualism. E.g., Spirit=Good, Matter=Evil.

Hedonism Ethical theory claiming pleasure is the highest good.

Human Being The non-tangible aspects that make humans unique from other living things, made in the image of God, composed of a physical body and an immaterial soul/spirit (logos/kardia/nous).

Idealism Reality is in the mind. Ideals = Reality. Plato is considered the father of Idealism.

Immanence God permeates the universe. God fills all things; there is no place where God is not. This emphasizes the omnipresent and omniscient qualities of the Godhead.

Innate Qualities or attributes that are part of a being at birth. Innate traits are givens, they are neither learned or acquired, rather they are pre-existing conditions of human beings e.g., the ability to learn or develop a language, the concepts of space and time, the ability to distinguish between this and that and to make value judgments.

Kantian Ethics Ethical theory developed by Emmanuel Kant in which reason (pure and practical) is the highest good.

Kardia The heart. Represents the seed of passion and emotion.

Logos Universal consciousness, mind and soul. Cosmic consciousness. Universal reason. That, which gives order, design and purpose to the cosmos. Sentient beings have the logos within e.g., their soul or consciousness. Minerals, planets and stars are directed by the logos externally.

Materialism Matter = Reality. Doctrine that all existence is reducible into matter or into an attribute or effect of matter. Matter is the ultimate reality; the phenomenon of consciousness is explained by physiochemical changes in the nervous system. Antithesis of idealism.

Metaethics Foundational presuppositions and questions concerning ethics.

Metaphysics Beyond physics. Above, after or beyond the physical. Metaphysics deals with everything outside the realm of the tangible, therefor concepts such as God, soul, spirit, mind etc. would all be included in metaphysics. Theology itself is a sub-category of Metaphysics. Origins also become a metaphysical topic since no one was around to see the creation or evolution of the world.

Monism All is One. Monism can also mean that reality only consists of one thing e.g., water, wind, earth fire etc. as in the case of the ancient Greeks.

Morality Applied ethics.

Mystic One who seeks union with God.

Naturalism Nothing supernatural or metaphysical. Everything can be understood by science, utilitarianism (good = right), all that exists is matter.

Natural Law Theory Ethical theory as established by Thomas Aquinas that combines human reason with Divine Command Theory, claims that faith and reason should be used together to determine right living.

Neonomian The new law.

Neo-Platonism Type of idealistic monism in which the ultimate reality of the universe is held to be infinite, unknowable, perfect One. From this One emanates nous (pure intelligence), which in turn is derived the world soul, the creative activity of which engenders the known world. Neo-Platonism is also known for its spiritual hierarchy and its development of the great chain of being.

Nihilism The belief in nothing, no authority, no absolutes.

Noetic effect Term referring to the application of consequences to day-to-day activities.

Nomian The law.

Normative Ethics Theories which apply ethics to human conduct.

Noumenon Things in and of themselves (as they are). Noumena cannot be perceived by the senses and are therefore unknowable at least to man. This way of thinking led Kant to believe that Metaphysics was an impossible study for human beings since we could only know what we could observe.

Nous Intellect, reason, pure intelligence, first principles.

Objective How God views things since he in all-knowing, absolute truth, detached, suspended judgment, reason and logic not influenced by emotions and feeling.

Omnibenevolence All Good, all the Time (the totality of Time, from the beginning to the end), absolute Goodness.

Ontology Study of being. Theory on being.

Panentheism All is in God. God is greater than the sum of His creation. God is in everything.

Pantheism All is god, nature is god, the world soul. "All is God, God is all, All is one, Everything exists inside God!" Came out of polytheism.

Paradigm Outlook, model, worldview.

Perception Interpreting and synthesizing our senses.

Phenomena That which is perceived, senses (as they appear), see Kant.

Philosophy Philo (love)/Sophia (wisdom). Love of wisdom.

Physics Tangible, scientific method, hypothesis, theory (Aristotle).

Pneuma Spirit.

Pneumanomian   Spirit law, the law of the Spirit.

Polytheism   Many gods. Evolved from the many spirits of Animism.

Postmodern   It is a rejection of metanarratives and emphasizes subjective perspectives and truth claims, complex concept used to describe a wide range of behavior and belief.

Predestination   God predisposes certain events to take place and specific courses for peoples' lives.

Presuppositions   Preconceived ideas.

Psyche   Soul.

Rationalist   Truth is the Rational.

Realism   What is out there is real; reality is self-existent apart from our perceptions.

Salvation   The act of being rescued or redeemed.

Sarx   The Greek term for flesh which can mean physical body or the appetites that come from having a physical body.

Scientific Panentheism   Equating Spirit with Energy.

Sin   That which is contrary to the will of God, or that which falls short of God's standard which is perfection.

Soma   The Greek term for the physical body.

Sovereignty   The qualities derived from God's omnipotence and omniscience, Divine control, absolute authority.

Stoicism   Opposed to Epicureanism, developed from Cynics, Socrates, divine reason, logos, duty is highest good. Follow the natural way. (Big bang)

Subjective   How everyone but God views things, viewed from my knowledge.

Teleological Ethics   Relativistic and consequential based ethical theories.

Theism   Personal God, immanence, transcendence.

Theosis   Deification, the process by which humans are knit together with the Divine.

Transcendence   God is not contained.

Truth (the True)   That which is whole, complete, and lacking nothing, eternal and perfect, not subject to change. (Throughout this book, the Truth = God's perfection, truth = humanity's insufficient conception of the perfect ideal).

Utilitarianism   Ethical theory developed by Jeremy Bentham and John Stuart Mill that seeks to produce the greatest good for the most people.

Virtue Ethics   Character based ethical theories.

Glossary of Important People

Aristotle. 384-322 B.C. - Greek philosopher, a student of Plato, Father of Realism; associated with Virtue Ethics.

Aquinas, St. Thomas. 1225-1274 A.D. – Integrated reason and faith, syncretized Christianity with Aristotelian reason (baptizing Aristotle's ideas and philosophy); associated with Natural Law Theory.

Augustine, Saint. 354-430 A.D. - Integrated idealism and faith, syncretized Christianity with Plato's idealism (baptizing Plato's ideas and philosophy; wrote *City of God*; his ideas related to Divine Command Theory with regards to the sovereignty of God and predestination.

Bentham, Jeremy. 1748-1842 A.D. – Founder of action-based Utilitarian ethics.

Boas, Frans. 1858 - 1942 A.D. - American anthropologist, whose work influenced the development of Ethical Relativism

Descartes, Rene. 1596-1650 A.D. – Developed Cartesian dualism (the mind-body distinction); advocated for radical doubt; Father of Modern Philosophy.

Gilligan, Carol. 1936-Present – American psychologist, feminist, and ethicist; Introduced Ethics of Care.

Kant, Immanuel. 1724-1804 A.D. – Syncretized realism and idealism; father of and associated with Kantian Ethics.

Kierkegaard, Soren. 1813-1855 A.D. – Christian existential philosopher; Father of Existentialism.

Mill, John Stuart. 1806-1873 A.D. – Developed rule-based Utilitarianism and hedonic calculus.

Nee, Watchman. 1903-1972 A.D. – Chinese Christian preacher and teacher, who was martyred for his faith; Wrote *The Normal Christian Life*.

Plato. 427-347 B.C. - Greek philosopher, a student of Socrates, Father of Idealism; recognized and explained Egoism.

Socrates. 469-399 B.C. - Greek philosopher that established the dialectical approach to knowledge; "Know thy self."

Tolstoy, Count Leo. 1828-1910 A.D. – In addition to being a famous Russian novelist (having written *War and Peace* and *Anna Karenina*), he wrote *The Kingdom of God is Within You*. He was a total pacifist and did not believe one should use violence for any reason.

Works Cited

Anaxagoras, and Patricia Curd, "Anaxagoras." *The Stanford Encyclopedia of Philosophy.* Winter 2019 ed., edited by Edward N. Zalta, www.plato. stanford.edu/archives/win2019/entries/anaxagoras/

Copleston, Frederick S. J. *A History of Philosophy.* New York: Doubleday, 1993.

Descartes René, Mike Moriarty. *Meditations on First Philosophy: With Selections from the Objections and Replies.* Oxford U P, 2008.

Geisler, Norman. *Christian Ethics.* 2nd ed., Baker Academic, 2010.

Kant, Immanuel. *Groundwork of Metaphysics of Morals.* Cambridge U P, 1998., https://cpb-us-w2.wpmucdn.com/blog.nus.edu.sg/dist/c/1868/ files/2012/12/Kant-Groundwork-ng0pby.pdf

Kant, Immanuel. *The Metaphysics of Morals. Cambridge Texts in the History of Philosophy,* 2nd edited by L. Denis, translated by M. Gregor, Cambridge: Cambridge U P (2017).

Kolak, Daniel. The Philosophy Source: 100 Classic Masterworks on CD-ROM. Belmont, CA: Wadsworth, 2000.

Nee, Watchman. *The Normal Christian Life.* Tyndale House P, reprinted edition, 4 Nov. 1977.

Palmer, Donald. *Looking at Philosophy: The Unbearable Heaviness of Philosophy Made Lighter.* 2nd ed. New York: Mayfield, 1994.

Pew Research Center, "The Religious Dimensions of the Torture Debate." *Religion and Public Life.* 7 May 2009, https://www.pewforum. org/2009/04/29/the-religious-dimensions-of- the-torture-debate/

Redding, Paul, "Georg Wilhelm Friedrich Hegel." *The Stanford Encyclopedia of Philosophy.* Spring 2020 ed., edited by Edward N. Zalta, www.plato.stanford.edu/archives/spr2020/entries/hegel/

Ryrie. C.C. *The Ryrie study Bible: King James Version*. Chicago: Moody Press. 1976.

Sayre-McCord, Geoff. "Metaethics." *The Stanford Encyclopedia of Philosophy*. Spring 2012 ed., edited by Edward N. Zalta, www.plato.stanford.edu/ archives/spr2012/entries/metaethics/

The Scofield Study Bible: King James Version. commentary by C.I. Scofield, New York: Oxford U P, 2003.

Thurston, Herbert. "Apostles' Creed." *The Catholic Encyclopedia*. vol. 1. New York: Robert Appleton Company, 1907. 30 May 2020, https://www. newadvent.org/cathen/01629a.htm.

Timmons, Mark. *Conduct and Character: Readings in Moral Theory*. Cengage Learning, 6th ed., 2011.

Tzu, Lao. *Tao Te Ching*. translated by Gia-fu Feng and Jane English. New York: Vintage, 1972.